My Daily Appointment

By
Dr. Michael Elliott

Vision Publishing ~ Ramona, California

My Daily Appointment

Copyright 2004 by Dr. Michael Elliott

ISBN # 1-931178-72-0

All rights in this book are reserved worldwide. No part of the book may be reproduced in any manner, whatsoever, without written permission of the author except brief quotations embodied in critical articles or reviews.

Vision Publishing

1520 Main Street, Suite C

Ramona, California 92065

www.vision.edu/publishing

Printed in the United States of America

Daily Reading God's Word

Dear Friend,

Many people lament that they never hear God speak to them. However, when asked, they readily admit they do not discipline themselves to read the Bible as part of their daily routine. It is a surprising confession considering that the primary way in which God will speak to His people is through His Word. My personal testimony is that my life and ministry have been radically impacted as a result of developing a daily Bible reading habit. It never ceases to amaze me what new truths the Holy Spirit reveals to me as I read passages over, and over again.

The Bible, without question, is the crown jewel of all literature, and yet it is not treasured, much less, read by so many Christians. Many read the Bible like they read no other work of literature. No one would consider making the claim they understood the contents of a novel if they read only a few paragraphs of the third chapter and then skipped to the last page. Yet, this is precisely how the majority of readers read the Bible. Many choose to read the Bible as a devotional tool as they meditate on selected passages and verses. Devotional reading is richly beneficial to spiritual growth; however, when it comes to systematically reading through the Scriptures, it is an undisputed fact that one cannot merely read selected passages and expect to gain the wisdom of the whole counsel of God's Word. No other subject, or discipline, is learned or grasped in this manner. Why should the Bible be approached differently?

I recognize that committing to a daily Bible reading habit is one of the most difficult habits you will ever develop. The spiritual warfare launched against anyone who seeks to develop this habit is a clue to its life-changing benefits. The devil doesn't mind that you own a Bible, but he is concerned that you will read it and apply its truth to your life. He is very much aware of its life-changing power if it is embraced.

You have been given 1,440 minutes in each day. You are in control of this time, and it is your choice of how this time will be budgeted. It takes approximately ten to fifteen minutes to read four chapters of the Bible, which if done daily, will accomplish the goal of reading through the Bible in one year. If you take ten minutes to systematically read, and ten minutes to read devotionally, you have only spent twenty minutes in the Word. Surely we can find ten to twenty minutes of a day for God's Word…the decision is yours, and yours alone.

Let me challenge you to read through the Bible at least once every year. There are many templates that you can follow that will enable you to achieve your reading goal. Whichever template you follow is not important, but what is important, is that you commit to daily read God's Word. As you renew your commitments, let the Lord speak the truths of His Word to your heart.

Reading Through the Bible Each Year

GOAL	PLAN	ACHIEVEMENT
One Time a Year	4 Chapters a Day	Every 298 Days
Three Times a Year	10 Chapters a Day	Every 119 Days
Six Times a Year	20 Chapters a Day	Every 60 Days
Nine Times a Year	30 Chapters a Day	Every 40 Days
Twelve Times a Year	40 Chapters a Day	Every 30 Days

Psalms 119: 9-11
How can a young man cleanse his way?
By taking heed according to Your Word.
With my whole heart I have sought You;
Oh, let me not wander from Your commandments!
Your Word I have hidden in my heart,
That I might not sin against You.

Psalms 119:105
Your Word is a lamp to my feet
and a light to my path.

~ ~ ~ JANUARY 1 ~ ~ ~

"Then they entered into a covenant to seek the Lord God of their fathers with all their heart and with all their soul; and all Judah rejoiced at the oath, for they had sworn with all their heart and sought Him with all their soul; and He was found by them, and the Lord gave them rest all around" (II Chronicles 15:12, 15).

The first day of the year is always laden with new resolutions, that when kept, promise that the year will be different than the previous one. Have your resolutions ever fizzled?

Hidden in the story of Asa, lies the answer in keeping your spiritual resolutions. The first thing Asa did was to call for the nation to repent and remove all the idols they were worshiping: we must do the same. An idol is anything that we pursue, or embrace, at the expense of God and His Word.

The second thing that Asa did was to restore worship as the first priority. Today, we make the mistake of relegating worship to a Sunday activity; however, worship encompasses the entirety of life and must be given our highest priority.

Finally, Asa and the people made a covenant before the Lord to keep their resolutions with their whole hearts. The secret lies in the involvement of our whole hearts.

Thought for Today

As you set your spiritual resolutions, embrace the secrets of Asa. Repent and remove all idols from your life. Restore your worship of God to the number one priority. Remember, talk is cheap! The proof of your desire is evidenced by the discipline of your pursuit.

Prayer Journal

_____

_____

_____

~ ~ ~ JANUARY 2 ~ ~ ~

"For You do not desire sacrifice, or else I would give it; You do not delight in burnt offering. The sacrifices of God are a broken spirit, a broken and a contrite heart—these, O God, You will not despise" (Psalm 51:16-17).

In the Old Testament sacrificial system of worship, brokenness through death was physically required of the animals that were slain. The broken sacrifice became the representation of the atonement for the sins of the worshiper, as well as, the symbolic sacrifice of one's self.

The Law of Moses required that the sacrifices must be spotless, without blemish, or sickness. A crippled or blemished animal that was worthless to the owner would reflect the perception of the worshiper as to the worthiness of God. Therefore, if it were to be offered as a sacrifice, it would reveal the insincerity of the worshiper and be a dishonor to God.

We no longer worship and serve God at a physical altar through the sacrifice of an animal, as in the Old Testament. Our altar of service and devotion to God is in our hearts, and God is worthy of our very best. Whether we are in our devotional times of worship and prayer, or in our service to Him, we must honor the Lord with our best and most sincere expressions and efforts. He is worthy!

Thought for Today

Consider the altar of your heart. What has been the quality of the sacrifices of your praise, prayer, worship, and service? Purpose to give Him your best and do not give the Lord your leftovers of time, energy, emotion, and strength. Remember, He is worthy!

Prayer Journal

_____

_____

_____

~ ~ ~ JANUARY 3 ~ ~ ~

"I call heaven and earth as witnesses today against you, that I have set before you life and death, blessing and cursing; therefore choose life, that both you and your descendants may live" (Deuteronomy 30:19).

You are a product of the choices that you make. You exercise your right of choice in every arena of your life: the type of car you drive; the house in which you live and its location; the person to whom you are married; and the work that you do to make a living. These are only a few of the important choices that you make which define who you are.

Scripturally, you are also the product of the choices you make. It is your choice whether or not to: read the Word, spend time in prayer, be faithful in church attendance, forgive offenses, and help those in need. These are but a few of many choices you make that will define you spiritually.

God has granted the right to choose things that promote life, or to choose what will destroy you. Often, you want God to give you a spiritual experience that will relieve you of the responsibility to make a choice. For example, if you are participating in an activity that goes against the counsel of the Word, and you pray that God will take the opportunity to participate away…God won't answer that prayer! He will always require you to make a choice!

Thought for Today

God will not make you do the right thing and the devil cannot make you do the wrong thing. What you do, and what you become, is your choice. Choose things that will enrich your life.

Prayer Journal

_____

_____

_____

~ ~ ~ JANUARY 4 ~ ~ ~

"Wisdom is the principal thing; therefore get wisdom. And in all your getting, get understanding" (Proverbs 4:7).

Solomon, the wisest man who ever lived, said that the most important thing you could pursue in life was the wisdom of God. Wisdom will unite God—Who is the source of all knowledge and understanding—with our daily living; we must make the choice to put God's principles of right living into practice.

Wisdom encompasses the proper application of your knowledge into the areas of your life. Without wisdom, you are reduced to making decisions based solely on what seems logical and right to you. Solomon warns that doing things apart from the wisdom of God will result in death. Proverbs 14:12 says, *"There is a way that seems right to a man, but its end is the way of death."*

The number one source from which to receive God's wisdom is His Word. The most important decision you will make, second only to the decision you must make regarding embracing Jesus as your Savior, is your decision regarding the place the Word is to be given in your life. The Word is not merely a collection of historical stories and ancient proverbs; it is the living and relevant source of all truth on which you can choose to build your life. Building your life on the solid foundation of the Word will anchor you when the storms of life come and will assure you of His promised victory.

Thought for Today

The decision you make regarding the application of the Word into the government of your life will determine the value system you will build upon. Renew your commitment to the Word.

Prayer Journal

_____

_____

_____

~ ~ ~ JANUARY 5 ~ ~ ~

"He guards the paths of justice, and preserves the way of His saints. Then you will understand righteousness and justice, equity and every good path" (Proverbs 2:8-9).

Every promise of God is predicated on meeting a condition or requirement; each condition and requirement will always demand that you make a choice. We are told of three wonderful promises that God made to us through His Word in Proverbs 2:8-9. The first promise is that God will help you discern fraudulent circumstances and the questionable motives of others. The second promise is that God will guard you in your choice to walk in His Word and will see to it that, as you are faithful, you will not become side-tracked. The third promise is that God will show you the right decision to make in every circumstance.

What great promises! However, there are conditions that must be met in order to realize these wonderful promises. You must place a top priority and value on the wisdom that can be derived from the Word. You will find in Proverbs 2:1-4 that you must meet the following requirements. First, you must embrace the Word of God with discipline and with delight. Secondly, you must be teachable and willing to put into practice the truths you have discovered. Thirdly, you must be passionate and tenacious in your pursuit of the truths found in the Word. Finally, you must place a high value on truth and pursue it with a high expectation of receiving it.

Thought for Today

The Word of God is your most precious resource. God is anxious to load your life with His abundant blessings. Discipline yourself to embrace His Word and do not procrastinate another moment!

Prayer Journal

_____

_____

~ ~ ~ JANUARY 6 ~ ~ ~

"Give ear to my words, O Lord, consider my meditation. Give heed to the voice of my cry, my King and my God, for to You I will pray. My voice You shall hear in the morning, O Lord; in the morning I will direct it to You, and I will look up" (Psalms 5:1-3).

Whether it was in singing songs of praise to Him, or sharing the meditation of his heart, David loved to commune with the Lord. Prayer was not optional to David, nor was it offered only when it was convenient—David started his day in prayer. Listen once more to his statements: *"I will pray," "My voice You shall hear in the morning, in the morning I will direct it to You."* Fellowship with his Lord was a driving priority in David's life. He never allowed his circumstances, whether good or bad, to dictate his sacred desire to speak intimately with God.

Whether the Lord spoke words of encouragement, instruction, or rebuke, David treasured each word within his heart. We need to pay heed to the example of David's devotion to the Lord and his commitment to spend time in prayer. So often, we are moved by our circumstances and fail to pray because of negative attitudes that are born out of our adversity. It is in these painful moments that we need to seek the compassion of the Lord. Sometimes, we may allow our busy schedule to become so crowded that we do not have time to pray. We may promise ourselves, and promise God, that we will pray later; however, in reality, later never comes.

Thought for Today

A day started in His presence is a day that is started right! Remember, God is waiting to spend time with you and speak to you if you are willing to take the time to sit with Him.

Prayer Journal

_____

_____

_____

~ ~ ~ JANUARY 7 ~ ~ ~

"For You are not a God who takes pleasure in wickedness, nor shall evil dwell with You. The boastful shall not stand in Your sight; You hate all workers of iniquity. You shall destroy those who speak falsehood; the Lord abhors the bloodthirsty and deceitful man" (Psalms 5:4-6).

David knew that prayer would assist him in remaining devotionally in tune with the Lord; however, he also knew that prayer was a great preventative to sin and would help him avoid moral failure. The word for *"evil,"* that David used, is a word describing self-destruction. David also believed that prayer would help him discern circumstances, or people, that would cause him to self-destruct. He knew that prayer would temper his foolish boasting and pride.

David wanted to avoid becoming a *"worker of iniquity"*—one who has yielded to idolatry. Idolatry constitutes anything that we pursue that takes God's place as the priority of our lives. Idolatry will bring about compromise with God's Word and His ways.

David believed that prayer would seal his lips with truth and prevent lying. The word for *"bloodthirsty"* carries the meaning of one who is a lover of violence. David believed prayer would keep his heart tender; therefore, his heart would not become hardened in the bloodshed that followed him as king.

Thought for Today

What prayer prevented in David's life, prayer can also prevent in your life if you will take the time to pray. You need to examine what David believed concerning what prayer would prevent in his life. Ask God, in faith, to do the same for you.

Prayer Journal

_____

_____

~ ~ ~ JANUARY 8 ~ ~ ~

"But as for me, I will come into Your house in the multitude of Your mercy; in fear of You I will worship toward Your holy temple" (Psalms 5:7).

Worship is a level of communion with God that is even more intimate than prayer. Worship speaks of the tender expression of "kissing towards," or perhaps better stated, "brush the lips against" God. Prayer is often spent using all of our energy to conform to the "will of God"; however, in worship we lay hold of the power of the Spirit that transforms us into the "image of God."

Tragically, we often relegate worship to a musical activity on Sunday that we participate in at church. While worship might occur during these times of sacred assembly, worship is much broader in its scope than just singing songs. Worship encompasses all of our tender expressions of affection and the adoration of our hearts towards the Lord. It envelops the sweet release of all of our pent-up emotions and our deepest devotion for Who the Lord is—not just what He has done, is now doing, or will yet do for us.

David knew that, just as with prayer, worship was a personal expression and no one could transact it for him. The meditations of David, concerning God's faithfulness and goodness, would always yield to his love for God and he expressed this in worship.

Thought for Today

If we are not careful, we will spend more time complaining to God about our circumstances than communing with Him in prayer. Meditate on the Lord's tender mercies. Allow your heart to express itself in love to the Lord for His faithfulness.

Prayer Journal

_____

_____

_____

JANUARY 9

"But let those rejoice who put their trust in You; let them shout for joy, because You defend them; let those also who love Your name be joyful in You. For You, O Lord, will bless the righteous; with favor You will surround him as with a shield" (Psalms 5:11-12).

While there are many things Christians need, "rejoicing in the Lord" has to be near the top of the list. Sometimes, we are the saddest acting people on the face of the earth. Even when God answers a "major prayer," we don't show very much emotion in the rejoicing department. It is no wonder, when we try to share our faith with those who don't know Jesus and tell them, "You need what I have," they reject our appeal concerning their spiritual needs. They don't want what we've told them we have—they have enough of their own problems. They definitely don't want to add to their lives whatever made us so unhappy.

David loved to "rejoice in the Lord," and he did so with great abandon to his pride and to the opinion of others. David believed that if you were going to put your trust in the Lord and claim that you love Him, you needed to rejoice in Him as well. He understood that rejoicing in the Lord released the Lord's protection over his life, and that alone was worth shouting about. He also knew the Lord would respond to his joy by surrounding his life with favor.

Thought for Today

Would there be anyone that is acquainted with you, who would want what you have? Would anybody be able to identify that you have joy in the Lord? Why not decide right now to do a little rejoicing today—come on, shout a little. He deserves our daily rejoicing!

Prayer Journal

_____

_____

_____

~ ~ ~ JANUARY 10 ~ ~ ~

"Do not fear any of those things which you are about to suffer. Indeed, the devil is about to throw some of you into prison, that you may be tested, and you will have tribulation ten days. Be faithful unto death, and I will give you the crown of life" (Revelation 2:10).

The devil loves to try and intimidate us with fear. He tempts us by getting us to assume the worst, and he wants us to believe his negative report about us. There are four things you can do to conquer the devil's attack of fear on your life. First, you must recognize that what is happening to you is not from the hand of God. II Timothy 1:7 tells us, *"For God has not given us a spirit of fear, but of power and of love and of a sound mind."* Secondly, recognize who the author of fear is, and resist him by submitting yourself to God. In James 4:7-8 we read, *"Therefore submit to God. Resist the devil and he will flee from you. Draw near to God and He will draw near to you."* Thirdly, place your focus on Jesus, Who gives you your faith and causes you to be victorious through your faith. We read in Hebrews 12:2, *"Looking unto Jesus the author and finisher of our faith, who for the joy that was set before Him endured the cross, despising the shame, and has sat down at the right hand of the throne of God."* Finally, read and search the scriptures, for through the Word your faith will be strengthened. We can see this principle clearly in Romans 10:17, *"So then faith comes by hearing, and hearing by the Word of God."*

Thought for Today

Do not allow yourself to yield to the fear tactics of the devil. Turn to God and stand on the promises of His Word. Offer Him praise as you stand on the factual truth that God is forever faithful to keep the promises of His Word.

Prayer Journal

_____

_____

_____

~ ~ ~ JANUARY 11 ~ ~ ~

"There is no fear in love; but perfect love casts out fear, because fear involves torment. But he who fears has not been made perfect in love" (I John 4:18).

The emotion of fear is a very natural response to negative circumstances. When we are gripped by fear, it weakens our physical and spiritual strength. Fear hinders our ability to think rationally; therefore, we are tormented in our emotions. Fear, that remains unchecked, can be very devastating. Fear is the number one weapon the devil uses to gain access to our lives. Fear is actually faith in reverse. They are the same energy flowing in opposite directions. Faith says, "I believe God's Word is true." Fear says, "I believe the report the devil is giving is true."

God, as well as the devil, dwell and operate in the spirit realm; therefore, they must have a means of access, like a bridge to the natural world. God seeks to build His bridge so He can gain access to us through our faith in His Word. The devil seeks to build his bridge so he can access our lives through developing a fear of circumstances. The Psalmist encourages us to build a bridge of faith in the Word; *"I have chosen the way of truth; Your judgments I have laid before me. I cling to Your testimonies; O Lord, do not put me to shame! I will run the course of Your commandments, for You shall enlarge my heart. Teach me, O Lord, the way of Your statutes, and I shall keep it to the end"* (Psalms 119:30-33).

Thought for Today

Remove fear from your life by placing your complete trust in the Word of God. Like the Psalmist David, determine you will remain standing on the Word to the end.

Prayer Journal

_____

_____

_____

~ ~ ~ JANUARY 12 ~ ~ ~

"Enter into His gates with thanksgiving, and into His courts with praise. Be thankful to Him, and bless His name" (Psalms 100:4).

When I was starting out in ministry, a wise and seasoned minister gave me a piece of advice. He said, "Son, never make the mistake of asking the people at church how they are feeling, they just might tell you!" I have often wished that I had heeded his advice. I guess it is just part of human nature to want to tell someone just how bad things are. I'm sure that in your life there are some people, that when you see them coming, you wish the earth would swallow you up whole. You know that they will moan and groan about how miserably life is treating them. It seems as if they never have anything good to report about anything. Listening to them drains you and frustrates you, for they never let you speak. They aren't interested in looking for an answer to their problem as they never take your advice.

It is amazing how much of our prayer time is spent complaining about what's wrong and how God needs to fix it—and we want it fixed NOW! We often fail to acknowledge all the wonderful things He has done. We are blinded by our lack of faith in Him, for we are so busy complaining, that we fail to see His faithfulness to us.

Thought for Today

Honestly, how thankful have you been lately? Do you spend more time complaining to Him than you do praising Him for the things He has already done? When God sees you coming, is He tempted to crawl in a hole and hide? When God sees you coming, does He brace Himself for another tongue lashing? Make your time with Him today a lasting time of loving fellowship in His presence.

Prayer Journal

_____

_____

_____

~ ~ ~ JANUARY 13 ~ ~ ~

"I am the true vine, and My father is the vinedresser...I am the vine, you are the branches. He who abides in Me, and I in him, bears much fruit; for without Me you can do nothing" (John 15:1, 5).

Sitting in the Upper Room, celebrating the Passover meal with His disciples, Jesus used the illustration of a vineyard to teach them a very important aspect of their relationship with God. Grapevines grew in abundance in Palestine and if carefully pruned, they produced an abundance of sweet grapes. However, if they were left unattended, the vines would fall and grow along the ground and as a result, they produced little or no grapes as they couldn't receive enough sunshine. Jesus spoke to the disciples concerning their relationship to Him. He told them they were the branches that were attached to the true and only vine; and everything they needed and wanted to promote and sustain life, was forever sourced in Him.

In pointing out that His Father was the vinedresser, Jesus established the rights of ownership within the vineyard. The Father owned the vineyard: thus, He was the sole owner of the vine and its respective branches. Hidden in this revelation, is the truth that the branches do not belong to themselves. The branches have no right to choose where they want to grow, nor do they have the right to choose if they will produce fruit.

Thought for Today

We are the branches attached to the vine within the Father's vineyard and we belong to the Father, not to ourselves. Therefore, it is our responsibility to allow the life of Jesus to flow through us so that we might produce fruit that is pleasing to the Father.

Prayer Journal

_____

_____

_____

~ ~ ~ JANUARY 14 ~ ~ ~

"By this My Father is glorified, that you bear much fruit; so you will be My disciples...You did not choose Me, but I chose you and appointed you that you should go and bear fruit, and that your fruit should remain, that whatever you ask the Father in My name He may give you" (John 15:8, 16).

Jesus used the illustration of a vineyard to teach the disciples of their responsibility concerning their relationship to the Father. Jesus spoke to them of their assignment of bearing fruit. They were to glorify the Father through the abundance of fruit that was produced from their lives. As they bore fruit, it would give evidence that they indeed were His disciples. The fruit that Jesus was interested in them bearing was to have lasting value; therefore, it would be able to stand the test of time.

The Apostle Paul further defined the manner of fruit that we, as disciples, are expected to bear in Galatians 5:22-23, *"But the fruit of the Spirit is love, joy, peace, longsuffering, kindness, goodness, faithfulness, gentleness, self-control. Against such there is no law."* A close examination reveals that the fruit of the Spirit actually has nine distinctive characteristics of the nature and character of Jesus. As branches connected to Jesus, Who is the Vine, His Spirit flows into us and through us. When we are healthy branches, we will then produce His nature and character through each of our lives.

Thought for Today

Submit to the life-flow and inner working of the Holy Spirit. Allow the Holy Spirit to form and reveal Jesus through you today. The result will give evidence to the fact that you are a disciple of Jesus and the Father will be glorified in the fruit you are bearing.

Prayer Journal

_____

_____

_____

~ ~ ~ JANUARY 15 ~ ~ ~

"Abide in Me, and I in you. As the branch cannot bear fruit of itself, unless it abides in the vine, neither can you, unless you abide in Me. I am the vine, you are the branches. He who abides in Me, and I in him, bears much fruit; for without Me you can do nothing" (John 15:4-5).

One of the wonderful things about God is that when He gives us an assignment, He never expects us to accomplish it with our own resources or strength. He makes available to us His resources, and His strength, to do whatever it is that He has asked of us. Jesus told the disciples that the Father expected them to bear fruit; thereby, they would glorify Him. Jesus revealed that the key to fruit bearing was to abide in Him for, in and of ourselves, we cannot accomplish such an assignment. Jesus repeatedly told the disciples: *"Abide in Me; Abide in My love; Let My words abide in you."* The word *"abide"* literally means, "take up residence."

So many Christians make the mistake of dividing their lives into two compartments—"sacred" and "natural." Abiding in Jesus means that we must let go of such a division in our lives and set up permanent residence with Him. Abiding demands that we don't just visit the Lord on Sundays; rather we live with Him on a daily basis. Jesus is not just a part of our everyday lives, He is our life, and the source of all that we hold dear.

Thought for Today

Stop trying to produce the fruit of the Spirit from your own strength—it will never happen. Don't just plan to quickly visit the Lord's presence; however, plan to stay in His presence throughout the day so you will be able to make right decisions.

Prayer Journal

_____

_____

_____

~ ~ ~ JANUARY 16 ~ ~ ~

"Every branch in Me that does not bear fruit He takes away; and every branch that bears fruit He prunes, that it may bear more fruit" (John 15:2).

One summer, when I was young, my grandfather invited me to help him prune the apple trees in his orchard. With indifference, I watched as he cut away the broken or dead branches; however, when he started cutting off what I deemed to be strong and healthy branches, I quickly became confused. My grandfather told me that the pruning would make it possible for the tree to bear even more apples—this was a mystery to my understanding. While today I understand the theory of pruning, it still mystifies the little boy within me.

Jesus told us that the Father prunes us to increase the yield of His harvest in our lives. Pruning is never pleasant. Repeatedly, the Father examines our lives and prunes everything that He deems an impediment to our producing more of the fruit of the Spirit. We will notice the result of His pruning in that some of our relationships suddenly, and for no apparent reason, change, or no longer exist. We awaken to find that the activities we enjoyed yesterday, suddenly do not hold any joy or interest for us anymore. When we are branches connected to the tree, God is committed to do whatever it takes to help us produce our full potential of fruit.

Thought for Today

There are only two choices in your response to the Lord's pruning: you can either "trust Him" or "cuss Him." If God is pruning, it can only mean that He sees something in your future that He is preparing you for. God will prune areas that impede your future.

Prayer Journal

_____

_____

_____

~ ~ ~ JANUARY 17 ~ ~ ~

"And he said, 'Listen all you of Judah and you inhabitants of Jerusalem, and you, King Jehoshaphat! Thus says the Lord to you: Do not be afraid nor dismayed because of this great multitude, for the battle is not yours, but God's'" (II Chronicles 20:15).

King Jehoshaphat and the people of Jerusalem were in serious trouble. They were surrounded by their enemies and were told to either surrender or die. Great fear gripped the peoples' hearts as King Jehoshaphat prayed to God for help. God answered by telling the king and the people that they need not worry, for He would fight this battle for them.

The Bible tells us that the devil's agenda is to steal, kill, and destroy everything that he can, and we need to understand why this is his goal. We must realize that the devil's real enemy is God; however, because he is powerless against God, he attacks that which is closest to God's heart—mankind.

Satan grieves God's heart by attempting to harm us, as well as, trying to stop God's purposes from coming to pass. The devil desires to pierce God's heart by challenging God's creation to doubt His integrity. When we doubt God's Word, we are in a sense calling God a liar. Our relationship with God is based on our believing Him to be truthful.

Thought for Today

We must decide that God is truthful as Moses relates in Numbers 23:19, *"God is not a man, that He should lie, nor a son of man, that He should repent. Has he said, and will He not do? Or has He spoken, and will He not make it good?"*

Prayer Journal

_____

_____

_____

~ ~ ~ JANUARY 18 ~ ~ ~

"Be sober, be vigilant; because your adversary the devil walks about like a roaring lion, seeking whom he may devour. Resist him, steadfast in the faith, knowing that the same sufferings are experienced by your brotherhood in the world" (I Peter 5:8-9).

The Bible warns us that the devil *"walks about like a roaring lion, seeking whom he may devour."* We are also instructed to, *"resist him, steadfast in the faith."* We are promised in the Word that we have already been made more than conquerors through Christ; wherein, through Christ, we are assured the victory over all the attacks of the devil. While there are various weapons the devil uses, the Word promises that not one of them will be successful.

One of the weapons that the devil uses is delays. He tries to abort or postpone your miracle, knowing that His delays will weaken your faith and desire. Another weapon is deceit, as he tries to get you to believe his lies about your circumstances and future. We are to remember that the devil is the father of lies and that there is absolutely no truth in him. One of the devil's favorite weapons is distractions. He tries to break your focus through things such as: unproductive friendships, unworthy criticism, and unexpected negative circumstances. Take heed to Proverbs 4:27, *"Do not turn to the right or the left; remove your foot from evil."*

Thought for Today

Remember, the Word says you are more than a conqueror through Christ Jesus. The Bible says the attacks of the devil will never be successful. Regardless of what weapon the devil has tried to use against you be encouraged in the Word, for the Prophet Isaiah says *"No weapon formed against you shall prosper"* (Isaiah 54:17).

Prayer Journal

_____

_____

_____

~ ~ ~ JANUARY 19 ~ ~ ~

"Therefore, in all things He had to be made like His brethren, that He might be a merciful and faithful High Priest in things pertaining to God, to make propitiation for the sins of the people. For in that He Himself has suffered, being tempted, He is able to aid those who are tempted" (Hebrews 2:17-18).

Immediately after His baptism, Jesus was driven into the wilderness to face the devil, "one-on-one," for a period of forty days. Some might be tempted to think that because Jesus was the Son of God, the temptations and trials He faced in the wilderness with the devil were easy for Him to overcome. Nothing could be further from the truth. Jesus robed Himself in the flesh of a man and took upon Himself the frailty of that flesh. The temptations and trials were both real and hard to deal with. Another important factor to remember is that these trials were not unique to Jesus, but within their scope, they encompassed things common to all of us.

A logical question to ask is, "Why did Jesus need to face such temptations and trials?" The answer to this question is laden with promise for all of us. In order to identify with the temptations and trials common to man, Jesus had to be tempted with the same things that face us. Coming successfully through His trials, Jesus emerged as our faithful High Priest. Now in our temptations and trials, we can turn to Jesus and know He fully understands what we are feeling; therefore, we are more than conquerors, and we can conquer the sin that is trying to control us.

Thought for Today

Jesus understands everything you are experiencing because He has been there. He can be trusted to lead you through to victory.

Prayer Journal

_____

_____

_____

~ ~ ~ JANUARY 20 ~ ~ ~

"Immediately the Spirit drove Him into the wilderness. And He was there in the wilderness forty days, tempted by Satan, and was with the wild beasts; and the angels ministered to Him" (Mark 1:12-13).

There is no escaping the fact that trials are a part of each and every one of our lives. What seems so unfair, and thus hard to deal with, is that they seem to come at the wrong times. Just when we are experiencing relief from the last trial, something negative unexpectedly hits our life. Just when we are walking closer to God than ever before, adversity comes and shatters our serenity. The honest cry from our heart to God is, "Why now?"

As the Lord submitted Himself to His cousin, John the Baptist, to be baptized in the Jordan River, something wonderful happened. The Scripture tells us that as Jesus was coming up out of the water the heavens opened, the Holy Spirit descended upon Him, and the voice of His Father declared His love and approval of His Son for all to hear. Then, IMMEDIATELY, the Holy Spirit drove Jesus into the wilderness to be tempted by the devil.

Just as with our trials, the timing of this trial for Jesus seems to be all wrong. Yet, we must remember that behind each trial there was the underlying purpose to make Jesus our merciful and faithful High Priest. There is a purpose behind every one of our trials. That purpose is not only to make us into the image of Jesus, but it also involves helping others come through their trials in great victory.

Thought for Today

God has scheduled someone to enter your life that will need your experience to know how to come through their trials with victory.

Prayer Journal

_____

_____

_____

~ ~ ~ JANUARY 21 ~ ~ ~

"In this you greatly rejoice, though now for a little while, if need be, you have been grieved by various trials, that the genuineness of your faith, being much more precious than gold that perishes, though it is tested by fire, may be found to praise, honor, and glory at the revelation of Jesus Christ" (I Peter 1:6-7).

The Scripture instructs us to greatly rejoice in our trials. Even though this appears on the surface to be an impossible assignment, we are to look at the benefits the trials bring to us, and ultimately, to the cause of Jesus Christ in the earth. We must understand that the fire of trials will test our faith in God and the integrity of His Word. It is only in the testing of our faith, through our trials, that we come to the realization that our faith in God and His Word is the most valuable asset we have in life.

All of the world's gold cannot accomplish for us what our faith in God will accomplish. Through our trials, we discover that our faith is powerful and a very effective weapon against the attacks of the enemy that are used to destroy us. The question, of whether the exercise of our faith will work to gain us victory over our trials, is forever answered. Through the exercise of our faith in God, and in the integrity of His Word, people will notice a marked difference in our attitudes concerning our trials and how we deal with them—we will not have a "woe is me" attitude. Ultimately, God will receive His praise, honor, and glory, through the revelation of Jesus Christ in us.

Thought for Today

Remember that your trials will not last forever. The Scripture promises you that your trials are but *"now for a little while."*

Prayer Journal

_____

_____

_____

~ ~ ~ JANUARY 22 ~ ~ ~

"But may the God of all grace, who called us to His eternal glory by Christ Jesus, after you have suffered a while, perfect, establish, strengthen, and settle you" (I Peter 5:10).

Our tendency to vacillate in our Christian walk will prove to be extremely frustrating. One day we are enjoying a spiritual high, and the next day we are in a deep spiritual valley. One moment we are full of faith, and the next moment we are void of faith. One day we are confident that we are in the center of God's will, and the next day we haven't a clue as to what the will of God is. We rise to staggering heights of joy, only to plunge into caverns of despair and depression. We cry out to God and ask Him to help get us off of this emotional and spiritual roller coaster. God hears our cry for help and allows a trial to come into our lives. While a trial is the last thing that we think we need, and may even deem it to be unfair, it is actually a work of God's grace on our behalf.

This will be impossible to understand apart from knowing how God uses our trials to help deliver us from the emotional and spiritual roller coaster on which we seem to have reserved seating. Through our trials, God promises to perfect us. The word *"perfect"* means to complete. In other words, God will add what is needed to make our lives complete. We will be established in God's Word and our faith will be strengthened.

Thought for Today

God allows our trials and He will work through them to develop us in our Christian walk. As we faithfully apply the principles of the Word against our adverse circumstances, we will be strengthened in our faith and encouraged to trust God for the victory.

Prayer Journal

_____

_____

~ ~ ~ JANUARY 23 ~ ~ ~

"Looking unto Jesus, the author and finisher of our faith, who for the joy that was set before Him endured the cross, despising the shame, and has sat down at the right hand of the throne of God. For consider Him who endured such hostility from sinners against Himself, lest you become weary and discouraged in your souls" (Hebrews 12:2-3).

There are basically three ways that God will deal with our adverse circumstances. One way, is to remove us from the circumstances. Another way is to change our circumstances. Predominately, He deals with circumstances by bringing us victoriously through them. This will give credence to our testimony of the faithfulness of God to us and to His Word; wherein, God will be honored and glorified.

Jesus is our example of how to deal with adverse circumstances. We are instructed by the Scriptures to look at His example, for He is the beginning and the end of our faith. When we walk in faith, Jesus will bring to completion what He started. Jesus endured adversity with joy. He derived His joy from looking beyond His trial to the victory that His endurance would bring. He saw the defeat of the devil through His obedience, as well as, the reconciliation of mankind to God through His full payment for man's sin penalty. Jesus saw that through His suffering, He would be able to meet every need of mankind. We need to follow Christ's example of enduring our trials with joy.

Thought for Today

We must look beyond our adversity to what His victory will accomplish in us, and in the lives of others around us. This will enable us to endure our trials with joy.

Prayer Journal

_____

_____

_____

~ ~ ~ JANUARY 24 ~ ~ ~

"A man who has friends must himself be friendly, but there is a friend who sticks closer than a brother" (Proverbs 18:24).

Finding a true friend, one who is genuinely interested in your well-being and wants to relate to you for who you are, and not just for what you can do for them, is hard to find these days. A great number of people are so wrapped up in themselves that they only connect to others when they need something. Often, this connection is hidden behind the veil of friendship; however, strip away the perceived asset and the self-serving heart is exposed.

The hymn writer of old penned these words in one of the great hymns of the church, "What a friend we have in Jesus, all our sins and griefs to bear." There never has been, nor will there ever be, a friend like Jesus. Jesus is truly interested in a relationship with us for who we are, and not for what we can do for Him.

When you consider this concept, you will quickly realize there is nothing we can bring in the asset department to the friendship Jesus wants to establish with us. He is the one with all of the assets, while we are only loaded with liabilities. The commitment of friendship Jesus offers is deeper in its commitment than the love of a brother. Jesus has vowed to love us and to "stick with us" no matter what the circumstances. He is not a "fair-weather" friend.

Thought for Today

There is nothing we can do to make Him love us more than He already does, and there is nothing we can do to make Him love us less. Jesus not only offers to be our Savior, but if allowed, He wants to be our best friend.

Prayer Journal

_____

_____

_____

~ ~ ~ JANUARY 25 ~ ~ ~

"Let your conduct be without covetousness; be content with such things as you have. For He Himself has said, 'I will never leave you nor forsake you'" (Hebrews 13:5).

No one can truly understand the pain of rejection and heartache that separation inflicts on ones' soul unless they have experienced it personally. Unfortunately, most all of us have experienced this pain at one time or another in our lives. A sad commentary on our society is the shallowness of our commitments to one another. Marriage vows, though pledged in sacred honor, are broken with frightening ease. Children rise up in defiance to parental authority and renounce their relationship with the very people who, in love, have sacrificed so much. Parents abandon their God-given responsibility to their children out of hearts consumed with selfishness. Friends walk out on us when they perceive that relating to us is a liability rather than an asset.

Jesus is the only One you can trust to never stop loving you. The strongest bond known on the earth is the love of a parent. Yet, even if this bond of love should be broken, the Lord promises to fill the need of our heart. The Psalmist said in Psalms 27:10, *"When my father and my mother forsake me, then the Lord will take care of me."* Jesus tasted the bitter cup of rejection and separation on the Cross when His Father rejected and separated Himself from His only Son; thereby, we will never face the rejection of God.

Thought for Today

We may lose every earthly friendship but we will never be rejected or separated from Jesus and His love. The Lord promises to fill the needs of our heart—He has vowed to stay close to us!

Prayer Journal

_____

_____

_____

~ ~ ~ JANUARY 26 ~ ~ ~

"Seeing then that we have a High Priest who has passed through the heavens, Jesus the Son of God, let us hold fast our confession. For we do not have a High Priest who cannot sympathize with our weaknesses, but was in all points tempted as we are, yet without sin. Let us therefore come boldly to the throne of grace, that we may obtain mercy and find grace to help in time of need" (Hebrews 4:14-16).

How many times have we heard someone say, or have maybe even said ourselves, "You just don't understand what I'm feeling and what I'm going through?" Often, this statement is defensible and true as the person who is speaking to us, or to whom we are speaking, may not be able to remotely relate to our circumstances or feelings. However, there is someone to whom we can never make this statement or claim—His name is Jesus. Jesus is the only person Who can truly relate to us and fully understand our hurts and problems. Jesus knows firsthand the boundaries of our strengths and the vastness of our weaknesses. He robed Himself in the frailty of human flesh and was tempted and tried in all things common to man. However, He emerged from every trial and every temptation without compromising Himself or committing sin. This truth is vitally important to us, as now we have in Jesus someone who understands what we are feeling and what we are going through. As Oral Roberts so often reminds us, "Jesus has been where we are and He's felt what we are feeling."

Thought for Today

Today, with confidence, tell Jesus where it hurts for He will understand and help you. Always remember, He has already been down the road you are traveling!

Prayer Journal

_____

_____

_____

~ ~ ~ JANUARY 27 ~ ~ ~

"But, He, because He continues forever, has an unchangeable priesthood. Therefore He is also able to save to the uttermost those who come to God through Him, since He always lives to make intercession for them" (Hebrews 7:24-25).

Among the many duties of a priest in the Old Testament, was the responsibility to offer sacrifices for the atonement of the peoples' sins, as well as, faithfully intercede in prayer on the peoples' behalf. Even the most devout of priests had to eventually yield to the ending of their active priesthood. If the frailty of their flesh didn't preclude them from continuing in their sacred duties, then death would ultimately bring their activities to an end. Therefore, change in the priesthood was inevitable and continual. Inevitable and continual that is, until Jesus assumed His priestly duties.

A number of distinctions are noticeable in the priesthood of Jesus. Jesus did not offer a yearly sacrifice for the atonement of the sins of the people. He willingly offered Himself on the Cross once and for all, for the atonement of man's sin. Another distinction in Christ's priesthood is seen in its duration. His priesthood, and thus, His sacred duties are continual, never-ending, and eternally unchangeable. Therefore, anyone who personally accepts the priestly sacrifice of Jesus will receive the atonement for their sins and be eternally saved. This very day, seated in Heaven at the right of God the Father, Jesus is pleading our case in intercessory prayer.

Thought for Today

This very moment, Jesus is calling your name before the Father in prayer. He is a faithful High Priest, and He is forever unchangeable in His commitment to you.

Prayer Journal

_____

_____

_____

~ ~ ~ JANUARY 28 ~ ~ ~

"Therefore Eli said to Samuel, 'Go, lie down; and it shall be, if He calls you, that you must say, Speak, Lord, for Your servant hears.' So Samuel went and lay down in his place. Now the Lord came and stood and called as at other times, 'Samuel! Samuel!' And Samuel answered, 'Speak, for Your servant hears'" (I Samuel 3:9-10).

Young Samuel was awakened to the sound of someone calling his name. Assuming it was Eli, the elderly priest, he arose and quickly made his way to Eli's chamber, only to find that he had not called for him. Again, Samuel heard his name called and rose to see what Eli wanted of him. Again, Eli denied calling for him and sent him back to bed. When Samuel made his third entrance into his bed chamber, insisting he had heard Eli call for him, Eli realized that it was the Lord calling Samuel's name in the night. Eli instructed Samuel that the next time he heard his name called, to answer, *"Speak, Lord, for Your servant hears."* A few moments later, Samuel responded to the Lord when He called his name. Samuel was learning to hear and distinguish the Lord's voice from the voice of men.

Samuel thought he heard Eli's voice calling to him, so he arose and sought to serve and please Eli. Developing a "hearing ear" is extremely important; for like Samuel of old, we must learn to distinguish the Lord's voice from all the other voices we hear.

Thought for Today

The voice you hear is the one you will seek to serve and please. Just as Samuel needed to learn to distinguish between Eli's voice and God's voice, you need to learn to recognize the Lord's voice. The Lord is calling your name—are you hearing Him?

Prayer Journal

_____

_____

_____

~ ~ ~ JANUARY 29 ~ ~ ~

"Call to Me, and I will answer you, and show you great and mighty things, which you do not know" (Jeremiah 33:3).

Many Christians have bought into the lie that God does not personally speak to people today. Nothing could be further from the truth. Our God is a talking God and what He speaks is both relevant and life-changing. According to Scripture, God makes an attempt to speak to us every day. We read in Hebrews 3:7, *"Therefore, as the Holy Spirit says: 'Today, if you will hear His voice'"* The problem is not with God's desire or ability to speak: it is our lack of desire and ability to hear His voice. God promises to answer everyone who calls to Him. He is a loving heavenly Father that is always willing to reveal even more than what we had initially requested of Him.

There are a number of ways the Lord will speak to our hearts, which include: dreams, visions, thoughts, impressions, and through the vocal gifts of the Spirit. However, the number one way God continues to speak to us today is through His written Word. As we read and meditate on His Word, the Holy Spirit will enlighten, instruct, and bear witness to the truth of the Word. He will also show us how we can apply it to our daily living experiences. Whatever instrument the Lord may choose to use when speaking, it is imperative that we learn to hear His voice.

Thought for Today

It is our ability to hear His voice that will determine the level of obedience in which we walk before Him. Take the challenge of the Lord from Jeremiah 33:3 and ask Him a question. If you will pause for Him to speak, you will be amazed at what you will hear.

Prayer Journal

_____

_____

_____

~ ~ ~ JANUARY 30 ~ ~ ~

"Then I will give them a heart to know Me, that I am the Lord; and they shall be My people, and I will be their God, for they shall return to Me with their whole heart" (Jeremiah 24:7).

God's greatest desire is for us to truly come to know Him. When Adam and Eve lost their revelation of God in the Garden of Eden through their disobedience, God set out to reveal Himself again to the heart of mankind. One of the tragic by-products of sin was that man developed an unfounded fear of God the Father. Adam and Eve heard God approaching them in the Garden of Eden and attempted to hide from Him. When confronted with their behavior, they admitted to being afraid of Him. Adam and Eve no longer lived in the security of the Lord's love, mercy, and grace. They were suspicious of His every word and thus, lived in the insecurity that fear brings. How this must have grieved the heart of the Lord. His highest creation and most prized possession were afraid of Him and didn't even want to know Him.

One day, God whispered a word into the spirit of a prophet named Jeremiah telling him of a promised work He would do in the hearts of men. He said He would remove the fear from the heart of man and replace it with a deep desire to truly know God and His ways. The greatest desire of God for His creation still has not changed. Just as with Adam and Eve, He wants us to truly know Him and live in the security of His love, mercy, and grace.

Thought for Today

God's greatest desire is for us to know Him and the greatest need of man is to know God. We must remove all fear and suspicion from our hearts and ask Him to give us a desire to truly know Him.

Prayer Journal

_____

_____

_____

JANUARY 31

"Therefore the Lord said 'Inasmuch as these people draw near with their mouths and honor Me with their lips, but have removed their hearts from Me, and their fear toward Me is taught by the commandment of men'" (Isaiah 29:13).

God challenged Israel for the integrity of their worship. While He acknowledged that they were doing and saying all the right things, He accused them of doing so apart from any loving action of their hearts. They were not responding to the Lord out of loving hearts; they were exacting religious ritual that had been taught to them out of the traditions of men. They were physically in the right place, doing and saying the right things, but their hearts were not in the right place.

Deuteronomy 6:5 says, *"You shall love the Lord your God with all your heart, with all your soul, and with all your strength."* To love God with every fiber of our being is the mandate of God's Word to us. Actually, we are to employ all of the cravings and passions of our hearts in loving the Lord. We are to expend the sum of our intellect, creativity, and emotions in expressing our love to the Lord. We are to exhaust the whole of our strength in our loving responses to God, for anything less than this is unacceptable to the Father. If we are not careful, we will fall into the same error as the Israelites. We can be in the right place, doing, and saying the right things, but our hearts can be absent from the Lord's presence.

Thought for Today

Do you love the Lord with all your heart, all of your soul, and with all of your strength? What is the Lord's opinion? We have not worshiped until our hearts have made contact with the Lord.

Prayer Journal

_____

_____

_____

~ ~ ~ FEBRUARY 1 ~ ~ ~

"For I know the thoughts that I think toward you, says the Lord, thoughts of peace and not of evil, to give you a future and a hope" (Jeremiah 29:11).

You were conceived in the heart of God long before you were conceived in your mother's womb. God has a wonderful plan for your life. He has given you an assignment that will accomplish His purposes, as well as, bring you into total fulfillment in life. The Prophet Jeremiah wrote in Jeremiah 1:5, *"Before I formed you in the womb I knew you; before you were born I sanctified you; I ordained you a prophet to the nations."* Long before your parents called out your name for the first time, God whispered it in the courtroom of heaven. Isaiah 49:1 says, *"The Lord has called me from the womb; from the matrix of my mother He has made mention of my name."* While your arrival on the scene might have been a surprise to your parents, your arrival did not surprise God; for God scheduled your arrival into this generation.

You are special to the heart of God and are uniquely gifted. There never has been, nor will there ever be, anyone like you. You get upset over things that others care less about. You find pleasure in things that others view with indifference. Your reactions to circumstances are clues to your assignment for which God has gifted you. You are a walking solution to someone else's problem.

Thought for Today

You are an answer to someone's prayer. No wonder the devil is working overtime to discourage you as he tries to persuade you to quit doing the right thing. There isn't anyone like you. God's plan for your life is rich and will give you hope and a future.

Prayer Journal

_____

_____

_____

~ ~ ~ FEBRUARY 2 ~ ~ ~

"Then He came to Bethsaida; and they brought a blind man to Him, and begged Him to touch him. So He took the blind man by the hand and led him out of the town. And when He had spit on his eyes and put His hands on him, He asked him if he saw anything. And he looked up and said, 'I see men like trees, walking.' Then He put His hands on his eyes again and made him look up. And he was restored and saw everyone clearly" (Mark 8:22-25).

We judge a man's worth by looking at his exterior, while God judges a man's worth by his heart. We see his problems: God sees his potential. We see his offenses: God sees an offender who needs help. We see what's wrong: God sees what can be made right. We see his past failures: God sees his future successes.

One day a blind man approached Jesus requesting His healing touch. Jesus touched him and asked about his ability to see, to which the first reply of the blind man was, *"I see men like trees, walking."* In other words, he couldn't see very clearly. His statement describes the difference between our ability to see people and God's ability to see people. The truth is, like the blind man, we need the Lord to touch our eyes and let us see men as He does. It is only through His divine touch that we will be able to see past peoples' problems and see their hurts, fears, and needs.

Thought for Today

Seeing people through the eyes of Jesus will unlock His love and compassion within us. We will then be motivated to reach out to them in His perfect love. The fate and the well-being of people need to matter as much to us as it does to God. How is your eyesight?

Prayer Journal

_____

_____

_____

~ ~ ~ FEBRUARY 3 ~ ~ ~

"As obedient children, not conforming yourselves to the former lusts, as in your ignorance; but as He who called you is holy, you also be holy in all your conduct, because it is written, 'Be holy, for I am holy'" (I Peter 1:14-16).

There are two subjects a preacher can choose to speak on that will cause the congregation to get nervous and quiet. One subject is tithing: the other is holiness. When we measure our holiness next to God's, we get very discouraged and agree with Samuel, when he said in I Samuel 2:2, *"No one is holy like the Lord."*

We live with a faulty definition of holiness. We so often equate it to a very serious form of self-denial. We assume that to achieve holiness, we have to embrace a never-ending list of "thou shalt nots." One must realize that holiness is not a "self-help" project. No matter what we do, or don't do, we will never be able to transform our unholiness into God's holiness. Holiness is actually a work of the Holy Spirit within us. Holiness will bring about change in our inner desires, which in turn, will change our outward behavior. Holiness will then be reflected in our "changed attitudes," rather than in our "controlled behavior." Holiness is traditionally viewed in a negative light, in that, we perceive that God expects us to become something that we know we can not possibly achieve. You can rest assured, without God's intervention, you will not be able to achieve holiness.

Thought for Today

The commandment of God in Scripture to be *"holy,"* also carries a wonderful commitment from God. God will never command us to be something that He will not enable us to become.

Prayer Journal

_____

_____

_____

~ ~ ~ FEBRUARY 4 ~ ~ ~

"Are not five sparrows sold for two copper coins? And not one of them is forgotten before God. But the very hairs of your head are all numbered. Do not fear therefore; you are of more value than many sparrows" (Luke 12:6-7).

It was the custom of the vendors in front of the Temple to offer a special deal that would entice the worshipers to purchase their sacrifices from them. Actually, four sparrows were sold for two copper coins, and then the fifth sparrow was a free one. The fifth sparrow had no apparent value, as it was the give-away item.

Jesus used the illustration of the fifth sparrow to proclaim a tremendous truth regarding the value God places on us. Problems tempt us to believe that God has forgotten us. Jesus said that God remembers the fifth sparrow, and if God remembers the fifth sparrow, surely He will remember us. We are also tempted to believe that somehow, even if God does remember us, He must not be aware of our circumstances. Jesus assured us that God is so intimately acquainted with us, that He knows when a new hair grows on our head and when an old hair falls out.

When trouble strikes our lives, we sometimes have the feeling that no one cares about us—including God. Jesus addressed this negative feeling by stating that we are more valuable to God than many sparrows.

Thought for Today

You may feel like the fifth sparrow—worthless, forgotten, and unloved. However, God remembers you. He knows your situation and He cares about you. Whatever touches us touches God.

Prayer Journal

_____

_____

~ ~ ~ FEBRUARY 5 ~ ~ ~

"And we have known and believed the love that God has for us. God is love, and he who abides in love abides in God, and God in him...We love Him because He first loved us" (I John 4:16, 19).

Amazingly, one of the hardest things for people to believe is that God loves them. They have no trouble believing that God loves the whole world, but many times that belief is based on the fact that everyone else says He does. However, when it comes to God being emotionally involved with them, well, that is another matter. Many believe God has merely intellectually determined to love them, even though He isn't excited about having them in the family. After all, we tend to make mistakes and are given to huge mood swings in our relationship with Him. We believe that if God really does love us, He must feel that somehow He has been trapped into the deal. After all, what choice does He have for He is God, and as God, He is supposed to be a loving God whether He wants to be or not. Nothing could be further from the truth.

God's love is not an action that He chooses to exercise towards us—*"God IS love."* If God loves us with an independent action, then that love is subject to being earned by what we do or by what we don't do. However, because *"God IS love,"* He cannot help but love us. He loves us just as we are and is not moved by our actions. We do not have the capacity, in and of ourselves, to make our actions virtuous enough to earn His love.

Thought for Today

Since *"God IS love,"* there is nothing that we can do to make God love us more than He does. Conversely, there is nothing that will make Him love us less. God loves you and that's that!

Prayer Journal

_____

_____

_____

~ ~ ~ FEBRUARY 6 ~ ~ ~

"Then Moses answered and said, 'But suppose they will not believe me or listen to my voice; suppose they say, "The Lord has not appeared to you."' So the Lord said to him, 'What is in your hand?' He said, 'A rod.' And He said, 'Cast it on the ground.' So he cast it on the ground, and it became a serpent; and Moses fled from it. Then the Lord said to Moses, 'Reach out your hand and take it by the tail' (and he reached out his hand and caught it, and it became a rod in his hand)" (Exodus 4:1-4).

God told Moses what part He wanted him to play in His plan to deliver the Israelites from the wicked hand of Pharaoh. Moses was convinced that God had the wrong man. Moses put up an argument as to why he was a poor choice. Yet, with all of his pleading, God was not moved and Moses continued to be God's chosen instrument for the deliverance of Israel.

God settled the argument by asking Moses a question, *"What is in your hand?"* To Moses, it was just a shepherd's staff, but to God, it was something more powerful. God commanded Moses to cast his staff to the ground, and when He obeyed, he watched in amazement as the rod turned into a snake. Then God gave Moses a very difficult instruction, *"Reach out your hand and take it by the tail."* Moses knew that to do so, would leave the "business end" of the snake unattended. However, upon obeying God, the snake in Moses' hand became the *"rod of God."* Moses used this rod to part the Red Sea and deliver the Israelites.

Thought for Today

What may seem inadequate to you becomes great, when it is freely released into the hands of God the Father.

Prayer Journal

_____

_____

_____

~ ~ ~ FEBRUARY 7 ~ ~ ~

"And He called the twelve to Himself, and began to send them out two by two, and gave them power over unclean spirits. He commanded them to take nothing for the journey except a staff—no bag, no bread, no copper in their money belt—but to wear sandals, and not to put on two tunics" (Mark 6:7-9).

Jesus called His disciples together and gave them specific instructions regarding the ministry assignment He was giving them. He instructed them not to worry about their daily provisions. He wanted them to stay focused on their primary assignment and not become encumbered worrying about how to make "ends meet."

In the Sermon on the Mount, Jesus said that we were not to worry about our daily provisions, for our Heavenly Father knows that we need these things and He will not fail to provide them for us. We often abort ministry opportunites because of our concern for provision. We need to step out in faith and remain focused on our assignment, and leave the providing up to God.

Another encumbrance we must guard against is that of becoming over-committed. If we are not careful, we will become so busy doing "good things," that we will not be effective at anything we are doing. There are times we need to learn to say "no." Over-commitment will drain your resources of strength that you will need to do the "right things" that the Father will ask of you.

Thought for Today

Over-commitment requires you to decide what is expendable on your list of priorities. If you do not learn to say "no," you will sacrifice something you hold as a sacred priority for your life.

Prayer Journal

_____

_____

_____

~ ~ ~ FEBRUARY 8 ~ ~ ~

"Also He said to them, 'In whatever place you enter a house, stay there till you depart from that place'" (Mark 6:10).

Jesus gave this instruction to His disciples as He was preparing them for their next assignment. In this particular verse, Jesus is addressing our human tendency to quit before the work is done. He told the disciples, that when they arrived at their place of assignment, they were to stay there until the work was completed.

There are various reasons we are tempted to quit before we complete our assignment such as; our circumstances are difficult and unbearable, or we get tired and don't see any visible results. Paul told young Timothy, *"Fight the good fight of faith, lay hold on eternal life, to which you were also called and have confessed the good confession in the presence of many witnesses"* (I Timothy 6:12). We would do well to remember that fighting the good fight of faith requires engaging in warfare and spiritual struggle. In spiritual warfare, circumstances often are unbearable; however, we need to remember the instruction of Paul to Timothy, *"You therefore must endure hardship as a good soldier of Jesus Christ"* (II Timothy 2:3).

If you are getting tired of fighting, draw on His strength. If you don't see any visible results, remember your sight is limited but God's sight is limitless. We need to achieve endurance and stay focused on our assignment, leaving the results to God.

Thought for Today

Don't quit—anybody can do that. Champions achieve endurance and go the distance.

Prayer Journal

_____

_____

_____

~ ~ ~ FEBRUARY 9 ~ ~ ~

"And whoever will not receive you nor hear you, when you depart from there, shake off the dust under your feet as a testimony against them. Assuredly, I say to you, it will be more tolerable for Sodom and Gomorrah in the Day of Judgment than for that city" (Mark 6:11)!

In preparing the disciples for their assignment, Jesus warned them that not everyone was going to receive ministry from them. He told them that whenever they encountered disagreement and rejection, they were to simply move on to the next place.

It is a basic human desire to be liked. However, when it comes to ministry, we must remember that some people will not like us or agree with us. They won't like what we say, or what we do. They won't agree with why we said what we said, or why we did what we did. Bottom line…they don't like us and refuse to receive ministry from us. Remember that opposition does not invalidate us. Rather, it often serves as an indicator that we are on the right track. Jesus said that people in the world would hate us for no other reason other than the fact that we are His disciples. We must remember that we are not assigned to everybody; therefore, when we encounter opposition, we need to move on to the next person or place. Don't waste your time or energy trying to argue your position. If they don't receive your witness, look for someone who will.

Thought for Today

Don't take the rejection of others, personally. If you are living according to the precepts of God's Word, you can stand tall. Remember, it is not you they are rejecting—it is Jesus.

Prayer Journal

_____

_____

_____

~ ~ ~ FEBRUARY 10 ~ ~ ~

"And He called the twelve to Himself, and began to send them out two by two, and gave them power over unclean spirits...So they went out and preached that people should repent. And they cast out many demons, and anointed with oil many who were sick, and healed them" (Mark 6:7, 12-13).

Just before Jesus sent His disciples out on an evangelistic ministry assignment, He empowered them to accomplish their mission. The disciples took heed to the instructions Jesus gave them and they achieved great success. Miracles accompanied their ministry, as they followed the Lord's instructions.

When it comes to following instructions, we have a tendency to lean towards doing things our own way instead of the prescribed way. We all, at one time or another, have tried to assemble something without paying much attention to the enclosed instructions. We discover that we waste an incredible amount of time, have parts left over, and what we have assembled doesn't look anything like the picture on the box. We usually have to dismantle things and start over. Sheepishly, we decide to read the instructions. To our utter amazement, we find that following the instructions is much easier and will produce the intended results.

When it comes to ministry, the Lord expects us to follow His prescribed way. He will not give us license to alter His instructions. God has a plan and He expects us to follow it without exception.

Thought for Today

Attempting to alter God's plan is our way of telling Him that we have a better idea.

Prayer Journal

_____

_____

_____

~ ~ ~ FEBRUARY 11 ~ ~ ~

"And Abraham stretched out his hand and took the knife to slay his son. But the Angel of the Lord called to him from heaven and said, 'Abraham, Abraham!' And he said, 'Here I am.' So He said, 'Do not lay your hand on the lad, or do anything to him; for now I know that you fear God, since you have not withheld your son, your only son, from Me'" (Genesis 22:10-12).

Isaac was the miracle son of promise to Abraham and Sarah. One day, God asked the unthinkable of Abraham. He asked him to offer Isaac, his son of promise, on an altar of sacrifice as an act of worship. No doubt, Abraham struggled with this request. He must have thought to himself, "Why would God grant a miracle in giving me a son, whom I love more than life itself, and then ask for him back?" Though laden with questions and his heart wrenched with sorrow, Abraham determined to obey God. With his knife raised over the body of his son, Abraham heard the Lord calling for him to stop—he had passed the test. God wanted to see if His provision had taken His place in Abraham's heart.

Tragically, we often treat God like a vending machine. We only come to Him when we want something and after getting it, we turn and walk away. How many have promised God a deeper walk with Him, if He would but grant a particular request? However, when they receive the answer, they never follow through on their promise. God is a jealous God and will not allow His provision for us to ever take His place in our hearts.

Thought for Today

You need to evaluate where God is on your list of pursuits. God did not create anything that would have the capacity to take His place.

Prayer Journal

_____

_____

_____

~ ~ ~ FEBRUARY 12 ~ ~ ~

"Now therefore, thus shall you say to My servant David, 'Thus says the Lord of hosts 'I took you from the sheepfold, from following the sheep, to be ruler over My people, over Israel. And I have been with you wherever you have gone, and have cut off all your enemies from before you, and have made you a great name, like the name of the great men who are on the earth"'" (II Samuel 7:8-9).

God had said "no" to David's request to build the Temple. God's denial of his request was disappointing to David for it had been a long-time dream. However, God helped David deal with his disappointment by reminding him of how blessed he was. God reminded David, that it was He who had lifted David from being a shepherd of sheep to being king. God reminded David of how He had always been right there at David's side, helping him defeat his enemies. God reminded David that his claim to fame was not of his own doing, for it was God who had raised him up.

Life is full of disappointments. If we are not careful, we will become so focused on what is wrong, that we will forget to look at the things in our life that are right. The old hymn of the church reminds us, "Count your blessings, name them one by one; count your blessings, see what God has done." We need to take time each day and reflect on God's blessings. Everything that we have or every hope to have, or have ever accomplished or hope to accomplish, has come from the hand of the Lord our God.

Thought for Today

Count the blessings the Lord has given you. Any disappointment that you may presently be experiencing will fade in the light of His abundance.

Prayer Journal

_____

_____

_____

~ ~ ~ FEBRUARY 13 ~ ~ ~

"Then King David went in and sat before the Lord; and he said: 'Who am I, O Lord God? And what is my house, that You have brought me this far? For Your word's sake, and according to Your heart, You have done all these great things, to make Your servant know them'" (II Samuel 7:18, 21).

David loved to sit before the Lord and commune with Him. In these times of intimate fellowship, David would reflect on God's goodness and grace in his life. On this occasion, David was humbly inquiring of the Lord as to the reason he had been blessed so abundantly. David knew without a doubt that God had been good to him and his family, and he wanted to know why he deserved such blessings. David drew the conclusion that he had done nothing to deserve such wonderful treatment. David realized that God had blessed him for two reasons; for the declared purposes of His Word in the earth, and because He loved him.

We need to take time to reflect on God's goodness and grace. We also need to be reminded, that we have done nothing worthy of the Lord's blessings to us. Like David of old, we are blessed by God to accomplish the purposes of His Word; one of which is to let the world know that God is good and full of grace. We are blessed, simply because the Lord loves us and loves blessing us. Truly, God has abundantly blessed us, in spite of ourselves.

Thought for Today

We have been blessed by God so we can accomplish His will for our lives. God will continue to be good to you in spite of your faults, failures, and weaknesses. Every one of your blessings is a testimony of God's merciful love for you.

Prayer Journal

_____

_____

_____

~ ~ ~ FEBRUARY 14 ~ ~ ~

"Therefore You are great, O Lord God. For there is none like You, nor is there any God besides You, according to all that we have heard with our ears" (II Samuel 7:22).

David knew firsthand of the greatness of his God. From his early childhood he had contemplated the Lord's greatness, as he cared for his father's sheep and gazed upon the Lord's handiwork within creation. Whether he was looking at the vast expanses of the starry universe, or caressing the tender petals of the flowers that grew on the hillside, David saw the greatness of his God. David recounted in his heart the Lord's faithfulness to help him in times of trouble. He remembered how God helped him protect his sheep from the lions and bears, and helped him kill Goliath, the giant. God's greatness had been demonstrated over and over again.

In becoming intimately acquainted with God, David was firmly convinced that of all the gods that the peoples of the earth worshiped, his God was the only true and living God. David believed that no matter what the false claims of the heathen were about their gods, no god could begin to compare with his God. Not only did David believe these things in his heart, but he also took advantage of every opportunity to openly declare God's greatness. David's great God is our God! We need to remind ourselves of the times the Lord's greatness has been made manifest in our circumstances and boldly proclaim His greatness.

Thought for Today

Reflecting on God's greatness will not only increase our appreciation of His faithfulness, but it will strengthen our faith in Him. Tell someone today of the greatness of God.

Prayer Journal

_____

_____

_____

~ ~ ~ FEBRUARY 15 ~ ~ ~

"And who is like Your people, like Israel, the one nation on the earth whom God went to redeem for Himself as a people, to make for Himself a name—and to do for Yourself great and awesome deeds for Your land—before Your people whom You have redeemed for Yourself from Egypt, the nations, and their gods" (II Samuel 7:23)?

David remembered God's faithfulness to Israel, when He delivered them from Egypt. The Israelites were the beneficiaries of God's actions, but David realized that God was redeeming Israel for Himself. Through the demonstration of His power, God was declaring His greatness to the Israelites, to the Egyptians, and to the Egyptian gods. God wanted the Egyptians to know the Israelites had a God who would hear and answer their cries for deliverance. God also wanted them to know, that with their armies and gods combined, they could not stop Him from redeeming His people.

One of the ways the devil seeks to discourage us is to constantly try to make us believe that he has gained absolute control over an area of our lives. He tries to convince us that God will not be able to deliver us from his hand. The devil works overtime trying to convince us that God has not shown His faithfulness to us in the past; therefore, He will not be faithful to us now. This is a lie! God WILL hear our cry for His help; and God WILL, without fail, deliver us because of His abiding faithfulness.

Thought for Today

God wants us to know, as well as, those within our circle of influence, that all of the devils of hell cannot stop Him from being faithful to deliver us—He is a faithful God!

Prayer Journal

~ ~ ~ FEBRUARY 16 ~ ~ ~

"For You have made Your people Israel Your very own people forever; and You, O Lord, have become their God. Now, O Lord God, the word which You have spoken concerning Your servant and concerning his house, establish it forever and do as You have said. So let Your name be magnified forever, saying, 'The Lord of hosts is the God over Israel.' And let the house of Your servant David be established before You" (II Samuel 7:24-26).

David understood that in delivering Israel from the hands of the Egyptians, God not only wanted to stop their oppression, but He desired to establish a loving relationship with them. This has been God's goal for mankind from the very beginning of time, starting with Adam and Eve in the Garden, to this present day. God wants to have a relationship with man; whereby, there is the mutual exchange of genuine love and respect. God has never been interested in having a relationship that is only activated when we want something.

As David contemplated God's faithfulness to Israel, he saw that God was desirous of a relationship with the Israelites. This relationship would enable Him to declare them to be His own people and in return, they would declare Him to be their God. God desires to be in a loving relationship where He is loved and appreciated for being Himself and not just for what He can do.

Thought for Today

We belong to God through His right of purchase at Calvary. The benefits that come from this relationship with Him are only realized through the openness and willingness of our hearts to respond to His love and the sacrifice He made on the Cross.

Prayer Journal

_____

_____

_____

~ ~ ~ FEBRUARY 17 ~ ~ ~

"And now, O Lord God, You are God, and Your words are true, and You have promised this goodness to Your servant. Now therefore, let it please You to bless the house of Your servant, that it may continue forever before You; for You, O Lord God, have spoken it, and with Your blessing let the house of Your servant be blessed forever" (II Samuel 7:28-29).

David's regular practice was to reaffirm God's Lordship over his life and plans. No doubt, David was extremely disappointed over God's rejection of his plan to build the Temple. Building the Temple was something that David longed to do and yet, the Lord told him that He was giving that assignment to his son, Solomon. We see the maturity of David's spiritual life in his response to God over this matter. Instead of complaining and throwing a fit, David ignored the pain of his bruised heart and declared that God was his Lord. David declared that His decision would not only stand, but it would be embraced. David told the Lord to do whatever He wanted, and to do it in such a way that would bring Him pleasure.

It is easy to declare that Jesus is Lord, until He tells us "no" about something we really wanted. As long as he is doing things our way, we are pleased with His Lordship. However, Lordship is not limited ownership. Making Jesus the Lord of our lives requires the absolute and complete surrender of every decision that needs to be made. We must commit everything into His hands.

Thought for Today

The evidence of His Lordship is seen in our willingness to release Him to do whatever pleases Him. As His disciples, we must learn to be content with His decision and/or action.

Prayer Journal

_____

_____

_____

~ ~ ~ FEBRUARY 18 ~ ~ ~

"Those who are planted in the house of the Lord shall flourish in the courts of our God. They shall still bear fruit in old age; they shall be fresh and flourishing" (Psalms 92:13-14).

There are many rewards mentioned in the Scriptures for our being found faithful, especially as it applies to the work of the house of the Lord. Consider the word *"planted."* There is a vast difference between one who merely "attends" church and one whose life and talent is *"planted"* therein. An "attender" is usually on the receiving end of ministry. They rarely, if ever, contribute their resources or gifts back into the church and the ministry that God has assigned to that place. However, the one who is *"planted"* has their life rooted and grounded in the life-flow of the church. They can be counted on to be involved and they cheerfully invest their time, talent, and resources, into the church.

The Lord promises that those who are planted in His house will *"flourish."* They will grow and mature spiritually, as well as, enjoy the blessings of God. The Lord also promises that they will *"bear fruit in old age."* There will never be a time, or an attained age, that they will not be productive in their work for God. The world may force one to retire at a certain age, but not God! Finally, the Lord promises that those who are *"planted," "shall be fresh and flourishing."* The Word promises that they will retain the strength of their youth as they remain faithful in service for the Lord.

Thought for Today

Are you just an "attender," or are you *"planted"* in the house of the Lord? What contribution are you making to the life-flow of the church?

Prayer Journal

_____

_____

_____

~ ~ ~ FEBRUARY 19 ~ ~ ~

"For thus says the Lord of hosts: 'He sent Me after glory, to the nations which plunder you; for he who touches you touches the apple of His eye'" (Zechariah 2:8).

It would be truthful to say that we will never really know how much the Lord loves us until we get to heaven. While the evidence of His love daily surrounds us, we cannot comprehend the breadth, width, or the depth of His love for us. It was the demonstration of His love that brought us into His family, in that, Jesus died and paid for our sins to prove that God loves us.

Not only are we drawn into the family of God through His love, but we are also kept safe within the family, by His love. It is the consistent expression of God's love for us that brings us our daily provisions, maintains our health, touches our hurts, and speaks peace to our hearts and minds. God sees us through the eyes of love; thus, He can see potential that we cannot see within ourselves.

The expression, *"the apple of His eye,"* is a reference to the pupil within the eye which is very sensitive and tender when touched. We are told that we are *"the apple of His eye."* God's love for us is so great, that as far as He is concerned, whenever someone touches us, they have touched Him. Zechariah presents the picture of an enemy who is coming against God's beloved, and in doing so, is actually sticking his finger in God's eye.

Thought for Today

You are *"the apple of His eye."* You can rest assured, that when the devil starts messing with you, he is sticking his finger in the eye of God. God will deal with him—all because He loves you.

Prayer Journal

_____

_____

_____

~ ~ ~ FEBRUARY 20 ~ ~ ~

"And being assembled together with them, He commanded them not to depart from Jerusalem, but to wait for the Promise of the Father, 'which,' He said, 'you have heard from Me; for John truly baptized with water, but you shall be baptized with the Holy Spirit not many days from now'" (Acts 1:4-5).

The New Testament places a great deal of emphasis on our being filled with, and our living in, the fullness of the Spirit. To help the disciples understand what it would mean to be filled with the Holy Spirit, Jesus used the word *"baptized."* The meaning of the word baptism is one being immersed, like unto a sunken ship. Baptism also denotes the dipping of a piece of bread into a bowl of liquid, thus, saturating it. Baptism can also describe a garment that is dipped into dye so that it takes on a new appearance.

These three above meanings, associated with being baptized into the Person of the Holy Spirit, wonderfully describe our entry into the Spirit's fullness. Like a sunken ship, God desires to flood every compartment of our lives with the presence of the Spirit. Just as bread becomes saturated with the liquid into which it has been dipped, so God wants our lives to become saturated with the Holy Spirit's wisdom and power. To be baptized into the Holy Spirit will bring a change in our appearance and behavior. Just as the dying of a garment will forever change the appearance, our appearance will be changed by the Holy Spirit as He makes us like Jesus.

Thought for Today

Take time right now and ask the Spirit of God to fill you with His presence today. As He fills your life, every area will be radically affected and others around you will notice you have changed.

Prayer Journal

_____

_____

_____

~ ~ ~ FEBRUARY 21 ~ ~ ~

"But you shall receive power when the Holy Spirit has come upon you; and you shall be witnesses to Me in Jerusalem, and in all Judea and Samaria, and to the end of the earth" (Acts 1:8).

Just before Jesus ascended back into heaven to be seated at the right hand of the Father's throne, He gathered His disciples and gave them a ministry assignment. This ministry assignment involved taking the message of the Gospel of Jesus Christ to the ends of the earth; and they were to make disciples of those who would receive their message.

In Luke 24:49 we read, *"Behold I send the Promise of My Father upon you; but tarry in the city of Jerusalem until you are endued with power from on high."* Jesus knew that apart from their partnership with the Spirit, the assignment He had given them to be witnesses would be impossible to fulfill.

To describe the Holy Spirit's role, Jesus used the term *"come upon,"* in Acts 1:8. This is the same word He used in Luke 24:49, *"endued with."* Jesus was disclosing to the disciples that when the Holy Spirit had *"come upon"* them, they would be clothed in the enabling power of the Spirit. Today, Jesus wants the Holy Spirit to *"come upon"* everyone of us. We will never be successful in reaching to the ends of the earth with His message of saving grace, without first being clothed with the enabling power of the Spirit.

Thought for Today

As we allow the Holy Spirit to *"come upon"* us, He will clothe us in His supernatural enabling power. Our passion for the lost and our perspective on world evangelism will be forever changed.

Prayer Journal

_____

_____

_____

~ ~ ~ FEBRUARY 22 ~ ~ ~

"And it shall come to pass in the last days, says God, that I will pour out of My Spirit on all flesh; your sons and your daughters shall prophesy, your young men shall see visions, your old men shall dream dreams. And on My menservants and on My maidservants I will pour out My Spirit in those days; and they shall prophesy" (Acts 2:17-18).

On the Day of Pentecost, Peter stood on the porch of the Temple and preached to the vast throng of people that gathered to see what the commotion was about. Some of the people accused the disciples of being drunk, while others thought them to be crazy. As Peter began to preach about the death and resurrection of Jesus, he went on to explain that they were witnessing the fulfillment of prophecy that had been given generations ago through the Prophet Joel. Joel had prophesied that the Holy Spirit would be poured out on all who would receive Him.

In order to fully understand this concept of being "poured out," think of a dam which holds back a large body of water. As water is suddenly released from behind the dam, it rushes through with great power, generating enough electricity to light the nearby city. On the Day of Pentecost, God released His Holy Spirit with demonstrations of great power on those gathered in the upper room. God desires that same powerful release in us, as we allow Him to *"pour out"* His Holy Spirit on us.

Thought for Today

Just as water released from a dam generates electricity to give light to the nearby city, so the Spirit's release in our lives will become a source of light to others who have no hope.

Prayer Journal

_____

_____

_____

~ ~ ~ FEBRUARY 23 ~ ~ ~

"Now when the Day of Pentecost had fully come, they were all with one accord in one place. And suddenly there came a sound from heaven, as of a rushing mighty wind, and it filled the whole house where they were sitting. Then there appeared to them divided tongues, as of fire, and one sat upon each of them. And they were all filled with the Holy Spirit and began to speak with other tongues, as the Spirit gave them utterance" (Acts 2:1-4).

While gathered in the upper room, one-hundred and twenty disciples prayed and waited for the promised arrival of the Holy Spirit. They were not even sure what, or who, they were waiting for; but Jesus said to wait, and wait they would. Suddenly, the Holy Spirit was there among them. He came to each one of them individually and *"filled"* them with Himself. As each one was *"filled"* with the Holy Spirit, He unlocked their tongues and they began to worship God on a level they had never dreamed possible. A holy fountain of joy and praise began to bubble up from within their beings, demanding that they pursue this avenue of expression.

The verb *"filled"* in this passage of Scripture describes an "overflow." Literally, the disciples were experiencing an overflow of the Holy Spirit and His abundant resources. We are to be *"filled"* with the "overflow" of the Holy Spirit on a daily basis if we desire to do the assigned will of God on the earth.

Thought for Today

Tell the Holy Spirit you are available. The Holy Spirit's fullness means that there will always be more than enough of His resources available to us. When these supernatural resources are at work, we will then be able to accomplish the purposes of God.

Prayer Journal

_____

_____

_____

~ ~ ~ FEBRUARY 24 ~ ~ ~

"While Peter was still speaking these words, the Holy Spirit fell upon all those who heard the word" (Acts 10:44).

Jesus told the story of the prodigal son in order to reveal how great the Father's love and desire is towards His children. A tender moment in the story was when the father saw his young son walking towards home. The father ran and fell on his son's neck in a loving, grace-filled embrace. The love and desire of the father to be in right relationship with the son outweighed the sin and guilt of his repentant son. The father's forgiving embrace restored the son to his fellowship with the father and to his place in the family. This is the picture that is portrayed as the above passage of Scripture, describes the Holy Spirit's "falling upon" those to whom Peter was speaking. The verb *"fell upon,"* used in this passage, is the same one Jesus used in the story of the prodigal son, when He said, the father *"fell upon"* his son's neck.

We have all known what it is to be separated from God's fellowship as a result of our sin. With fellowship broken, God's purposes for our lives come to a grinding stop. We are robbed of our sense of self-worth, burdened with guilt, and void of His fulfilling joy. We need the Holy Spirit to "fall upon" us in His loving embrace and restore us to fellowship with God. When fellowship has been restored, He re-establishes our self-worth, lifts the load of guilt, and fills us with joy.

Thought for Today

The Holy Spirit has a great desire to "fall upon" us. His desire is to capture us in heaven's loving, grace-filled embrace which will bring us back into the fullness of God's intended purposes.

Prayer Journal

_____

_____

_____

~ ~ ~ FEBRUARY 25 ~ ~ ~

"Then they laid hands on them, and they received the Holy Spirit" (Acts 8:17).

In this passage of Scripture, a wonderful revival had broken out among the people in Samaria. The report of people receiving Jesus as their Lord and Savior so stirred the hearts of the apostles, they sent Peter and John to Samaria to minister to them.

Arriving in Samaria, Peter and John soon realized that while many had been saved, none had yet been baptized in the Holy Spirit. They laid their hands on them and the Scriptures tell us that they received the Holy Spirit. This passage of Scripture describes the "giving and receiving" process by which we interact with the Holy Spirit; thereby, we allow the Holy Spirit to interact with us.

Everything in our life ultimately relates to an act of our will. We have to choose, through an act of our will, to be faithful to our mates, honest with our employers, accessible to our children, and the list just begins there. This is especially true of our spiritual lives. Our openness to the will of God is determined solely by an act of our will. We have to allow the Holy Spirit access to the inner-most recesses of our heart for He wants to work the intended purposes of God within us. "Receiving" the Holy Spirit, and His intended work, will determine the level of His abundant life we will enjoy.

Thought for Today

Living in the fullness of the Holy Spirit, requires more than an experience with Him. It demands that we adopt an interactive lifestyle. This lifestyle is a direct result of an act of our will.

Prayer Journal

_____

_____

_____

~ ~ ~ FEBRUARY 26 ~ ~ ~

"But we all, with unveiled face, beholding as in a mirror the glory of the Lord, are being transformed into the same image from glory to glory, just as by the Spirit of the Lord" (II Corinthians 3:18).

On the Day of Pentecost, the same Holy Spirit that "over-shadowed Mary," resulting in the incarnation of Jesus, was made available to all who would willingly receive Him. There in the upper room, God poured heaven's glory into imperfect human vessels through the Holy Spirit. What the Spirit did in a biological sense within Mary, He wants to do in a spiritual sense within each of us. When we repent of our sins and receive Jesus as our Savior, the Holy Spirit gives birth to the "life of Christ" within our hearts. Then through the process of discipleship, the Spirit causes the "life of Christ" to grow within us; whereby, He is enabled to release the "power of Christ" through us in ministry.

"Beholding as in a mirror the glory of the Lord," is a reference to the full revelation of Jesus. This revelation encompasses, both the Old and New Testaments. It is in the "mirror of the Word," that we can see ourselves in comparison to the light of Jesus. This is not intended to embarrass us or to render us hopeless; nor is it meant to motivate us to imitate Jesus in the strength of our flesh. This comparison does, however, reveal to us the promise that we are being made into the image of Jesus, as our current state of progress is revealed.

Thought for Today

Only the Holy Spirit can make you into the image of Jesus. Quit working yourself into a frenzy. Submit yourself to the Holy Spirit and let Him do His perfect work!

Prayer Journal

_____

_____

_____

~ ~ ~ FEBRUARY 27 ~ ~ ~

"But we all, with unveiled face, beholding as in a mirror the glory of the Lord, are being transformed into the same image from glory to glory, just as by the Spirit of the Lord" (II Corinthians 3:18).

The term, *"unveiled face,"* has two dynamic meanings. First, it means "being totally honest" before the Lord. Often, we make the mistake of telling the Lord what we think He wants to hear from us, instead of telling Him what we are really feeling or thinking. If we are angry with Him, we are hesitant to express that sentiment for fear of the Lord's response to us. We must understand that God already knows exactly how we are feeling and whether or not we are telling Him the truth. Until we get totally honest, He cannot deal with our feelings and release us from the negative emotions that have enslaved us. Our honesty before the Lord is a key to the healing of our emotions.

The second meaning of *"unveiled face"* speaks of our being "completely open" before the Lord. The Holy Spirit's work is to conform us into the image of Jesus; thereby, reproducing His nature and character in our lives. The work of the Holy Spirit can only be accomplished if we are willing; therefore, we are called to a lifestyle of remaining open to the working of the Holy Spirit. We must always guard against the tendency to shut-down and retreat when the work of the Holy Spirit gets too uncomfortable.

Thought for Today

The job of the Holy Spirit is to make us into the image of Jesus. At times we may be tempted to be indifferent and/or disobedient to Him. That is a dangerous place to be, as it is the same as telling Him to "be quiet and leave me alone."

Prayer Journal

_____

_____

_____

~ ~ ~ FEBRUARY 28 ~ ~ ~

"And it happened, while Apollos was at Corinth, that Paul, having passed through the upper regions, came to Ephesus. And finding some disciples he said to them, 'Did you receive the Holy Spirit when you believed?' So they said to him, 'We have not so much as heard whether there is a Holy Spirit'" (Acts 19:1-2).

It was of deep concern to the Apostles that every believer would not only receive Christ as their Savior, but that they would also receive the Holy Spirit and live in His fullness. At Ephesus, Paul found believers who had received Christ and had been baptized, but they had not received the infilling of the Spirit. In essence, Paul asked if they had received the Holy Spirit, for he knew that this would empower them for ministry and everyday living. Paul's question is still relevant today. Perhaps, you know you are saved, but you haven't asked Jesus to fill you with the Holy Spirit. His infilling is received in the same manner you received Christ as your Savior. You must ask Jesus to fill you, and then believe that you will receive this gift which will enable you to live in His power.

In either case, take a moment and pray the following: "Dear Lord Jesus, I want to follow You and know both the 'power of the Cross' and the 'power of the Spirit.' I want to grow in the dimensions assigned for my life as I move in the Spirit's power. I want to receive Him as Your Word instructs; and I ask You to fill me with the Holy Spirit and let my life flow with His power. As I enter into praise, I gratefully receive Your gift—Thank You!"

Thought for Today

Renew your commitment to walk with the Holy Spirit in all of His fullness and gifts. He wants to reveal His power to you.

Prayer Journal

_____

_____

_____

~ ~ ~ MARCH 1 ~ ~ ~

"For You, Lord, have made me glad through Your work; I will triumph in the works of Your hands. O Lord, how great are Your works! Your thoughts are very deep" (Psalms 92:4-5).

The Psalmist David knew his frailties and acknowledged that within himself, he was limited in the scope of his ability to work things out. Yet, the Psalmist knew that the works of God on his behalf were great, and they caused him to rejoice. David lived in the assurance that he would triumph over every enemy and every challenge that he faced, or ever would face in the future.

The secret to David's confidence was rooted in his ability to focus on what the Lord was doing on his behalf. David chose not to focus on what the devil was attempting to work against him. We must place our gaze on Jesus, the author and finisher of our faith, and on what He is doing for us. We will then be enabled to rejoice in the works of His hands. Hebrews 12:1-2 tells us, *"Therefore we also, since we are surrounded by so great a cloud of witnesses, let us lay aside every weight, and the sin which so easily ensnares us, and let us run with endurance the race that is set before us, looking unto Jesus, the author and finisher of our faith, who for the joy that was set before Him endured the cross, despising the shame, and has sat down at the right hand of the throne of God."*

Thought for Today

Remember, in every battle you face, God is on your side. Like David of old, take a moment to remember His faithfulness to you. Spend time and rejoice in His mighty works, for He will help you triumph over every one of your enemies and over every one of your challenges.

Prayer Journal

_____

_____

_____

~ ~ ~ MARCH 2 ~ ~ ~

"But God, Who is rich in mercy, because of His great love with which He loved us, even when we were dead in trespasses, made us alive together with Christ (by grace you have been saved), and raised us up together, and made us sit together in the heavenly places in Christ Jesus, that in the ages to come He might show the exceeding riches of His grace in His kindness toward us in Christ Jesus" (Ephesians 2:4-7).

At one time or another, we have all heard someone say to us, or to someone we know, "Don't worry, keep looking up." This statement is usually a tenderhearted attempt to lift someone's spirits as they go through tough times. If this has ever been said to you, you know that it brings about as much encouragement as someone saying, "Every cloud has a silver lining."

Our spirits can only be lifted when we learn that the Lord invites us to view our problems in light of His ability to solve them. The Bible says that God *"raised us up together, and made us sit together in the heavenly places."* We may not fully understand what all that means, but one thing is for sure, we should begin to see our problems from His divine perspective. Our perspective of our challenges will change if we take advantage of seeing things from God's viewpoint. What appears to be gigantic and unsolvable to us, is tiny and of no challenge to God.

Thought for Today

No matter how large your problem looks to you at this moment, it is small when compared to God's ability. See your problem from God's perspective. Measure your problem against His ability. Trust Him—He has everything under control!

Prayer Journal

_____

_____

_____

~ ~ ~ MARCH 3 ~ ~ ~

"For when we were still without strength, in due time Christ died for the ungodly. For scarcely for a righteous man will one die; yet perhaps for a good man someone would even dare to die. But God demonstrates His own love toward us, in that while we were still sinners, Christ died for us" (Romans 5:6-8).

God loves us; and considering who we are and what we have done, it is utterly amazing and will never be comprehended. Beginning with Adam and continuing through the generations, God has been rejected and ignored; cursed and blamed; and yet, He still loves us. This kind of love is a mystery. No one would blame God if He threw up His hands in disgust and walked away, never looking back. Fortunately, God never asks us to understand why He loves us, He just wants us to rest assured that He does.

When it comes to punishment, no one wants to stand in another's stead: no one, that is, except Jesus. God didn't just give lip service to His claim of loving us; He proved it in one dynamic demonstration that will stand as proof for all of eternity. He gave His Son, Jesus, to pay our sin penalty so we could escape His judgment of wrath on our sin. How can you explain such an action? Why would Jesus trade places with us? While we will never comprehend why God loves us, we can rejoice in the fact that we are loved by Him.

Thought for Today

It does not matter what you have done in the past, or how many times you have failed God; remember that God loves you! He is waiting for you to make a decision. Sing again the little song, "Jesus loves me, this I know!" Then smile.

Prayer Journal

___

___

___

~ ~ ~ MARCH 4 ~ ~ ~

"Christ has redeemed us from the curse of the law, having become a curse for us (for it is written, 'Cursed is everyone who hangs on a tree')" (Galatians 3:13).

God never intended for the Israelites to live under the Old Testament Law. He knew that in the strength of man's flesh, it would be impossible for them to keep the Law. God's ultimate desire for man was that he would perpetually live under His covenant of grace. The Israelites quickly discovered that keeping the Law was an impossible task; for to fail at one point of the Law, would render one guilty of transgressing the entirety of the Law.

The failed Law commanded a three-pronged curse: poverty, sickness, and death. Jesus came to redeem us from the curse of the failed Law. He loosened poverty's grip with every stinging blow He received from the whip of the Roman soldiers. He purchased our healing by virtue of those stripes. *"Beloved, I pray that you may prosper in all things, and be in health, just as your soul prospers"* (III John 2). The ultimate penalty of the failed law from which Jesus redeemed us, was death. Death not only encompassed the physical body, but the spiritual man as well. However, through the shed blood of Jesus, the curse of death has been broken. We must make the choice to receive His gift of eternal life.

Thought for Today

If poverty, sickness, and death are stalking your life, they are trespassing on God's property! Boldly rebuke their presence in the name of Jesus and stand on the promises of God's Word. God sent His Son, Jesus, so that you would be redeemed from curse of the Law and its consequences.

Prayer Journal

_____

_____

_____

~ ~ ~ MARCH 5 ~ ~ ~

"Christ has redeemed us from the curse of the law, having become a curse for us (for it is written, 'Cursed is everyone who hangs on a tree'), that the blessing of Abraham might come upon the Gentiles in Christ Jesus, that we might receive the promise of the Spirit through faith" (Galatians 3:13-14).

Through the death of Jesus we are redeemed from the curse of the Law. Now through Christ, and the exercise of our faith, we can be free from the hopelessness of poverty, the pain of sickness, and free from the fear of death. In redeeming us, Jesus liberated us from the evils of the curse; and positioned us to receive the blessings of Abraham; and enabled us to walk in victory.

In Genesis 24:1 we read, *"Now Abraham was old, well advanced in age; and the Lord had blessed Abraham in all things."* God blessed Abraham's health, his finances, his family, his business dealings, and everything else that was of concern to Abraham. This verse opens the floodgates of possibilities for enjoying the blessings of God in our life. God abundantly blessed Abraham in every area of his life, and the Scriptures tell us that it is God's intention to have the abundant blessings of Abraham come upon us. Therefore, we should not settle for anything less, for God wants to bless us just as He blessed Abraham. The blessings that Abraham enjoyed throughout his life were the direct result of his faith in God and his daily obedience to God's instructions.

Thought for Today

Jesus' death on the Cross positioned us to receive Abraham's blessings; but like Abraham, we must walk by faith and in absolute obedience to make them a reality.

Prayer Journal

_____

_____

_____

~ ~ ~ MARCH 6 ~ ~ ~

"To console those who mourn in Zion, to give them beauty for ashes, the oil of joy for mourning, the garment of praise for the spirit of heaviness; that they may be called trees of righteousness, the planting of the Lord, that He may be glorified" (Isaiah 61:3).

The Holy Spirit supernaturally showed the Old Testament Prophet, Isaiah, the life and ministry of Jesus the Messiah. In doing so, Isaiah became acquainted with the tender compassion that would characterize Jesus' life. Jesus came so He could take all the things that were wrong, and not in line with the Word of God, and make them right. Except among the people of His own hometown, Jesus touched and changed the lives of people everywhere He ministered: He healed the sick, raised the dead, fed the hungry, lifted guilt and shame from those who had failed, gave hope where all hope was gone, replaced sighing with a song of praise, and so much more.

We could never list everything Jesus said or accomplished in His brief lifetime. The expressions of God's love for us, exceeds the scope of our understanding. The gifted songwriter of yesterday, so clearly expresses the love of God: "Could we with ink the oceans fill and were the skies of parchment made; Were every stalk on earth a quill and every man, a scribe by trade; To write the love of God above, would drain the oceans dry; Nor could the scroll contain the whole, though stretched from sky to sky." Oh, how great and vast is God's love for us!

Thought for Today

We cannot speak with authority of everything Jesus has done for others, but we can proclaim the difference His love has made in our own lives.

Prayer Journal

_____

_____

_____

~ ~ ~ MARCH 7 ~ ~ ~

"My son, give attention to My words; incline your ear to My sayings. Do not let them depart from your eyes; keep them in the midst of your heart; for they are life to those who find them, and health to all their flesh" (Proverbs 4:20-22).

Most of us have faced the harsh reality that we need to do something about controlling our weight for the sake of our health. As a young man, I was concerned that I did not weigh enough because I could actually see my ribs. No matter how much I ate, I couldn't gain a single pound. Then something changed and the few pounds that I had been seeking came and brought a lot of "friends." As we all know, the secret to weight management is largely reliant upon developing a proper diet, coupled with consistent exercise, which will result in enjoying better health.

Spiritual health is derived in much the same way. We must discipline ourselves to develop a proper diet of "feeding" on the Word of God. Our diet of "feeding" must be coupled with a consistent exercise program of "heeding" the Word we have fed on. For many Christians, the only time they read or hear the Word is in the sermon on Sunday. They are starving themselves spiritually, and as a result, they are very weak spiritually. Spiritual health also has an impact on our physical health. A daily diet of the Word promotes good health in our minds and bodies.

Thought for Today

The challenge is not in recognizing the benefit that can be derived from a proper and balanced diet of daily "feeding" on the Word. The challenge always lies in disciplining ourselves to develop a DAILY HABIT of "feeding" and "heeding" the Word of God.

Prayer Journal

_____

_____

_____

~ ~ ~ MARCH 8 ~ ~ ~

"Through Your precepts I get understanding; therefore I hate every false way. Your Word is a lamp to my feet and a light to my path" (Psalms 119:104-105).

There are a multitude of benefits derived from daily interacting with the Word of God. The Psalmist declared that he received the direction for his life from studying God's Word. It was through the Word that he came to understand the difference between the ways that were right in the Lord's eyes and, consequently, the ways that were displeasing to Him. He believed the Word directed one's immediate steps, as well as, reveal the distant future.

The Word serves as *"a lamp to my feet and a light to my path."* This represents a picture of one walking down a dark path and holding a lantern to his side at arm's length. There is enough light cast to allow one to take the next step in safety, as well as, allowing one to see far enough down the path so that he may choose his direction wisely. The Word details for us specific instructions for daily living. In the light of the Word, we are shown each step to take that will keep us in the center of God's will. Through the Word, we are also shown the course in which the Lord will direct our lives. Without our interaction with the Word, we would be void of direction for today and discernment for tomorrow. We must always keep in mind that steps taken today, determine how safely we reach tomorrow's destination.

Thought for Today

When we daily read God's Word, we make a statement to God, "Your Word is a foundational priority in all matters of my life." To walk in the Word, is to walk in perpetual safety.

Prayer Journal

_____

_____

_____

~ ~ ~ MARCH 9 ~ ~ ~

"The law of the Lord is perfect, converting the soul; the testimony of the Lord is sure, making wise the simple" (Psalms 19:7).

You probably don't remember what you ate for lunch three months ago. Whether or not you remember your specific meal, you do know that it provided nourishment to get you through that day; and unseen to the eye, it promoted the process of life that provides for the needs of your body. Daily feeding on the Word works in much the same way, for it promotes spiritual health and well-being. We may not remember what we read in the Word three months ago; however, what was read was taken by the Holy Spirit and hidden in our hearts in the form of "wisdom on deposit" and this provides our daily spiritual nourishment. This wisdom also becomes a resource from which the Holy Spirit can bring the Word to our remembrance in times of need.

When David used the words, *"making wise the simple,"* he was not demeaning anyone in the sense of calling them ignorant; rather, he was making an honest reference to one who is "inexperienced." *"Making wise the simple,"* is a promise to us from God. This wonderful promise assures us, that in matters in which we are inexperienced, the Word will supernaturally give us wisdom to respond correctly.

Thought for Today

If we will commit to daily reading and meditation of the Word, we will place "wisdom on deposit." The Holy Spirit will bring this wisdom to our remembrance when needed in our life experiences. "Wisdom on deposit" nourishes our spirits and provides spiritual strength and wisdom for living.

Prayer Journal

_____

_____

_____

~ ~ ~ MARCH 10 ~ ~ ~

"Only be strong and very courageous, that you may observe to do according to all the law which Moses My servant commanded you; do not turn from it to the right hand or to the left, that you may prosper wherever you go. This Book of the Law shall not depart from your mouth, but you shall meditate in it day and night, that you may observe to do according to all that is written in it For then you will make your way prosperous, and then you will have good success. Have I not commanded you? Be strong and of good courage; do not be afraid, nor be dismayed, for the Lord your God is with you wherever you go" (Joshua 1:7-9).

Joshua understood that the promise of God's presence and the fulfillment of His promises, were directly tied to His precepts found in the Word. Joshua knew that the Lord would not accept partial obedience, nor would the Lord allow him to alter His Word to make it fit his desires. It was clear from the Lord's instructions to Joshua, that in order for the Word to work out the designed purposes in his life, it must dominate his thoughts and words. When Joshua allowed the Word to be the dominate force in his life, then, and only then, would he be led by the Word into the success and prosperity in life which God had promised.

It is undeniable that the Word of God promises us prosperity and success in life; however, these promises will be determined by our willingness to walk in absolute obedience to God's Word.

Thought for Today

The promise of our success in life will be realized on the same terms as given to Joshua. We are to perpetually keep the Word of God in our thoughts and on our lips, and then, let it work.

Prayer Journal

_____

_____

_____

~ ~ ~ MARCH 11 ~ ~ ~

"Oh, that my ways were directed to keep Your statutes! Then I would not be ashamed, when I look into all Your commandments... How can a young man cleanse his way? By taking heed according to Your word. With my whole heart I have sought You; Oh, let me not wander from Your commandments! Your Word I have hidden in my heart that I might not sin against You" (Psalms 119:5-6, 9-11)!

We have all made mistakes that have brought pain and shame to ourselves, and sometimes to those we love the most. While we cannot go back in time and undo what has been done, we can set some disciplines in place that will help prevent our making future mistakes and suffering the shame of our failures. We must make a significant decision and follow it through as we make a commitment to embrace the application of God's Word to every area of our lives. If we will consult the Word of God regarding every decision, every thought, and for the determination of every action, we will avoid the confusion that surrounds us when making embarrassing mistakes.

God's Word will keep us pure in our pursuits. The Word acts as a searchlight that shines inward: prompting, exposing, adjusting, correcting, and instructing us. If we will persistently pursue the Word it will purify us from the stain and residue of sin, and will act as a preventative against our participation in sin.

Thought for Today

The evangelist, Dwight L. Moody once stated, "The Bible will keep you from sinning and sinning will keep you from the Bible." These are wise words for the soul concerning the Word of God and its power in your life.

Prayer Journal

_____

_____

_____

~ ~ ~ MARCH 12 ~ ~ ~

"Assuredly, I say to you, this generation will by no means pass away till all things take place. Heaven and earth will pass away, but My words will by no means pass away. But take heed to yourselves, lest your hearts be weighed down with carousing, drunkenness, and cares of this life, and that Day come on you unexpectedly. For it will come as a snare on all those who dwell on the face of the whole earth. Watch therefore, and pray always that you may be counted worthy to escape all these things that will come to pass, and to stand before the Son of Man" (Luke 21:32-36).

When instructing His disciples in the matters pertaining to His second coming, Jesus reminded them to pay strict attention to His Word. He revealed the value of heeding His Word, in that, if the disciples would do so, it would keep them from becoming entangled in the moral decline that would grip all of the earth.

We are living in a time in history where spiritual darkness has fallen over the entire earth like a smothering blanket. The indulgence and acceptance of carnal lusts has almost completely erased the lines of decency and morality upon which our nation was founded. As Christians, we are not immune to carnality. However, our only hope of remaining pure and alert to Christ's return will be found in the Word of God.

Thought for Today

The Word keeps us sensitive and alert in our expectation of the Lord's promised return. Our daily participation in the Word is our only hope of escaping the temptation of being lulled into carnality and the sensual indulgences that our society declares to be normal.

Prayer Journal

~ ~ ~ MARCH 13 ~ ~ ~

"Surely He shall deliver you from the snare of the fowler and from the perilous pestilence. He shall cover you with His feathers, and under His wings you shall take refuge; His truth shall be your shield and buckler" (Psalms 91:3-4).

The Psalmist David was completely confident of the Lord's ability to protect him at all times. *"He shall cover you with His feathers and under His wings you shall take refuge,"* is a picture of a mother hen gathering her young chicks under her wings for their protection. Jesus used this comforting analogy as He overlooked the city of Jerusalem and He described His desire towards the people within that beloved city. David also knew that the secret of living in the Lord's constant and protective care was tied to his own personal embrace and acceptance of the Word.

The exercise of our faith is the fundamental means by which we resist and shield our lives from the devil's attacks. Our faith is a gift from God; however, it is forged and fashioned in only one way—by hearing His Word. Paul tells us in Romans 10:17, *"So then, faith comes by hearing and hearing by the Word of God."* We must make the Word the foundational footing on which we build. It must become the standard of measurement by which everything in life, both now, and for all of eternity, is gauged.

Thought for Today

When we hear something from the Word, we are guilty of saying, "Oh, I've heard that before." Faith doesn't come from our having "heard" but from our continually *"hearing."* To keep *"hearing"* the Word, will perpetuate the building of your faith. There is no other way for faith to be built! Set your heart to hear His Word!

Prayer Journal

_____

_____

_____

~ ~ ~ MARCH 14 ~ ~ ~

"Watch therefore, for you do not know what hour your Lord is coming...Therefore you also be ready, for the Son of Man is coming at an hour you do not expect" (Matthew 24:42, 44).

Jesus' first sermon and His last sermon, share the same themes. Jesus spoke of the certainty of His return, the finality of His judgment, and the need to be prepared for His return. Christ's words of warning to the disciples, *"Watch therefore,"* are still relevant. We must remain in a state of readiness for the Lord's return. We must be prepared to miss hell and gain heaven.

The story is told of Sir Ernest Shackleton and his Antarctic expedition, and due to difficulties, he had to return to England. He left some of his men on Elephant Island with the promise of his speedy return. Circumstances beyond his control delayed his return and by the time he was able to make the journey, the sea was frozen; thereby, closing his access to Elephant Island. He made three, unsuccessful attempts to rescue his men. On his fourth attempt, the ice broke and he navigated a narrow channel to the island. To his amazement, he found his men packed and ready to leave. When asked how they knew the day of his return, they replied, "We didn't know when you would return, we just knew you would. So every morning, we packed our gear thinking today might be the day you would return and take us home."

Thought for Today

Are you ready for the Lord's return? Don't let the delay in His return dull your anticipation and preparation for this promised event. Like Shackleton's men, live as though today is the day He is coming back to take us to our eternal home.

Prayer Journal

_____

_____

~ ~ ~ MARCH 15 ~ ~ ~

"When the Son of Man comes in His glory, and all the holy angels with Him, then He will sit on the throne of His glory. All the nations will be gathered before Him, and He will separate them one from another, as a shepherd divides his sheep from the goats" (Matthew 25:31-32).

Jesus spoke often of His return to earth to gather His people unto Himself and fulfill His promise to take them to their new home in heaven. In speaking of His return, Jesus left no room for debate as to the certainty of this fact. Approximately, $1/20^{th}$ of the New Testament addresses His return. There are over 300 specific references to His return, while 23 out of the 27 books of the New Testament contain proclamations of it. The return of Jesus Christ is not a "maybe," His return is "absolutely—for sure!"

Jesus does not reveal the time or day of His return, but He does describe what that precious day will be like when He returns in all of His splendor and majesty. On this great day, everyone who has ever drawn a breath will be represented in this gathering out of every nation, tribe, tongue, color, and creed. Standing side by side will be kings and peasants, the rich and poor, as well as, the young and the old. What a sight this will be to behold. As intriguing as the gathering of the nations will be, it will not begin to match the regal splendor of Christ, Himself. Jesus will be radiant in glory, magnetic in power, and attended by angels.

Thought for Today

In that glorious and long awaited moment, our eyes will behold the return of our Savior and we will hail Him as King of Kings and Lord of Lords. Jesus is coming back. Don't ever doubt it!

Prayer Journal

_____

_____

_____

~ ~ ~ MARCH 16 ~ ~ ~

"All the nations will be gathered before Him, and He will separate them one from another, as a shepherd divides his sheep from the goats. And He will set the sheep on His right hand, but the goats on the left. Then the King will say to those on His right hand, 'Come, you blessed of My Father, inherit the kingdom prepared for you from the foundation of the world.'...Then He will also say to those on the left hand, 'Depart from Me, you cursed, into the everlasting fire prepared for the devil and his angels'" (Matthew 25:32-34, 41).

On the day of the Lord's return, there will be great rejoicing on one hand and on the other hand, there will be great sorrow. Jesus said that on this day, He will divide the people as one separates the sheep from the goats. One group will stand on His right side and He will usher them into heaven where they will enjoy their eternal rewards. The group standing on His left side will be banished to their eternal punishment in hell.

On this day, great cries of anguish and sorrow will fill the air; husbands and wives will be separated, parents and children will be separated, as well as, brothers, sisters, and friends. Every man, woman, and child, that has reached the age of accountability, will be granted their choice regarding eternity. Our eternal destiny is solely our choice, and God loves us enough not to overrule it.

Thought for Today

Are all of your loved ones saved? Will they be standing by your side at Christ's right hand, waiting to be ushered into Heaven's eternal reward? If not, recommit your heart to make sure they are eternally secure in the saving love of Christ Jesus our Lord.

Prayer Journal

_____

_____

_____

~ ~ ~ MARCH 17 ~ ~ ~

"For God did not appoint us to wrath, but to obtain salvation through our Lord Jesus Christ, who died for us, that whether we wake or sleep, we should live together with Him" (I Thessalonians 5:9-10).

The Scriptures tell us that it is not God's will for anyone to suffer His wrath. He desires that everyone would receive His gift of love and salvation through receiving Jesus as their Lord and Savior. However, while it may be God's desire for us to receive salvation, it still remains our choice. God invites us to love Him. In the Word, God explains the benefits of loving Him; He outlines the promises associated with loving Him; and spells out the consequences for not loving Him. God sent His Son to pay our sin penalty for He wanted us to understand the Father's love for us and how we are to love Him in return.

The freedom of choice is a God-given right to everyone. We are free to choose whether we will spend eternity in heaven with God, or in hell without God. Someone can survive the wrong choice of a job, a mate, a friend, or a career; but no one will survive the wrong choice of eternal destiny. Some accuse God of being an unjust God because He allows people to go to hell. Yet, how can God be any more just than He is? He is simply honoring the choices we have personally made.

Thought for Today

We cannot be casual concerning the eternal destinies of our loved ones and friends. We must ask God to present us with an opportunity to tell them about Jesus. Eternal issues must be taken seriously, for there is a judgment coming.

Prayer Journal

_____

_____

_____

~ ~ ~ MARCH 18 ~ ~ ~

"And the Lord said: 'I have surely seen the oppression of My people who are in Egypt, and have heard their cry because of their taskmasters, for I know their sorrows. So I have come down to deliver them out of the hand of the Egyptians, and to bring them up from that land to a good and large land, to a land flowing with milk and honey, to the place of the Canaanites and the Hittites and the Amorites and Perizzites and the Hivites and the Jebusites'" (Exodus 3:7-8).

The Israelites were enslaved by the Egyptians and their cry for help was heard. Their bondage bothered God and He called a leader, Moses, to deliver them. The goal of God was not just to deliver them from Egyptian bondage, but it was to lead them to the promised land of abundance *"flowing with milk and honey."*

In Scripture, Egypt is symbolic of a life that is lived in bondage and oppression; and the Promised Land represents God's plan of abundant blessings for us. God wants to miraculously deliver us: out of the bondage of sickness, and deliver us into the promised land of health; from the bondage of sin, into the promised land of forgiveness; from the bondage of poverty, into the promised land of prosperity; from the bondage of despair, to the promised land of hope; from the bondage of sadness, to the promised land of joy; and from the bondage of fear, to the promised land of peace.

Thought for Today

We are the objects of God's affection and He never looks away from us—not even for a moment. The cry of our heart gets His full and undivided attention. In the moment we cry out to Him, nothing is more important to Him than reaching out to help us.

Prayer Journal

_____

_____

_____

~ ~ ~ MARCH 19 ~ ~ ~

"And it came to pass, when Joshua was by Jericho, that he lifted his eyes and looked, and behold, a Man stood opposite him with His sword drawn in His hand. And Joshua went to Him and said to Him, 'Are you for us or for our adversaries?' So He said, 'No, but as Commander of the army of the Lord I have now come.' And Joshua fell on his face to the earth and worshiped, and said to Him, 'What does my Lord say to His servant?' Then the Commander of the Lord's army said to Joshua, 'Take Your sandal off your foot, for the place where you stand is holy.' And Joshua did so" (Joshua 5:13-15).

Joshua had been appointed by God to lead His people, the Israelites, into the Promised Land. As Joshua sized up the fortress city named Jericho, suddenly, a Man stood before him with His sword drawn. Not recognizing this Man, Joshua asked His identity and questioned Him as to what side He represented. This Man's answer caused Joshua to fall on his face and worship Him. Joshua called Him *"my Lord,"* which revealed that he understood that this Man was God, Himself. Joshua realized Jericho could not be conquered until the question of Lordship had been settled in his heart. When Joshua called Him *"my Lord,"* he was acknowledging the Lord to be the absolute ruler of every area of his life. Joshua understood that Lordship placed God on the throne of his heart. Hence, God would make decisions concerning every area of Joshua's life, as it pleased Him.

Thought for Today

Jesus asked, "Why do you call me Lord, and yet you won't do what I tell you to do?" Calling Jesus, *"Lord,"* demands our absolute obedience to His every instruction.

Prayer Journal

_____

_____

_____

~ ~ ~ MARCH 20 ~ ~ ~

"Now Jericho was securely shut up because of the children of Israel; none went out, and none came in. And the Lord said to Joshua: 'See! I have given Jericho into your hand, its king, and the mighty men of valor'" (Joshua 6:1-2).

The walled city of Jericho looked like it was impossible for the Israelites to defeat. The city walls were thick and tall, as well as, the people within the city were known to be fierce warriors. The Israelites could not move any further into the future blessings that had been promised by God until the people of Jericho were defeated. As much as the Israelites probably wanted to go around them and simply move on, the Lord would not let them. Jericho had to be dealt with and conquered. God wanted the Israelites to see the city of Jericho as He did—already defeated!

Jericho represents the strongholds of the enemy in our lives; those problems that stand between us and Gods promised best. We may be tempted to ignore our "Jerichos" and move on, but the Lord will not allow us to. Our "Jerichos" must be conquered, because God will never allow us to cohabitate with the enemy. The fear of our "Jerichos" will dissipate if we will choose to see our "Jerichos" from God's perspective—already defeated. We must understand that God has put the fear of us within the hearts of our enemies. God is on our side—no stronghold can remain standing!

Thought for Today

Satan fears believers who walk in the fullness of the Spirit. Hell trembles when believers see challenges from God's perspective—already defeated. Strongholds are broken when believers apply their faith and expect to be set free by the power of God.

Prayer Journal

~ ~ ~ MARCH 21 ~ ~ ~

"You shall march around the city, all you men of war; you shall go all around the city once. This you shall do six days. And seven priests shall bear seven trumpets of rams' horns before the ark. But the seventh day you shall march around the city seven times and the priests shall blow the trumpets. It shall come to pass, when they make a long blast with ram's horn, and when you hear the sound of the trumpet that all the people shall shout with a great shout; then the wall of the city will fall down flat. And the people shall go up every man straight before him" (Joshua 6:3-5).

Everything about God's instructions, as to conquering Jericho, defied all of Joshua's military training and logic. There was nothing about God's plan that bore witness to his understanding. Joshua was not convinced that God's instruction, *"You shall march around the city,"* and *"When you hear the sound of the trumpet, that all the people shall shout,"* would work on such a fortified city. Joshua found himself at the crossroads of doing things God's way, or altering God's plan to fit his understanding.

Every one of us has stood at the same crossroads. We cannot see how following God's instructions will work and therefore, have ignored Him. However, we found that doing things our way caused us to fail. Let's make a decision once and for all—God's plan always works.

Thought for Today

God wanted Jericho defeated His way and with His plan. He wanted the Israelites to know He was the One Who gained them the victory, and that it was not in their strength. God knew that doing things His way would build faith for their next battle.

Prayer Journal

_____

_____

_____

~ ~ ~ MARCH 22 ~ ~ ~

"The Lord your God, who goes before you, He will fight for you, according to all He did for you in Egypt before your eyes, 'and in the wilderness where you saw how the Lord your God carried you, as a man carries his son, in all the way that you went until you came to this place' Yet, for all that, you did not believe the Lord your God" (Deuteronomy 1:30-32).

Moses had led the Israelites out of Egypt and the Promised Land lay just before them. Due to Israel's disobedience and unbelief, they wandered aimlessly in the wilderness for forty years. Most of the generation who had not believed in the faithfulness of God had died. Now, Moses wanted to impress on the new generation the tender faithfulness of God to them, and to their parents. As a father to a son, Moses pleaded with them to believe God and not follow in the unbelief of their parents.

There is one thing that God's heart desires—He wants us to "believe Him," no matter what the circumstances. One of the deepest pains imaginable is inflicted on the heart of God when we, through our words and actions, say to Him, "I don't believe You." God's love for us is a pure love and His intentions concerning us are above reproach. His actions on our behalf are without fail and always in our best interest. His Word will always establish codes of conduct and a proper attitude in order to release us to reach our potential. Tragically, we simply do not believe Him.

Thought for Today

We accuse God of being unfaithful and unloving; and worst of all, we accuse Him of being unable to do what He says He will do. How this must grieve God's heart, as He has been faithful.

Prayer Journal

_____

_____

_____

~ ~ ~ MARCH 23 ~ ~ ~

"God is not a man, that He should lie, nor a son of man, that He should repent. Has He said, and will He not do? Or has He spoken, and will He not make it good" (Numbers 23:19).

The evil king, Balak, hired a prophet named Balaam to prophesy doom over the Israelites as they marched through the land. Balaam responded to King Balak, telling him that whatever God had purposed could not be reversed—*"Has He said, and will He not do?"* In recording this event, Moses wanted the Israelites to fully understand the faithfulness of God to them and to their children. He stressed that God was not like men who have a nature to lie when cornered, or when it will serve their interests. Moses wanted them to know that God has done everything, and has not failed to do anything that He promised to do. Therefore, God has no failures that would necessitate His repentance.

God does not make idle promises to anyone. If God has said that He will do something, you can be sure He will do it. There has never been a time that He failed to keep the promises of His Word. It does not matter how difficult our circumstances may be, or how seemingly impossible our problems may appear to us, God is able to keep His promises on our behalf. We must not allow the negativity of our circumstances to dictate our level of faith in God and His power. Let us establish our hearts so that we will not allow unbelief to be the only thing that stops God from helping us.

Thought for Today

We live in an ever-changing and confusing world. The only constant we have is to allow God to be our anchor. He will never lie to us, nor will He fail to keep the promises He has made to us.

Prayer Journal

_____

_____

_____

~ ~ ~ MARCH 24 ~ ~ ~

"The entirety of Your Word is truth, and every one of Your righteous judgments endures forever" (Psalms 119:160).

One of the most important decisions you will ever make is whether or not you believe the Word of God to be the absolute truth. If you take the position that His Word is not the absolute truth, you will allow yourself to treat its mandates as optional and changeable depending on the circumstances in your life. You will see within the Word perceived "gray areas" to which you will apply your own interpretation; which in turn, will govern your conduct. The laws and commands of the Word will be reduced to suggestions at best. If you hold that the Word is not the absolute truth of God, then how do you know that the part you believe is not also bogus? How do you know whether or not the promises on which you are standing are actually true or not?

The Psalmist proclaimed that the entirety of the Word is truth. The Bible doesn't just contain the truth of God—it IS the truth of God. The truth of the Word will stand for all of eternity and will never be changed. The truth of the Word is not based on society, time, or our opinion. Consider Psalms 119:89, *"Forever, O Lord, Your Word is settled in heaven."* Jesus said *"Heaven and earth will pass away, but My words will by no means pass away"* (Luke 21:33). God's Word is an anchor for you in the storms of life. God's Word is a sure foundation on which to build your life. Don't worry…the truth of God's Word is absolute!

Thought for Today

You must settle this matter once and for all. The Word of God is absolute truth and its precepts are relevant to every area of life.

Prayer Journal

_____

_____

_____

~ ~ ~ MARCH 25 ~ ~ ~

"You believe that there is one God. You do well. Even the demons believe—and tremble" (James 2:19).

The Apostle James was basically saying, "You claim to believe God—big deal. The demons believe the same thing and it makes them tremble." The devil does not have one single doubt about the truth contained in a single verse of Scripture. This is why he spends so much of his time trying to convince you to doubt God's Word, and therefore, God's ability to keep His Word. The devil knows that if we truly believe the Word of God, and we stand in faith on its promises, his work against us is certainly doomed for defeat.

Unbelief is not just dangerous—it's deadly! Our unbelief calls God a liar according to I John 5:10, *"He who believes in the Son of God has the witness in himself; he who does not believe God has made Him a liar, because he has not believed the testimony that God has given of His Son."* When we doubt God, we are basically saying, "I don't believer Your Word is true;" "You are not Who You say You are;" and "You cannot do what You say You can do." When we walk in unbelief, we break God's heart for the Word says that unbelief makes it *"impossible"* to please God, *"But without faith it is impossible to please Him for he who comes to God must believe that He is, and that He is a rewarder of those who diligently seek Him"* (Hebrew 11:6).

Thought for Today

Put your faith to work and believe God! Your faith in His Word will determine what He can accomplish through you. *"Now He did not do many mighty works there because of their unbelief"* (Matthew 13:58).

Prayer Journal

_____

_____

_____

~ ~ ~ MARCH 26 ~ ~ ~

"Then Peter said, 'Silver and gold I do not have, but what I do have I give you: In the name of Jesus Christ of Nazareth, rise up and walk.' And he took him by the right hand and lifted him up, and immediately his feet and ankle bones received strength. So he, leaping up, stood and walked and entered the temple with them—walking, leaping, and praising God" (Acts 3:6-8).

A man, lame from birth was laying daily at the Temple gate begging for alms. Peter and John were on their way into the Temple when they noticed him. The lame man was begging as he sought something that would help him with his circumstances. However, Peter and John gave him something that forever changed his life and conquered his circumstances.

We have been given a sphere of influence. The needs within our realm of influence include those who are unsaved, backslidden, sick, and oppressed. We have a responsibility to give them something that will change their lives. We have two things we can give to everyone which will create an impact for change in their lives. First, we have our testimony about what Jesus has done for us. People can argue with religion and doctrine, but they cannot argue with our personal experience with Christ. Secondly, we have the prayer of faith. We can pray in faith believing for their needs and know that God answers our prayers.

Thought for Today

List the people in your sphere of influence and begin to pray for them. Ask God to open a door for you to touch them with your testimony and prayers of faith. When the door opens, walk with boldness knowing God has provided the opportunity.

Prayer Journal

_____

_____

_____

~ ~ ~ MARCH 27 ~ ~ ~

"One of the two who heard John speak, and followed Him, was Andrew, Simon Peter's brother. He first found his own brother Simon, and said to him, 'We have found the Messiah' (which is translated, the Christ). And he brought him to Jesus" (John 1:40-42).

Andrew was a disciple of John the Baptist and when Jesus was baptized in the Jordan River, Andrew witnessed the glorious confirmation of God. These events so impacted him that he became a follower of Jesus. Andrew was so convinced that Jesus was the long-awaited Messiah that he tried to convince his brother, Simon Peter, to become a follower of Jesus as well.

In this story, there is a simple strategy that we can follow for winning the lost. The first step is to be convinced that a relationship with Jesus is the only hope of escaping hell and gaining heaven. Andrew was convinced that Jesus was the Messiah. The second step involves finding someone to share with—like Andrew did in finding his brother. Unfortunately, some wait for the Lord to give them a "word and a burden" about sharing their faith. Don't fall into this trap for we are to be His witnesses; and as for a burden—pick one. Some are concerned that perhaps the devil might be leading them to share their faith with an individual in an attempt to run them away from God. This is not possible…the devil will never lead you to share your faith.

Thought for Today

You can be assured the devil will never inspire you to share your faith—at anytime! It is too dangerous, for they might get saved. Go and tell—today!

Prayer Journal

_____

_____

_____

~ ~ ~ MARCH 28 ~ ~ ~

"For 'whoever calls on the name of the Lord shall be saved'" (Romans 10:13).

We are often guilty of making salvation more complicated than it really is; whether personally, or through our denominational affiliations. We get too theological, even though not intending to muddy the waters, we often do. Remember that it is the purity and the simplicity of the Gospel that makes it attractive. With this verse, you can lead someone to the saving knowledge of Jesus.

This verse tells us that "anyone" can be saved. This opens the door for everyone! You do not need to be rich or poor, educated, employed, married or single—or anything else to qualify. Everyone falls into the category of being a *"whoever."* It also tells us that the only thing we have to do is "ask." We don't have to pay anything, or do anything, or become anything. Since salvation is a gift from God, it cannot be earned—only received. This verse explains that we are to ask Jesus to save us: we do not have to ask the preacher, the church, the church leaders, or the denominational headquarters—the only One we have to communicate with is Jesus. This verse also promises us that if we ask, Jesus will save us. There are no questionnaires to fill out and no waiting period to find out if we have been accepted. We do not have to be any place special or feel anything unusual. Our request of Jesus is answered with a guaranteed, "yes!"

Thought for Today

You do not need to expound on the Bible's doctrines to win someone to Christ. You need to get them into the presence of the Lord—alone with His Word, and the Holy Spirit will do the rest.

Prayer Journal

_____

_____

_____

~ ~ ~ MARCH 29 ~ ~ ~

"And the king and his men went to Jerusalem against the Jebusites, the inhabitants of the land, who spoke to David, saying, 'You shall not come in here; but the blind and the lame will repel you,' thinking, 'David cannot come in here.' Nevertheless David took the stronghold of Zion (that is, the City of David)" (II Samuel 5:6-7).

The story of David's conquest of the Jebusites at Jerusalem is an exciting one. God had promised that He would give Israel that land and drive out all of their enemies. David knew firsthand of the Lord's help in times of trouble; and he was convinced that no matter who the enemy was, or how great their number, God would fight the battle for them. David penned these words, *"When I cry out to You, then my enemies will turn back; This I know, because God is for me"* (Psalms 56:9).

When David and his men arrived at Jerusalem, they taunted him, *"You shall not come in here; but the blind and the lame will repel you."* These words are familiar; the devil tells us that we are too weak to do battle. He tries to persuade us that we will never be victorious because we will never be able to break through his strongholds. However, the Bible says that, *"Nevertheless David took the stronghold of Zion."* The threats and taunting of the enemy didn't faze David. He became a *"nevertheless"* man by putting his full and complete trust in God; therefore, He conquered his enemy.

Thought for Today

God is looking for *"nevertheless"* men and women who will not be deceived by the taunting of the devil. These *"nevertheless"* men and women will put their trust in God and, in His strength, defeat the enemy.

Prayer Journal

_____

_____

_____

~ ~ ~ MARCH 30 ~ ~ ~

"Now therefore, fear the Lord, serve Him in sincerity and in truth, and put away the gods which your fathers served on the other side of the River and in Egypt. Serve the Lord! And if it seems evil to you to serve the Lord, choose for yourselves this day whom you will serve, whether the gods which your fathers served that were on the other side of the River, or the gods of the Amorites, in whose land you dwell. But as for me and my house, we will serve the Lord" (Joshua 24:14-15).

Joshua had been a great leader and was deeply loved by the people. In his farewell address, Joshua rehearsed the faithfulness of God to the nation of Israel. He reviewed how God had granted victory after victory. However, there was something weighing very heavy on his heart. Joshua was concerned about the willingness of the people to continue to serve the Lord after his death. He pleaded with them to remove all idols from their lives and from the lives of their families. He pleaded for them to make a decision to serve the Lord, and serve Him only.

If serving the Lord was not pleasing to the people, Joshua challenged them to choose which god they would serve. They could choose to serve the true and living God; or serve the god of their forefathers, which were the traditions of men; or they could serve the god's of the Amorites, which equated to the popular gods of society. In any event, Joshua told the Israelites his position, *"But as for me and my house, we will serve the Lord."*

Thought for Today

God is a jealous God and will not share you with other gods. Reaffirm, *"But as for me and my house, we will serve the Lord!"*

Prayer Journal

_____

_____

_____

~ ~ ~ MARCH 31 ~ ~ ~

"According to the glorious gospel of the blessed God which was committed to my trust. And I thank Christ Jesus our Lord who has enabled me, because He counted me faithful, putting me into the ministry" (I Timothy 1:11-12).

Paul was very grateful that *"He counted me faithful, putting me into the ministry."* To Paul, the message of the Gospel (and the ability to communicate it), was a priceless treasure that was to be guarded by his integrity and faithfulness. The burning and driving desire of every faithful Christian should be that the Lord Jesus would consider them to be faithful and true to His Word.

Let me share four words that help us define the word faithfulness. The first word is "commitment." Commitment will drive one to accomplish a task regardless of circumstances. The second word is "dependable." Your ability to keep your word and promises are vital to your being found faithful. Can you be counted on to be where you are supposed to be, and doing what you promised you would do? The third word is "consistent." Success in life doesn't happen because of one day of consistency. Success only comes to those who, day in and day out, do the right things the right way, according to the Word. The fourth word is "accomplishment." Accomplishment is the result when one is committed to stay the course, go the distance, and finish the task. The faithful will progress no matter what obstacles they have to face.

Thought for Today

Does Jesus count you faithful? Are you "committed?" Are you "dependable" and "consistent?" Are you "accomplishing" your God-given assignment in life?

Prayer Journal

_____

_____

_____

~ ~ ~ APRIL 1 ~ ~ ~

"As for you, my son Solomon, know the God of your father, and serve Him with a loyal heart and with a willing mind; for the Lord searches all hearts and understands all the intent of the thoughts. If you seek Him, He will be found by you; but if you forsake Him, He will cast you off forever. Consider now, for the Lord has chosen you to build a house for the sanctuary; be strong and do it" (I Chronicles 28:9-10).

King David knew that his time of departure from this life was drawing near. He gathered all the people together and told them of God's plan to have his son, Solomon, build the Temple. David charged Solomon to become intimately acquainted with the Lord and to *"serve Him with a loyal heart and a willing mind."* David warned Solomon, that God searches the hearts of men and knows the intents of a man's thoughts, and that He would know the difference between lip service and true worship. David reminded Solomon that the Lord had chosen him for the honored task of building the Temple; therefore, he should *"be strong and do it."*

Each of us has been chosen by God for a specific assignment in the establishment and advancement of the Lord's Kingdom on earth. Together, we are building a spiritual house for the Lord's presence among men. We need to set our hearts to serve the Lord out of desire, not out of mere duty.

Thought for Today

In and of our own strength, we will never accomplish the assignment the Lord has for us. We must ask the Holy Spirit to infuse our lives with His mighty power. Then, with willing minds and loyal hearts, do whatever it takes to get the assignment done.

Prayer Journal

_____

_____

_____

~ ~ ~ APRIL 2 ~ ~ ~

"Therefore, my beloved brethren, be steadfast, immovable, always abounding in the work of the Lord, knowing that your labor is not in vain in the Lord" (I Corinthians 15:58).

Someone wisely said, "I'd rather be a dim light in a secluded hallway, faithfully shining for the Lord, than to be the most fantastic display of fireworks ever imagined; seen in splendor for a few seconds and then gone forever." Unfortunately, this is how many have served the Lord. They come on the scene with an explosion of ideas, energy, and boasting of commitment, only to fizzle out a short time later. They started out serving the Lord with fervor, only to tire of the daily grind, or they become discouraged by challenges. The demands for consistency wearied them and they dropped down the ladder of commitment, one rung at a time.

Consistency in our spiritual life is crucial, and it should be the seat of government for all areas of our life. Remember that where spiritual matters are concerned, consistency is totally dependent on one's level of commitment to the task at hand and to their personal discipline to stay focused on their objectives. Often, the lack of visible results tempts us to re-evaluate the worth of our efforts. We wrongly assume that just because we don't see immediate results, God isn't doing anything. Nothing could be further from the truth—God is ALWAYS at work!

Thought for Today

Remember, that in spiritual matters only God can give the results to our labor. We don't know all that God is doing behind the scenes. However, we do know that our consistency in serving Him is necessary for us to reap the rewards of our labor.

Prayer Journal

_____

_____

_____

~ ~ ~ APRIL 3 ~ ~ ~

"Children, obey your parents in the Lord, for this is right. 'Honor your father and mother,' which is the first commandment with promise: that it may be well with you and you may live long on the earth. And you, fathers, do not provoke your children to wrath, but bring them up in the training and admonition of the Lord" (Ephesians 6:1-4).

Raising a family in our society is not easy. Television sitcoms and cartoons mock Christian ethics that used to be the standard for conduct. Our children are exposed to school curriculum which directly opposes what the Bible teaches. While this angers us, some of the blame lies with parents who have abandoned God-given responsibilities to train their children in the ways of the Lord. A recent newspaper cartoon depicted two little boys lamenting about the inconsistencies of their parents. One said, "Just about the time I learn what the rules are, Dad says, 'rules are made to be broken.'"

We must address the consistency issue in the home first. Parents must be consistent in holding to their values and guard against sending mixed messages. If a parent is passive and indifferent to a child's behavior, then disciplines the child for the same behavior the next day; the child will be confused as to where the lines are that govern his behavior. For example: If the family attending church together is valuable for part of the year, why isn't it valuable the rest of the year?

Thought for Today

Where there is inconsistency confusion sets in, stability of behavior is lost, and productivity grinds to a halt. Parents, we are to establish the values, and then be consistent to live out those values.

Prayer Journal

_____

_____

_____

~ ~ ~ APRIL 4 ~ ~ ~

"But Noah found grace in the eyes of the Lord. This is the genealogy of Noah. Noah was a just man, perfect in his generations. Noah walked with God" (Genesis 6:8-9).

Living the Christian life in today's society subjects one to ridicule. It is not popular to espouse Christian ethics and moral values today and anyone who does, is considered to be out of touch with reality and thus, dangerous to society. We have outlawed God's presence in the White House, the school house and in some cases, even the church house. Bible clubs on the school campus have at times been replaced with the open practice of witchcraft. Teachers who even hint at their faith in God in the classroom are rebuked and disciplined; while teachers who openly teach New Age dogma are championed.

Today's spiritual darkness is fast approaching the darkness that reigned in Noah's day. Talk about loneliness…Noah was the only man left that God considered to be righteous. He preached against the rampant sin and wickedness of his generation; yet, to no avail for no one listened. Noah was ridiculed and rejected by everyone, including his closest friends; no one wanted to embrace his values or his God. However, his relationship and fellowship with God was more important than all of his friends combined. He would rather have God's approval concerning his life, than the friendship of man that often changes with the seasons.

Thought for Today

Noah made a decision to walk with God, even if it meant that he would have to walk through his life alone. His friendship with God was the most important factor in his life.

Prayer Journal

_____

_____

_____

~ ~ ~ APRIL 5 ~ ~ ~

"Thus Noah did; according to all that God commanded him, so he did" (Genesis 6:22).

God's heart was grieved at the wickedness of Noah's generation. Lawlessness was championed, while righteousness was ridiculed and rejected. God found Noah to be the only righteous man on the earth. God shared with Noah how grieved He was over the sin of the people and what He planned to do about them. God made the decision to cleanse the earth of sin by destroying mankind from the face of the earth with a flood. God revealed to Noah a detailed plan by which, Noah and his family would be spared the coming judgment. This plan involved the building of a large boat that God referred to as the Ark. God was specific with His instructions to Noah concerning the dimensions of the Ark. He also instructed Noah to enter the ark with his family and the animals that the Lord had assigned.

When God spoke to Noah of the coming rain, it was something that Noah did not understand, for it had never rained on the earth. Also, in asking Noah to build the Ark, God was asking Noah to build something that he had never heard of, much less seen. However, Noah obeyed the instructions of God. The reason for Noah's level of obedience to things unknown rose out of his trust in the Lord. So intimate was his fellowship, that whatever God spoke he obeyed, whether he understood or not. Partial obedience was not obedience; therefore, Noah obeyed God's instructions.

Thought for Today

Intimate fellowship with God will develop our trust in God; which, in turn, will result in our obedience.

Prayer Journal

_____

_____

_____

~ ~ ~ APRIL 6 ~ ~ ~

"Then Noah built an altar to the Lord, and took of every clean animal and out of every clean bird, and offered burnt offerings on the altar. And the Lord smelled a soothing aroma. Then the Lord said in his heart, 'I will never again curse the ground for man's sake, although the imagination of man's heart is evil from his youth; nor will I again destroy every living thing as I have done'" (Genesis 8:20-21).

God's judgment of mankind and their sin was now complete, and the waters from the flood began to recede. As soon as the earth was sufficiently dry, Noah opened the Ark and descended to the dry ground with his family and all of the animals that God had instructed him to carry on the Ark. The very first thing that Noah did when leaving the Ark, was to build an altar and offer sacrifices as an expression of his worship. The Lord was well pleased with Noah's offering and made a vow that He would never again bring His judgment upon mankind in this manner.

It is important to note that before Noah sought shelter for his family or did anything else, he worshiped the Lord. Worship was the number one priority in his life. The more time Noah spent in the worship of God, the deeper and more intimate his relationship with God grew. Noah's worship was not merely an event—it was a lifestyle choice. He worshiped and served God out of the cravings and desires of his heart; not out of duty or obligation.

Thought for Today

We are not worshipers because we choose to worship; we worship because we are worshipers. Who we are in God's sight, will determine what we do in His presence.

Prayer Journal

_____

_____

_____

~ ~ ~ APRIL 7 ~ ~ ~

"And Noah began to be a farmer, and he planted a vineyard" (Genesis 9:20).

After the flood, Noah became a farmer. As the earth dried, Noah planted his seed and waited for his harvest. There is something revealing about Noah in this verse. The Scripture tells us that Noah *"began to be a farmer"* and that *"he planted a vineyard."* In this passage, we are reminded that Noah had an incredible trust in God; after all, what seed he had in his possession, was the only seed left on the entire earth. What if his seed did not bring a harvest? Noah remembered what the Lord had said at the conclusion of his sacrifice on leaving the Ark. God had promised that as long as the earth remained, there would be seedtime and harvest, and Noah believed God. Noah knew down in his heart, that his whole future rested in his planting of seed. If the seed did not get planted, Noah could not expect to receive a harvest. However, Noah had developed such a high level of trust in God that releasing his seed, based on God's promise to him, was easy.

Giving and faith are always tied together. Your action of giving will either validate your confession, or will invalidate what you say you believe. The only way you can develop trust in someone is to develop a relationship. The depth of your relationship with God, determines the level of your trust in God.

Thought for Today

When you set your heart to give, you will never release your seed to someone in whom you have no trust. Your failure to give your seed offerings to the Lord is the equivalent of telling Him, "I don't have trust in Your ability to provide for me."

Prayer Journal

_____

_____

_____

~ ~ ~ APRIL 8 ~ ~ ~

"There is a way that seems right to a man, but its end is the way of death" (Proverbs 14:12).

In the U. S. Naval Institute Proceedings (the magazine of the Naval Institute), the following story was recorded and it concisely illustrates the danger of having things our own way. It seems that two battleships were at sea on a training mission and the fog was extensive. Shortly after dark, a lookout reported seeing a light on the starboard bow. The captain asked "Is the light steady, or is it moving astern?" The lookout replied, "The light is steady." This meant they were on a collision course with another ship. The captain gave the order for the signal man to signal and advise the other vessel to change course twenty degrees. The reply came back advising that the captain be the one to change course twenty degrees. An angry captain ordered that the signal man reply, "I'm a battleship. Change course twenty degrees." To which came the reply, "I'm a lighthouse. Change course twenty degrees." The captain wisely changed his course.

We live in a generation and society that promotes people who are "self-made," "self-improved," and "self-motivated." In Proverbs 12:15 we read, *"The way of a fool is right in his own eyes, but he who heeds counsel is wise."* We are headed for a shipwreck if we ignore the warnings from the lighthouse of God's Word.

Thought for Today

Let me shock you: your way isn't always the right way. Your insistence on having things your way, could lead to a catastrophe in your life. Begin today and check your way against the perfect ways of God and His Word, and if you are wise, you will yield.

Prayer Journal

_____

_____

_____

~ ~ ~ APRIL 9 ~ ~ ~

"Now David was greatly distressed, for the people spoke of stoning him, because the soul of all the people was grieved, every man for his sons and his daughters. But David strengthened himself in the Lord his God" (I Samuel 30:6).

David joined his army of six-hundred men to the army of the Philistines. David then discovered the Philistines were planning to go to war against Saul and the Israelites. God spared David from fighting the Israelites by having the Philistine leaders reject David and his army from fighting with them. David and his men returned home to Ziglag only to find that the city had been burned and their wives and children taken captive by the Amalekites. David was not participating in some great sin or living in rebellion when this terrible thing happened. Had he known the enemy was coming, he would have taken preventative measures. David grieved over the pain of this tremendous loss.

Things got worse! The men decided to blame David and talked of stoning him to death. Understandably, David became distressed and discouraged. There was no one to comfort him or to encourage him; yet, David refused to stay down. He began to *"strengthen himself in the Lord his God."* When we are under attack, it is normal to become distressed and discouraged. People might be mad at you and not care enough to encourage you. Follow David's example— *"strengthen yourself in the Lord."*

Thought for Today

Do not rely on other people to encourage you. Learn to encourage yourself in the Lord. Turn to His Word and offer the sacrifice of praise. Your spirit will be lifted as you focus on His faithfulness.

Prayer Journal

_____

_____

_____

~ ~ ~ APRIL 10 ~ ~ ~

"So David went, he and the six-hundred men who were with him and came to the Brook Besor, where those stayed who were left behind. But David pursued, he and four-hundred men; for two-hundred stayed behind, who were so weary that they could not cross the Brook Besor" (I Samuel 30:9-10).

David's home and city had been burned. His wives and children, as well as the wives and children of his men, had been taken captive by the Amalekites. David refused to remain in a discouraged state; he immediately began to strengthen himself in the Lord. He knew that he had to do whatever was necessary to get back everything that the enemy had stolen from him. David rallied six-hundred men under his command and led them to the Brook Besor. Arriving at the Brook Besor, two-hundred men said that they were just too tired to go and fight. David's army was reduced to four-hundred men who were in agreement with him to fight the enemy. They were determined to get back everyone and everything that had been stolen.

There is always power in agreement. David knew that he could accomplish more with four-hundred men who were in agreement with him, than he could with six-hundred men, some of which were not in unity with the agenda. The Bible speaks of the power of agreement in Deuteronomy 32:30, *"How could one chase a thousand, and two put ten-thousand to flight."*

Thought for Today

Realize that not everyone will want to, or care enough, to fight your battle with you. Find someone who will get into spiritual agreement with you concerning the victory needed in your life.

Prayer Journal

_____

_____

_____

~ ~ ~ APRIL 11 ~ ~ ~

"And when he had brought him down, there they were, spread out over all the land, eating and drinking and dancing, because of all the great spoil which they had taken from the land of the Philistines and from the land of Judah. Then David attacked them from twilight until the evening of the next day. Not a man of them escaped, except four-hundred young men who rode on camels and fled. So David recovered all that the Amalekites had carried away, and David rescued his two wives. And nothing of theirs was lacking, either small or great, sons or daughters, spoil or anything which they had taken from them; David recovered all" (I Samuel 30:16-19).

David was not indifferent about what the Amalekites had done in burning his city and taking captive all the women and children. As a matter of fact, while his men were getting mad and blaming him, David spent his efforts getting mad at the enemy. David would not rest until the enemy was defeated and until everything that had been stolen was recovered. David didn't get mad at God, nor at his men; he got mad at the source—the Amalekites.

Far too often, when we come under attack from the enemy and things are stolen from us such as our health, finances, or families, we end up getting mad at the wrong person; we get mad at God and blame Him for what the devil has done. We must get angry at the devil, and get angry enough to fight back until we win.

Thought for Today

Nothing will change until you get mad at the devil for trying to steal your God-given promises. You must purpose to fight until you get everything back that he has stolen.

Prayer Journal

_____

_____

_____

~ ~ ~ APRIL 12 ~ ~ ~

"However, other boats came from Tiberias, near the place where they ate bread after the Lord had given thanks—when the people therefore saw that Jesus was not there, nor His disciples, they also got into boats and came to Capernaum, seeking Jesus. And when they found Him on the other side of the sea, they said to Him, 'Rabbi, when did You come here?' Jesus answered them and said, 'Most assuredly, I say to you, you seek Me, not because you saw the signs, but because you ate of the loaves and were filled'" (John 6:23-26).

When Jesus multiplied the loaves and fish to feed the multitudes a number of people were impressed, as were His disciples. The next day, Jesus and the disciples left by boat to travel to the other side of the lake. Noticing that Jesus and His disciples were gone, a crowd sought passage to the other side to rejoin Jesus and the disciples. You would think that Jesus would have been pleased with His new-found popularity. However, when the people arrived and greeted Him, He rebuked them saying, you're only here *"because you ate of the loaves and were filled."*

Today, the reason many go to church is for what they think the church can do for them. They expect everything to revolve around their needs, and they don't care about anyone else. They never consider that God has gifted them with something to give that will be a blessing—all they care about is getting blessed.

Thought for Today

What is your motivation for going to church and being a part of God's family? Has anyone in this last year said that you have been a blessing to their life? Don't just be on the take, give back.

Prayer Journal

_____

_____

_____

~ ~ ~ APRIL 13 ~ ~ ~

"Two men went up to the temple to pray, one a Pharisee and the other a tax collector. The Pharisee stood and prayed thus with himself, 'God I thank You that I am not like other men—extortioners, unjust, adulterers, or even as this tax collector. I fast twice a week; I give tithes of all that I possess.' And the tax collector standing afar off, would not so much as raise his eyes to heaven, but beat His breast, saying, 'God, be merciful to me a sinner'" (Luke 18:10-13)!

Everybody has met them and nobody likes them. Everybody has met someone at one time or another that really believe they are better than everyone else around. They raise their nose in judgment and disgust, for no one is good enough for their fellowship and no one can measure up to their standards.

Unfortunately, this problem is among God's family. Some have forgotten where they have come from and according to the Scriptures, we have all come from the same place—we are sinners saved by grace. However, some consider themselves spiritually superior to everyone around them. They think they know more about the Scripture than anyone in their circle and that they have their "act together"; therefore, they are spiritually superior. They develop a critical spirit and judge everyone they know and assume them to be inferior in every way.

Thought for Today

You must guard against self-righteousness, for it will promote the false belief of spiritual superiority. When you become aware of someone else's failure, you would be wise to always keep in mind the old saying, "but by the grace of God, there go I."

Prayer Journal

_____

_____

_____

~ ~ ~ APRIL 14 ~ ~ ~

"Then some came and told Jehoshaphat, saying, 'A great multitude is coming against you from beyond the sea, from Syria; and they are in Hazazon Tamar' (which is En Gedi). And Jehoshaphat feared, and set himself to seek the Lord, and proclaimed a fast throughout all Judah. So Judah gathered together to ask help from the Lord; and from all the cities of Judah and they came to seek the Lord" (II Chronicles 20:2-4).

Jehoshaphat, the King of Judah, was completely surrounded and about to be attacked by the enemy. Jehoshaphat did several things that are not normal for people to do when they find themselves in trouble. First, he did not consult with the generals of his army to strategize for battle. Secondly, he did not call his political cabinet to convene and give him their counsel. And thirdly, Jehoshaphat sought God for the help and direction he needed to win this battle.

Many in the church claim to be seeking God. However, they are not seeking Him as a first priority and God is, more often than not, an afterthought. God is the One turned to only when desperation has set in and all hope of dealing with the problem is gone. Usually, people seek out God's help after they have exhausted their energies, their resources, and their influence. Then, when all has failed, they turn to God as a last resort in seeking an answer to their problem. Thank God for His mercy; but take a moment to consider how your actions must insult Him.

Thought for Today

Make the pursuit of God and His ways the number one priority. When trouble comes (and it surely will), make the decision to seek God first for the answer and solution to your problems.

Prayer Journal

_____

_____

_____

~ ~ ~ APRIL 15 ~ ~ ~

"And now, here are the people of Ammon, Moab, and Mount Seir—whom You would not let Israel invade when they came out of the land of Egypt, but they turned from them and did not destroy them—here they are, rewarding us by coming to throw us out of Your possession which You have given us to inherit. O our God, will You not judge them? For we have not power against this great multitude that is coming against us; nor do we know what to do, but our eyes are upon You" (II Chronicles 20:10-12).

Jehoshaphat was outnumbered by the enemy and there was no way his people could survive the attack. Trapped by the enemy and enslaved to natural fear, Jehoshaphat turned to God and acknowledged that there was nothing from a natural standpoint that could be done to solve his problems. Jehoshaphat simply asked God what He was planning to do about this situation. He admitted to God, that even with their collective wisdom, they didn't know what to do about gaining victory over the enemy.

We live in a society that demands we have answers for every situation. This is especially true among Christians. We have a fear of being perceived as less than spiritual if we do not have an answer to our dilemma. We need to realize that it is all right not to know what to do in every circumstance. We need to admit this and realize that what really matters is that we know the Lord, the source of all the answers.

Thought for Today

Get honest and admit that your problem is bigger than you and get your eyes on the Lord for an answer. Ask God what He plans to do about your situation—He is waiting and would love to talk to you.

Prayer Journal

_____

_____

_____

~ ~ ~ APRIL 16 ~ ~ ~

"Now all Judah, with their little ones, their wives, and their children, stood before the Lord. Then the Spirit of the Lord came upon Jahaziel the son of Zechariah....And he said, 'Listen, all you of Judah and you inhabitants of Jerusalem, and you, King Jehoshaphat!' Thus says the Lord to you: 'Do not be afraid, nor dismayed because of this great multitude, for the battle is not yours, but God's'" (II Chronicles 20:13-15).

As God looked on this scene, His heart must have been overwhelmed by what His eyes beheld. The entire nation of Judah, every man, woman, and child, stood before the Lord waiting for His answer to their problem. If God did not answer them, they knew it was certain death, and that those who escaped the sword would be enslaved in a foreign land. They had offered their prayer, and now they humbled themselves waiting for His answer. God answered them with the greatest news their ears would ever hear, *"Do not be afraid nor dismayed because of this great multitude, for the battle is not yours, but God's."*

We are often guilty of "sending God a prayer" that is about as effective as a telegram. We rattle off what we need Him to do; then, without waiting for Him to speak to us, we immediately go back to our routine and get lost in our business. We subject ourselves to fear because we are too busy to wait. We ask God a question, but then are too rude to wait for His answer.

Thought for Today

Don't be guilty of sending God a "telegram" prayer. Make your request and discipline yourself to wait for His answer—*"Do not be afraid or dismayed...for the battle is not yours, but God's."*

Prayer Journal

_____

_____

_____

~ ~ ~ APRIL 17 ~ ~ ~

"And Jehoshaphat bowed his head with his face to the ground, and all Judah and the inhabitants of Jerusalem bowed before the Lord, worshiping the Lord. Then the Levites and of the children of the Kohathites stood up to praise the Lord God of Israel with voices loud and high...Now when they began to sing and to praise, the Lord set ambushes against the people of Ammon, Moab and Mount Seir, who had come against Judah; and they were defeated" (II Chronicles 20:18-19, 22).

On the night before the battle, Jehoshaphat led the people in a season of praise and worship to the Lord for the victory that He had promised to give them. So confident were Jehoshaphat and the people in God's ability to keep His promises, that they lifted their voices in praise and bowed their hearts to worship before the battle took place. In doing so, they were declaring their confidence and faith in their God.

We have no problem offering God praise after He answers our prayers, or opens His hands and meets the need. When the need is met we openly shout the victory. However, our victory has nothing to do with the absence of the problem. Victory comes when you can shout and sing in the midst of the problem. Shouting the victory after the problem is solved does not require faith. Anyone can shout victory when everything is taken care of.

Thought for Today

Either God is Who He claims to be—or He isn't. His Word and promises are either true—or they are not. Openly declare your faith in God through praise, even while you are yet in your problem. God has promised that He will not fail you, so shout the victory.

Prayer Journal

_____

_____

_____

~ ~ ~ APRIL 18 ~ ~ ~

"Your right hand, O Lord, has become glorious in power; your right hand, O Lord, has dashed the enemy in pieces. And in the greatness of Your excellence You have overthrown those who rose stubble against You; You sent forth Your wrath; it consumed them like rubble" (Exodus 15:6-7).

Moses and the children of Israel had just witnessed the miracle of a lifetime. Pharaoh had released them and just when they thought they were free, they saw the dust clouds of Pharaoh's army rising in the distance. Fear gripped their hearts as they realized that the Red Sea was in front of them and Pharaoh's army was quickly closing in behind them. There was no way out, and there wasn't any place for them to hide. It was in this setting that God continued to reveal His greatness to the Israelites. The waters of the Red Sea parted as Moses held his rod over them and the children of Israel walked across on dry ground. As Pharaoh's army followed them into the Red Sea, the walls of water collapsed and killed them. Moses was then responsible to lead the people in a celebration of God's greatness.

Remember that we serve a great and mighty God, with Whom nothing is impossible. The God of greatness that Moses celebrated so many years ago is our God. We are connected to greatness, because the God Who created the universe lives within us.

Thought for Today

There is no challenge so great, that God cannot cause us to overcome it. There is not an enemy so powerful, that God cannot deliver us from his hand. We need to renew our awareness of the greatness of God.

Prayer Journal

_____

_____

_____

~ ~ ~ APRIL 19 ~ ~ ~

"Yours, O Lord, is the greatness, the power and the glory, the victory and the majesty; for all that is in heaven and in earth is Yours; Yours is the kingdom, O Lord, and You are exalted as head over all. Both riches and honor are from You, and You reign over all. In Your hand is power and might; in Your hand it is to make great and to give strength to all. Now therefore, our God, we thank You and praise Your glorious name" (I Chronicles 29:11-13).

David took the responsibility of gathering the necessary materials from which the Temple would be built. For David, the Temple would stand as a visible tribute to the greatness of God. David proclaimed that all of *"the greatness, the power and the glory, the victory and the majesty"* belonged solely to the Lord. David wanted the people to know that any *"riches and honor"* that they enjoyed had come from the hand of the Lord. David was fully aware, from personal experience, that it was the Lord's hand that places men in various positions in life. The Lord then gives them the strength to carry out the responsibilities that have been assigned to them.

God declares Himself to be unequaled as we find in Isaiah 40:25-26, *"To whom then will you liken Me, or to whom shall I be equal? says the Holy One. Lift up your eyes on high, and see Who has created these things, Who brings out their host by number; He calls them all by name, by the greatness of His might and the strength of His power; not one is missing."*

Thought for Today

There truly is no god, like our God, for He gives strength and wisdom to fulfill our assignments. *"Your way, O God, is in the sanctuary; who is so great a God as our God"* (Psalms 77:13)?

Prayer Journal

_____

_____

_____

~ ~ ~ APRIL 20 ~ ~ ~

"Oh, how great is Your goodness, which You have laid up for those who fear You, which You have prepared for those who trust in You in the presence of the sons of men! You shall hide them in the secret place of Your presence from the plots of man; you shall keep them secretly in a pavilion from the strife of tongues" (Psalms 31:19-20).

David knew firsthand of the goodness and the protection of God that had been displayed on his behalf. David knew that it was the Lord who had delivered him every single time from the hands of his enemies. No matter how close in proximity his enemies appeared to be, David was well aware that it was God who delivered him from their hands.

Every victory you have ever celebrated over your enemy has been the direct result of God getting involved in your trouble. Just when it looked like the enemy had you cornered and beat, there stood God on your behalf, delivering you from the enemy's wicked plan. When people have spread lies and false rumors about you, in an attempt to defame your character and integrity, the Lord lifted you into His presence and hid you away from the ensuing strife of their lying tongues. How foolish we have been at times to assume that we can fight our own battles. There never has been, nor will there ever be, an enemy strong enough to reach into the *"secret place of Your (His) presence"* and touch us.

Thought for Today

The Lord bids us to come to Him in times of trouble. When we come to Him in these times, He promises in His Word to hide us from our enemies. In the *"secret place of Your (His) presence,"* the Lord will reveal His faithfulness and abiding goodness to us.

Prayer Journal

_____

_____

_____

~ ~ ~ APRIL 21 ~ ~ ~

"Praise the Lord, all you Gentiles! Laud Him, all you peoples! For His merciful kindness is great toward us, and the truth of the Lord endures forever. Praise the Lord" (Psalms 117:1-2)!

We love to sing the line from the song that says, "If it had not been, for the Lord on my side; tell me where would I be?" When we begin to re-examine God's goodness, we see just how rich our lives really are and how many blessings we enjoy from His hands. We need to stay focused on what the Lord has done for us if we want to remain in a consistent state of thankfulness and gratitude.

The Word serves as a constant reminder to the goodness and mercy of God towards us. The Psalmist reminds us in Psalms 145:8, *"The Lord is gracious and full of compassion, slow to anger and great in mercy."* Where would you be today, if the Lord had not shown you His mercy instead of giving you what you rightfully deserved? In Psalms 147:5 we read, *"Great is our Lord, and mighty in power; His understanding is infinite."* Where would you be today, if the Lord had not demonstrated His power against your enemies? And finally, in Lamentations 3:22-23 we read, *"Through the Lord's mercies we are not consumed, because His compassions fail not. They are new every morning; great is Your faithfulness."* Where would you be today, if the Lord had not been faithful to keep His Word concerning you?

Thought for Today

Where would you be, if the Lord hadn't rescued your life from the snares the devil had set for you? Where would you be, if the Lord hadn't answered your cries for help? Take a moment and thank Him. Offer your heart's gratitude to Him for being so kind to you.

Prayer Journal

_____

_____

_____

~ ~ ~ APRIL 22 ~ ~ ~

"Great is the Lord, and greatly to be praised in the city of our God, in His holy mountain" (Psalms 48:1).

It is one thing to know about the greatness of God; however, it is yet another thing to properly respond to this knowledge. The Bible declares God's greatness, and the whole of creation is stamped with the proof of it. We have witnessed His greatness on our behalf in the various stages of our lives. Our daily response to the greatness of God is very crucial to our walking with Him in obedient and absolute faith.

We are clearly instructed in the Word to acknowledge the manifold greatness of God through our praise. As we offer up our praise, we openly declare our faith in God. If we fail to acknowledge the Lord's greatness through our praise, we are demonstrating our indifference to Him through our lack of gratitude. In conjunction with acknowledging God's greatness through our praise, we are instructed to reverence Him. In Psalms 96:4 we read, *"For the Lord is great and greatly to be praised; He is to be feared above all gods."* To fear the Lord encompasses the concept of God's ability to bring judgment on the rebellion in each of our lives. However, to fear the Lord lends to a broader application of truth in that, we are to reverence Him. Our reverence of Him will keep our rebellion against Him in check.

Thought for Today

The Bible is full of the greatness of our God. We read in Psalms 145:3, *"Great is the Lord, and greatly to be praised; and His greatness is unsearchable."* We can rest in our faith because of God's greatness. Our praise and reverence give rise to faith.

Prayer Journal

_____

_____

_____

~ ~ ~ APRIL 23 ~ ~ ~

"The eyes of your understanding being enlightened; that you may know what is the hope of His calling, what are the riches of the glory of His inheritance in the saints, and what is the exceeding greatness of His power toward us who believe, according to the working of His mighty power" (Ephesians 1:18-19).

The prayer of Paul is a powerful reminder of who we are in Christ and that we are to live within the boundaries of the greatness of our God. Why would we settle for anything less in life? Why would we settle for defeat and despair, when we are guaranteed absolute victory? II Corinthians 2:14 says *"Now thanks be to God who always leads us in triumph in Christ."* Why would we settle for living with guilt, when we are guaranteed absolute forgiveness? In I John 1:9 we are promised, *"If we confess our sins, He is faithful and just to forgive us our sins and to cleanse us from all unrighteousness."* Why would we settle for living in doubt and unbelief, when we can live with absolute certainty about God? II Timothy 1:12 says, *"For this reason I also suffer these things; nevertheless I am not ashamed, for I know whom I have believed and am persuaded that He is able to keep what I have committed to Him until that Day."* Why would we settle for living in fear, when we can live by absolute faith? Galatians 2:20 says, *"I have been crucified with Christ; it is no longer I who live, but Christ lives in me; and the life which I now live in the flesh I live by faith in the Son of God, who loved me and gave Himself for me."*

Thought for Today

If we settle for anything less than what we are promised we can have in the Word, we insult the Lord's graciousness to us. Do not live beneath your privilege as a child of God.

Prayer Journal

_____

_____

_____

~ ~ ~ APRIL 24 ~ ~ ~

"Then Zacchaeus stood and said to the Lord, 'Look, Lord, I give half of my goods to the poor; and if I have taken anything from anyone by false accusation, I restore fourfold.' And Jesus said to him, 'Today, salvation has come to this house, because he also is a son of Abraham'" (Luke 19:8-9).

Zacchaeus was despised among his own people; not only because he collected taxes for Rome, but because he was a liar, a cheat, and a thief. He overcharged his own people on their taxes and pocketed the difference. While for the time being, he was getting away with this behavior in public, he wasn't getting away with it in his heart—he knew what a despicable man he had become. He hadn't always treated people this way, but something had happened along the way that soured him on life and twisted his understanding. His eyes were cold as steel and his heart had been closed to others due to a lack of compassion; yet, Zacchaeus sensed that something deep within him was unfulfilled.

What drew him that day to climb the tree to see Jesus as He passed through town? He was not drawn there because of idle curiosity concerning someone who was gaining notoriety. However, the magnet that pulled on his heart was the various rumors that he had heard concerning how Jesus had miraculously changed the lives of others. In his heart, he knew that he had become lost to the higher purposes of God to which he had been born.

Thought for Today

Zacchaeus's life was changed as he encountered Jesus. Have you lost your way like Zacchaeus? Invite Jesus to talk with you. You won't be disappointed and you will never be the same.

Prayer Journal

_____

_____

_____

~ ~ ~ APRIL 25 ~ ~ ~

"And Jesus, walking by the Sea of Galilee, saw two brothers, Simon called Peter, and Andrew his brother, casting a net into the sea; for they were fisherman. Then He said to them, 'Follow Me, and I will make you fishers of men.' They immediately left their nets and followed Him" (Matthew 4:18-20).

Jesus called Simon Peter and Andrew, his brother, to leave their fishing business and follow Him. Jesus told them that in doing so, He would make them fishers of men. The call of Jesus to Simon Peter and to his brother, Andrew, is the same call that He gives to us. We are to follow Him, and as we follow, He will make us *"fishers of men."* A *"fisher of men"* is someone who wins souls for God by introducing them to the life-changing love of Jesus.

There is a law about following Jesus hidden in this passage that is much like the present day law of gravity. If we throw a ball into the air ten times, ten times it will return to the earth because of the law of gravity. The law of gravity, very simply stated is, "whatever goes up, must come down." The law of following Jesus operates much the same way. Jesus said *"Follow Me, and I will make you fishers of men."* Simply stated; if we are following Jesus, we are fishing for men. If we are not fishing for men, we are not following Jesus. The good news is that we don't have to know how to fish for men for Jesus will teach us everything we need to know. Our only responsibility is to follow Him.

Thought for Today

As you follow Jesus He will lead you to people who need His love and grace, for He desires the world to be saved. All He needs is for you to introduce them to Him—He will do the rest.

Prayer Journal

_____

_____

_____

~ ~ ~ APRIL 26 ~ ~ ~

"The Spirit of the Lord is upon Me, because He has anointed Me to preach the gospel to the poor; He has sent Me to heal the brokenhearted, to proclaim liberty to the captives and recovery of sight to the blind, to set at liberty those who are oppressed; To proclaim the acceptable year of the Lord...And He began to say to them, 'Today this Scripture is fulfilled in your hearing'" (Luke 4:18-19, 21).

Jesus stood in the synagogue and began to read from the writings of the Prophet Isaiah. This passage outlines His agenda for ministry and His purpose in coming to earth. He then states that this prophecy was now being fulfilled before their eyes. In other words, what Isaiah promised in prophecy, Jesus was now fulfilling and making it a living reality. Jesus wanted them to know that He was sent from God to give an answer to their dilemmas and problems. He had come to break every form of bondage that was common to mankind. What the devil had done in taking God's highest creation captive, Jesus came to undo by setting every captive free.

The ministry of Jesus touches us in all three areas of life: He touches our physical bodies with His healing power; He touches our souls, by which, He cleanses our minds and molds our wills; and He touches our spirits with His eternal life. Jesus drives back the darkness that comes about by the devil's work against us and introduces us to God's mercy, grace, hope, and power.

Thought for Today

Jesus holds the answer to every problem that we will ever have. We can turn to Him and have the assurance that His touch will liberate us from every enemy, and from every form of bondage.

Prayer Journal

_____

_____

_____

~ ~ ~ APRIL 27 ~ ~ ~

"For I have come down from heaven, not to do My own will, but the will of Him who sent Me" (John 6:38).

Jesus gave us the perfect example of what it means to walk in obedience to the Father's will. In speaking to this gathering of would-be-followers, Jesus made it very clear that everything He did, and everything He said, was an expression of the will of the Father. On another occasion, Jesus said that He didn't do anything that He didn't first see the Father doing, and that He didn't say anything that He didn't hear the Father saying. We know that Jesus came to seek and to save everyone that had been lost through Adam's sin, *"For the Son of Man has come to seek and to save that which was lost"* (Luke 19:10). The life and ministry of Jesus can be summed up and characterized by His efforts to recover everything that had been lost. His mission was to recover what had been lost to God and to God's original intent.

Prior to His ascension, Jesus gave His disciples the commission to go to the ends of the earth with the good news of the Gospel of Jesus. They were to lead people to a saving knowledge of Christ, baptize them, and teach them, so that these converts could become disciples. In carrying out this commission, the disciples were continuing the ministry of Jesus. Jesus told His disciples that just as He had been sent by the Father, He was now sending them; *"As the Father has sent Me, I also send you"* (John 20:21).

Thought for Today

The same commission that Jesus gave to the first century disciples continues as our commission—nothing has changed. Like Jesus, we must determine to obey the will of the Father.

Prayer Journal

_____

_____

_____

~ ~ ~ APRIL 28 ~ ~ ~

"But you be watchful in all things, endure afflictions, do the work of an evangelist, fulfill your ministry" (II Timothy 4:5).

The primary work of an evangelist is to win souls to Christ. The evangelist proclaims the love and saving power of Jesus to those who are lost. His daily passion involves finding opportunities to share his faith. Paul told young Timothy to be careful and mindful in all things and to endure hardships. Paul also told him to win souls, and in doing so, he would fulfill his ministry.

Soul winning is often thought of as a ministry that belongs to someone else other than to us. We love to hear stories of how people shared their faith with someone and led them to Christ, but we don't consider ourselves responsible to do any sharing. We want our family and friends to be saved, but we want someone else to tell them how. We want our altars at church to be filled with people of all ages giving their lives to Jesus Christ, but we want the pastors and the church leaders to be the ones responsible to tell them. We need to change our mindset about the lost and ask ourselves the question, "If I don't tell them, who will?" When it comes to the souls of people who are dear to us, we cannot assume that someone will accept our responsibility to introduce them to Jesus. We must realize it is our responsibility.

Thought for Today

We are to do the work of an evangelist and win souls to Christ. Failure to do so will impede the fulfillment of our ministries. There is too much at stake not to set our hearts to win souls. No one is in our lives by accident, for God has placed them within our sphere of influence by His divine appointment.

Prayer Journal

_____

_____

_____

~ ~ ~ APRIL 29 ~ ~ ~

"Then the master said to the servant, 'Go out into the highways and hedges, and compel them to come in, that my house may be filled'" (Luke 14:23).

Use your imagination: you are walking along the docks and notice a beautiful fishing vessel tied up. There is a lot of activity on board and you assume that they are preparing to embark on a fishing expedition. You are invited aboard and given a tour of the vessel. You notice how well-dressed the crew appears and the sophistication of the vessel's equipment. You are impressed with the captain's knowledge of the industry, but you see and hear something that disturbs you. The crew and captain have moved to the bow of the boat with their faces toward the sea; they cup their hands over their mouths and shout, "Come here, all you fish, and jump into our boat. We have the finest boat in the area and are equipped to process you. Our crew will help you make the transition from the sea to the ship." Their actions disturb you for you know this is foolish. The only way to catch fish is to leave the safety of the harbor and launch into the deep where the fish live.

This imaginary episode seems ridiculous until you consider that we described the majority of American churches. We pride ourselves on our buildings, trained staff, and finely-tuned programs. We sit in our pews every Sunday and call for the lost to come and jump into our church. This simply will not work.

Thought for Today

Jesus said to go bring them to His house. This requires us to leave the safety of our homes and churches. We are required to go where the lost live and bring them into the church's fellowship.

Prayer Journal

_____

_____

_____

~ ~ ~ APRIL 30 ~ ~ ~

"But at midnight Paul and Silas were praying and singing hymns to God, and prisoners were listening to them. Suddenly there was a great earthquake, so that the foundations of the prison were shaken; and immediately all the doors were opened and everyone's chains were loosed" (Acts 16:25-26).

Paul and Silas were arrested, tried, found guilty, beaten, and placed in the Philippian jail. You remember the story: Paul looked at Silas and asked him if he was in pain and what he was thinking. Silas bitterly replied that he had never hurt so much in his life and he told Paul that he wanted to resign from ministry. He complained that Paul had never told him that things like this could happen to people who were serving Jesus. Paul told him not to worry, for he was contemplating resigning himself, as he was angry at God for not protecting them. Paul then called for the guard to bring him a pen and parchment so they could compose their resignation letters. He demanded to see a lawyer so they could review their rights concerning their future freedom.

You know the story didn't happen that way. I guess I got Paul and Silas confused with you and me, for we are the ones that complain and quit. Paul and Silas didn't complain about being mistreated or for not having anyone to pay attention to their pain. They didn't complain to each other, to the guard, to the other prisoners, or to God. They didn't want to resign from their job; they wanted to sing, and sing they did.

Thought for Today

Discipline yourself to praise the Lord and trust Him in the midst of your adversity. You will be surprised by the results.

Prayer Journal

_____

_____

_____

~ ~ ~ MAY 1 ~ ~ ~

"The Lord God has given Me the tongue of the learned, that I should know how to speak a word in season to him who is weary. He awakens me morning by morning, He awakens my ear to hear as the learned" (Isaiah 50:4).

God is looking for anyone who is willing to tell His story of love to a hurting world. So many Christians do not share their faith on a regular basis. Some have gone years between the times they have led someone to a saving knowledge of Jesus. An alarming number of Christians have never led someone to Christ, and for that matter, they have never even tried. There are a plethora of reasons why we don't share our faith, which range from our fear of rejection, to feeling inadequate in our knowledge of the Scripture. Probably the the most prominent reason is that we are afraid we won't know what to say or how to say it.

God is not looking for theologians or speakers with "no one can offend me" personalities. God is looking for anyone who is willing to speak on His behalf. To the willing one, God promises that He will enable them to speak and it will be as if they were professionally trained. Not only will God give the ability to speak as one knowledgeable and trained, but He will also put the right words into their mouths and stand close enough to place His hand on them. Isaiah 51:16 tells us, *"And I have put My words in your mouth; I have covered you with the shadow of My hand."*

Thought for Today

Whatever our excuse for not sharing Jesus with others—it's not good enough. God promises us that if we are merely willing, He will provide the opportunity and give us the words to say.

Prayer Journal

_____

_____

_____

~ ~ ~ MAY 2 ~ ~ ~

"Just as the Son of Man did not come to be served, but to serve, and to give His life a ransom for many" (Matthew 20:28).

D-Day was set into motion as three-million soldiers were deployed to invade Hitler's Atlantic Wall in France. The responsibility for the invasion fell on the shoulders of one man, General Dwight D. Eisenhower. The general spent the night before the invasion with the men of the 101st Airborne, known as the "Screaming Eagles." As the men checked their equipment, he went to each one and offered his words of encouragement and gratitude. The next morning, as planes departed, General Eisenhower stood with his hands in his pockets and with tears in his eyes. After the last C-47 disappeared into the morning darkness, he returned to his quarters and penned the following message which was to be delivered to the White House in the event of defeat: "Our landings have failed. The troops did all that bravery and devotion to duty could do. If any blame or fault attaches itself to the attempt, it was mine alone."

General Eisenhower was a man of great character. The man at the very top was taking the blame for every man below him—before blame even needed to be taken. What General Eisenhower did was noble; however, he was not the first to consider such a thing. Jesus did the same thing for us. He took the blame for sin and suffered our punishment, even though our blame was undeniable and our punishment deserved.

Thought for Today

Before mistakes were made, forgiveness was already offered. Jesus, the One at the top, willingly took the blame for sins He did not commit and paid the penalty for every man below Him.

Prayer Journal

_____

_____

_____

~ ~ ~ MAY 3 ~ ~ ~

"Behold, we are going up to Jerusalem, and the Son of Man will be betrayed to the chief priests and to the scribes; and they will condemn Him to death, and deliver Him to the Gentiles to mock and to scourge and to crucify. And the third day He will rise again" (Matthew 20:18-19).

Newspapers all over the country carried the story of the tragic death of the skydiving instructor. Harnessed together with his student, they jumped out of the plane for a routine skydiving lesson; however, the parachute didn't open. The instructor repositioned himself beneath the student to take the blunt of the fall's impact so that the student would survive the fall. Though it is tragic, this story beautifully portrays what Jesus came to do.

The term, *"Son of Man"* carried the same meaning to the Jews as the term, "General" carries for us—one with authority and a great conqueror. When Jesus referred to Himself as the *"Son of Man,"* the people cheered as they saw in Him the one who would deliver them from Rome's tyranny. When Jesus said that the *"Son of Man"* was going to be crucified, the disciples became confused, for how could the conqueror be the one conquered. They did not understand that the cross was the assignment of destiny for Jesus, the *"Son of Man."* They couldn't grasp the promise of life that was extended to them through the death of the *"Son of Man."*

Thought for Today

God had prepared the cross where His judgment would collide with His mercy; where His sovereignty would be confronted by His love; where His hatred of sin would wrestle with His grace for the sinner. Jesus the teacher died, so we the student could live.

Prayer Journal

_____

_____

_____

~ ~ ~ MAY 4 ~ ~ ~

"He has made everything beautiful in its time. Also He has put eternity in their hearts, except that no one can find out the work that God does from beginning to end. I know that nothing is better for them to rejoice, and to do good in their lives, and also that every man should eat and drink and enjoy the good of all his labor—it is the gift of God" (Ecclesiastes 3:11-13).

The concert was sold out and every seat was occupied with people waiting for the great pianist, Paderewski, to take his seat at the piano and fill the air with his glorious talent. Slipping away from the watchful eye of his mother, a nine-year-old boy ascended the stairs to the stage and ran to the piano. Still unnoticed, he began to pound out the tune of "Chopsticks." The crowd hushed and then began to "boo" and demand that someone remove the boy from the stage at once. Paderewski, hearing the commotion, walked out from the wings and approached the boy. Instead of removing him from the piano, he sat down next to him and smiled and started playing a counter melody. The jeering crowd turned their "boos" to "cheers" as a somebody, sat down next to a nobody, and they made beautiful music together.

Did you see yourself in this story? You were there! Except the stage wasn't hidden behind the walls of a beautiful theater; instead it was exposed to the harsh realities of life. The song of your life was out of tune and therefore, it was irritating at best. That is until Jesus sat beside you and made something beautiful.

Thought for Today

Jesus, who was a somebody, sat down next to you, a nobody, and a beautiful life was made.

Prayer Journal

_____

_____

_____

~ ~ ~ MAY 5 ~ ~ ~

"What is man that You are mindful of him, and the son of man that You visit him? For You have made him a little lower than the angels, and You have crowned him with glory and honor" (Psalms 8:4-5).

As David contemplated the majestic works of God's hands, he was amazed at God's loving-kindness towards mankind. In a sense, he was asking God what it was that caused Him to focus on man and what redeeming factor motivated Him to love man as He did? The answer is simple—in God's masterpiece of creation, man is His greatest and highest achievement. The trees on the hillside and the lilies of the valley were patterned one after the other. The beasts of the field and the birds of the air were also fashioned accordingly. However, when it came to man God used Himself as the pattern. In God's image, man was created. While created in God's image, each is unique in appearance and ability.

While we are the same, in that we were all created in the image of God, and while we are unique in our appearance and abilities, we share a common need to be loved. People may search their entire lives for someone to love them. The desire to be accepted and needed drives us to find unconditional love. We want to be loved for who we are, and not merely for what we can do. We desire to be loved in spite of our faults because we hold on to the hope, that with love, we will be given help to overcome them.

Thought for Today

God loves each of us and He accepts us just as we are. Yet, He loves us too much to leave us as He found us. Through His loving grace, He helps us change.

Prayer Journal

_____

_____

_____

~ ~ ~ MAY 6 ~ ~ ~

"'Come now, and let us reason to together,' says the Lord, 'Though your sins are like scarlet they shall be as white as snow; though they are red like crimson, they shall be as wool'" (Isaiah 1:18).

The nation of Israel had sinned against God—again! Yet, God was merciful and reached out to them, pleading with them to at least come and discuss the matter with Him. He promised them that no matter how vile their sin or how deep the stain, He would forgive and cleanse them of their unrighteousness. All they were required to do was to seek His forgiveness.

Perhaps the number one misconception people have about establishing a relationship with God, centers around their inability to believe that He actually loves them, personally. They assume that they have made too many mistakes and that they have demonstrated too much indifference towards God for Him to even be remotely interested in them. Their lives are loaded with the guilt of sin, thus, they are convinced they are unworthy to receive the love of God. They are painfully aware of the personal habits and cravings that bind them and with haunting clarity, yesterday's failure is remembered. Oh, if we only knew the depth of the love of God. A line within one of the hymns says, "There is a fountain filled with blood; drawn from Emmanuel's veins. And sinners plunged beneath that flood, loose all their guilty stains."

Thought for Today

The greatest cleansing agent is the blood of Jesus as its application redeems and restores. Come with a repentant heart and seek forgiveness—He is waiting to forgive and cleanse.

Prayer Journal

_____

_____

_____

~ ~ ~ MAY 7 ~ ~ ~

"And Pharaoh said to his servants, 'Can we find such a one as this, a man in whom is the Spirit of God?' Then Pharaoh said to Joseph, 'Inasmuch as God has shown you all this, there is no one as discerning and wise as you'" (Genesis 41:38-39).

Pharaoh woke in the night from a nightmare. He tried to go back to sleep, but as soon as he did, he was visited with another dream. The next morning he called all of the wise men of his counsel to be gathered to interpret his dreams. The wise men listened intently to Pharaoh as he recounted in detail his two dreams, and yet, they could not interpret his dreams. Pharaoh was told that a man in prison, named Joseph, had the ability to interpret dreams. Pharaoh ordered that he be brought to him; and he asked Joseph if he indeed could interpret dreams. Joseph replied that, in and of himself, he couldn't, but that God would give him the answers he desired. Pharaoh recounted his dreams and Joseph interpreted them as God revealed them to him. Pharaoh was so impressed, that he turned to his wise men and asked, *"Is there anyone in all of my kingdom like this man, in whom dwells the Spirit of God?"*

Pharaoh recognized that the difference between his wise men and Joseph was the presence of the Spirit of God. The same is still true today. It is the presence of the Holy Spirit in one's life that makes the difference between victory and defeat; between power and no power; and between wisdom and no wisdom.

Thought for Today

Throughout the Bible, the Spirit of the Lord is the one that makes the difference in the everyday lives and circumstances of men. Is the Holy Spirit making a difference in you?

Prayer Journal

_____

_____

_____

~ ~ ~ MAY 8 ~ ~ ~

"Then the Spirit of the Lord will come upon you, and you will prophesy with them and be turned into another man. So it was, when he had turned his back to go from Samuel, that God gave him another heart; and all those signs came to pass that day" (I Samuel 10:6, 9).

When Samuel anointed Saul to be King over the Israelites, he prophesied that the Holy Spirit would come upon him in such a measure, that he would literally, *"be turned into another man."* Just as Samuel had prophesied, King Saul received a new heart and was supernaturally changed by the power of the Holy Spirit.

The most exciting reading in the Bible is found in the "before and after stories." When Moses stood before the burning bush, he was weak and full of excuses as to why he couldn't do what God had assigned him to do. Yet, when we see Moses standing before Pharaoh, we see him looking the most powerful man in the world in the eye and telling him to let God's people go. What happened that was responsible for making the difference?

Before the crucifixion we find Peter to be weak in loyalty and afraid; however, on the Day of Pentecost, he preached Jesus from the Temple porch. What made the difference? The difference came when they were touched by the Holy Spirit. God is looking for people who are willing to *"be turned into another man."*

Thought for Today

The Holy Spirit so radically changes us that we are never the same again. He overrules our excuses and enables us to successfully accomplish our assignments.

Prayer Journal

~ ~ ~ MAY 9 ~ ~ ~

"Now a certain man was there who had an infirmity thirty-eight years. When Jesus saw him lying there, and knew that he already had been in that condition a long time, He said to him, 'Do you want to be made well?' The sick man answered Him, 'Sir, I have no man to put me into the pool when the water is stirred up; but while I am coming, another steps before me.' Jesus said to him, 'Rise, and take up your bed and walk.' And immediately the man was made well, took up his bed, and walked. And that day was the Sabbath" (John 5:5-9).

On the five porches surrounding the Pool of Bethesda, people laid suffering with every form of infirmity. Jesus, while visiting the pool, noticed one particular man and He asked what appears on the surface, to be a ridiculous question; *"Do you want to be made well?"* It may sound like a ridiculous question until you hear the man's response. He didn't directly answer the question; instead, he complained about how unfairly he was being treated and how no one cared enough to help him get into the water. He pointed out how someone else always got what he deserved. His self-pity blocked his ability to see that Jesus wanted to heal him.

It is a fact that not everyone wants to get well for they have learned to use their sickness and/or problems to gain attention and sympathy. They are afraid that if they get well, they will lose the extra attention they have grown accustomed to receiving.

Thought for Today

Some are so attached to their bitterness that they would rather complain and blame others than to exercise their faith and believe for healing. Don't become blinded by self-pity.

Prayer Journal

_____

_____

_____

~ ~ ~ MAY 10 ~ ~ ~

"Brood of vipers! How can you, being evil, speak good things? For out of the abundance of the heart the mouth speaks. A good man out of the good treasure of his heart brings forth good things, and an evil man out of the evil treasure brings forth evil things. But I say to you that for every idle word men may speak, they will give account of it in the Day of Judgment. For by your words you will be justified, and by your words you will be condemned" (Matthew 12:34-37).

While the eyes may be the window to man a man's soul; his words will reveal his heart. In rebuking the scribes and Pharisees, Jesus told them that whatever was abundant and dominant within a man's heart, would be revealed through the words of his mouth. Jesus also told them if a man's heart was wholesome, his words would be the verification; and by the same token, if a man's heart was evil, his words would give him away. And finally, Jesus told them that every man would give an account for his words on the Day of Judgment. It would be through the man's words that he would be justified in God's eyes, or condemned. Actually, our words are the end product of our focus. Whatever you focus on long enough, you will internalize; whatever you internalize, you will eventually verbalize; whatever you verbalize, will be established unto you. Your words either give permission for God to do His redeeming work of grace in your heart, or it will release the devil to work his corruption within you.

Thought for Today

If you want to know what someone is like, listen to the way they talk and listen to what they talk about. By the way—what do people assume you are like based on the words you speak?

Prayer Journal

_____

_____

_____

~ ~ ~ MAY 11 ~ ~ ~

"Be anxious for nothing, but in everything by prayer and supplication, with thanksgiving, let your requests be made known to God; and the peace of God, which surpasses all understanding, will guard your hearts and minds through Christ Jesus. Finally, brethren, whatever things are true, whatever things are noble, whatever things are just, whatever things are pure, whatever things are lovely, whatever things are of good report, if there is any virtue and if there is anything praiseworthy—meditate on these things. The things which you learned and received and heard and saw in me, these do, and the God of peace will be with you" (Philippians 4:6-9).

The mind has long been known to be the battle ground for spiritual matters for it is there, that we wrestle with doubts about God and the validity of His Word. Every action, as well as, every word we speak, begins with a thought. Paul addressed the need to master our thought life. He warned that the devil would try to twist our thoughts to contemplate imaginary circumstances; and if successful, our thoughts would then have the power to torment us. The devil will entice the lusts of our flesh as he brings about compromise through an undisciplined thought life. We don't have to be the victim of our thoughts; but rather, we can have the power over them. Paul told us to discipline ourselves to think about good things and then we would know the peace of God, and the God of peace would be with us, and in us.

Thought for Today

You cannot be held responsible for the thoughts that knock on your mind's door. However, you are held accountable for the ones you invite to sit in your parlor and socialize with.

Prayer Journal

_____

_____

_____

~ ~ ~ MAY 12 ~ ~ ~

"Now we exhort you, brethren, warn those who are unruly, comfort the fainthearted, uphold the weak, be patient with all. See that no one renders evil for evil to anyone, but always pursue what is good both for yourselves and for all. Rejoice always, pray without ceasing, in everything give thanks; for this is the will of God in Christ Jesus for you. Do not quench the Spirit. Do not despise prophecies. Test all things; hold fast what is good. Abstain from every form of evil" (I Thessalonians 5:14-22).

Consider Paul's list of responsibilities for living a Christian life that is victorious. We are to warn the undisciplined of the consequences of their rebellion against God. We are to be a source of comfort to the hurting and be consistent in our encouragement of those who are struggling. We are to be patient with everyone, regardless of how much they irritate us. We are to stop anyone's attempt to harm another, regardless of how justified it might be. In pursuing our own interests, we are to make sure we don't harm another's well-being. We are to be joyful regardless of our circumstances. We are to pray about everything and maintain an attitude of gratitude. We are to remove any compromise that will grieve the Holy Spirit. We should not be critical of the Holy Spirit's instructions to us. We are to test everything against the Word and only embrace what the Word confirms to be true. We are to guard our conduct so that there isn't the slightest appearance of wrong doing.

Thought for Today

Paul's list is not for fanatics. It very simply describes what a normal Christian is to be like and how they are to respond to the daily issues of life. What areas do you need to work on to be able to say you are normal?

Prayer Journal

_____

_____

_____

~ ~ ~ MAY 13 ~ ~ ~

"I will bless the Lord at all times; His praise shall continually be in my mouth. My soul shall make its boast in the Lord; the humble shall hear of it and be glad. Oh, magnify the Lord with me, and let us exalt His name together. I sought the Lord, and He heard me, and delivered me from all my fears...This poor man cried out, and the Lord heard him, and saved him out of all his troubles...Oh, taste and see that the Lord is good; blessed is the man who trusts in Him! Oh, fear the Lord, you His saints! There is no want to those who fear Him. The young lions lack and suffer hunger; but those who seek the Lord shall not lack any good thing" (Psalms 34:1-4, 6, 8-10).

David wasn't devoid of negative feelings; he just refused to let negative feelings control him. David chose to bless the Lord in the good times and in the bad times, for his praise to God was not conditional. Instead of whining about what God had not done, David chose to boast about what God had done and would yet do. He praised God's faithfulness, as God never failed to deliver him.

David was convinced that God was good all the time and that God was not the source of his problems. David declared his faith in God's promises, believing that regardless of how things appeared, God would satisfy his longings and desires. He knew his choices, concerning his attitude and conduct, would have an affect on his own life, as well as, the lives of people around him.

Thought for Today

David knew his response to problems would have influence on others and their opinions of his God. David wanted everyone to see God's goodness and faithfulness.

Prayer Journal

_____

_____

_____

~ ~ ~ MAY 14 ~ ~ ~

"A wise man will hear and increase learning, and a man of understanding will attain wise counsel" (Proverbs 1:5).

Life demands that we learn to adapt to new things, done in new ways, even if it means embracing the dreaded word "change." Everything around us is changing at a very rapid pace. Technology has made the computer that you just purchased an antique before you even get it out of the store and into the trunk of your car. We are bombarded with advertisements boasting of new and improved products. When it comes to our health, no one is content to use medical methods that were developed a century ago. Yet, it is the nature of man to resist change. Once we get set in our ways, it is almost impossible to get us to change what we have grown comfortable with. We want things to be done the same way throughout the entirety of our lives. Some of the most serious disagreements we encounter, center on someone's attempt to change something we have grown accustomed too.

Resistance to change is a difficult problem in spiritual matters. The Bible tells us that a wise man will listen, continually learn new things, and seek out the counsel of others. The most dangerous person around the church is the one who believes they have the answer for everything. They don't listen to counsel, because they have an unteachable spirit. An unteachable spirit is full of pride, and therefore, one that God will resist.

Thought for Today

God will resist the proud, but gives grace to the humble. Don't allow yourself to develop an unteachable spirit. Don't resist the Holy Spirit when He seeks to change you.

Prayer Journal

_____

_____

_____

~ ~ ~ MAY 15 ~ ~ ~

"Do not be rash with your mouth, and let not your heart utter anything hastily before God. For God is in heaven, and you on earth; therefore let your words be few...When you make a vow to God, do not delay to pay it; for He has no pleasure in fools. Pay what you have vowed—better not to vow than to vow and not pay" (Ecclesiastes 5:2, 4-5).

It is amazing how spiritual we become when we get into trouble. We turn to God and make all sorts of promises if He will just get us out of the current jam. Our promises range from better attendance in church to giving more money in the offering. Then, equally amazing, is how quickly we forget the promises that we have made to God. We rationalize that we just got caught up emotionally in the circumstance and then when our heads clear, we realize that we had spoken and made the promise too quickly. We assume that God understands and we avoid talking to Him about it, just in case He doesn't understand. The result of not following through on our promises to God is a deep sense of guilt.

The Bible gives instructions concerning our vows or promises to God. We are warned not to let our mouths overload our capacity to follow through on promises. Actually, it is not our capacity that is overloaded by our mouth; rather, it is our level of commitment. In a sense, we are trying to manipulate God by our promises, even when we know we have no intention of keeping them.

Thought for Today

It is much better not to not make a promise to God than to make a promise, and not keep it. God takes us at our word, just as He expects us to always take Him at His Word—keep your vows.

Prayer Journal

_____

_____

_____

~ ~ ~ MAY 16 ~ ~ ~

"He who walks with wise men will be wise, but the companion of fools will be destroyed" (Proverbs 13:20).

It really is true that you are known by the company you keep. Over the course of our lifetime, we will have a large number of people who will come in and out of our lives, and to one degree or another, have an influence on us. According to Scripture, not everyone is qualified to have access to us, much less, have a relationship. Only the Holy Spirit can be the One to guide us as to who is qualified and who is not. Lest you think that I am speaking of some sort of elitism that we as Christians are entitled to enjoy, I am not! I am talking about having wrong associations in our lives. We should not be giving access to our hearts, our values, our time, our resources, and our dreams, to just anyone.

As parents, we tell our children not to hang out with the kids that are rebellious; because we know that good values can be eroded over time; *"Do not be deceived, evil company corrupts good habits"* (I Corinthians 15:33). The problem is that while we want our children to heed this Biblical advice, we do not want to heed this advice as adults. Everyone in your life is either taking you closer to your God-given assignment, or they are pulling you away from everything you hold dear. They are either adding to your spiritual strength, or they are draining it from you. They are either sharpening your focus, or they are breaking your focus.

Thought for Today

One who does not share your values regarding God, His Word, or His ways, will never be able to truly value you as a person. Ask the Holy Spirit to qualify every relationship.

Prayer Journal

_____

_____

_____

~ ~ ~ MAY 17 ~ ~ ~

"But let him ask in faith, with no doubting, for he who doubts, is like a wave of the sea driven and tossed by the wind. For let not that man suppose that he will receive anything from the Lord; he is a double-minded man, unstable in all his ways" (James 1:6-8).

The longest lines at any amusement park are to be found at the roller coaster ride. There is something insane within all of us who ride roller coasters. Our hearts pound with anticipation as the car chugs up the steep incline, and then we yell and scream as it plunges rapidly into the depths below. We do not have time to recover from the last plunge before the next one sucks the breath from our lungs. The butterflies in our stomach turn into buffalos and our heart lodges in our throat. We exit rubber-legged, nervous in the stomach, with hair standing on end, and our eyes glazed over. Then we smile and claim to have enjoyed the ride.

Riding a roller coaster in an amusement park may be fun while it lasts, but riding one in regard to the commitments necessary to life can be disastrous. The Bible tells us that *"he is a double-minded man, unstable in all his ways."* A double-minded person is one who is emotionally on a roller coaster—up one day and down the next. They are living in faith one day and out of faith the next as they make promises that they never keep. They have nothing in their life to give evidence that they even understand the meaning to the word consistency, much less, exhibit any.

Thought for Today

How stable are you in your commitments to God, your spouse, your family, your church, and your work? If you are riding a roller coaster, get off at the next stop.

Prayer Journal

_____

_____

_____

~ ~ ~ MAY 18 ~ ~ ~

"Even so the tongue is a little member and boasts of great things. See how great a forest a little fire kindles! And the tongue is a fire, a world of iniquity. The tongue is so set among our members that it defiles the whole body, and sets on fire the course of nature; and it is set on fire by hell" (James 3:5-6).

One day, a mother took her young son to the edge of the cliff overlooking the deep ravine. She wanted to teach him a lesson about the power of hurtful words. Holding a feather pillow in one hand, she sliced it with a knife and began to shake the feathers into the wind. Catching the feathers on its wings, the wind carried them deep into the ravine and scattered them a great distance from each other. Turning to her son, the mother asked him if he thought it would be possible for him to find and gather every feather from the pillow. The son laughed and said that while he might be able to get most of them, there would no way possible to get all the feathers back. The mother then used his answer to explain the truth of hurtful words. Once spoken, like the feathers scattered in the wind, there will be no way to get them all back.

We have all said things that we wish we hadn't said and we would give anything if we could get our words back, but we can't. Far more damage can be done with our words than with our fists. Blows from a fist will eventually heal, but hurtful words will wound the heart, and a bruised heart is very difficult to heal.

Thought for Today

With our words, we are building someone up or tearing someone down. We must learn the discipline of bridling our tongues! Renew your commitment to speak words that heal, not hurt.

Prayer Journal

_____

_____

_____

~ ~ ~ MAY 19 ~ ~ ~

"Even so the tongue is a little member and boasts great things. See how great a forest a little fire kindles! And the tongue is a fire, a world of iniquity. The tongue is so set among our members that it defiles the whole body, and sets on fire the course of nature; and it is set on fire by hell. For every kind of beast and bird, of reptile and creature of the sea, is tamed and has been tamed by mankind. But no man can tame the tongue. It is an unruly evil, full of deadly poison" (James 3:5-8).

James minces no words in warning us of the dangers of an unbridled tongue. If unbridled, the tongue, though it is small, has the capacity to boast of things greater than we are able to fulfill. The tongue can destroy people much like a forest fire, and if left alone, can destroy the forest. James tells us that it is easier to tame a wild beast then it is to tame the tongue. He likens the tongue to a deadly poison and notes that it is ruled by a rebellious nature.

How much trouble has your tongue gotten you into? It is amazing how our tongues are willing to shade the truth to serve our own purposes. Most of the problems we have can be traced back to an unbridled tongue. We get into a heated argument with someone and before we know it, we are saying words that we really don't mean and would give anything not to have said. Truthfully, the problem with the tongue is always rooted in our hearts. Jesus said that the tongue only repeats what it hears the heart saying.

Thought for Today

We need the help of the Holy Spirit. Only through the discipline and strength of the Holy Spirit can we turn our tongues from being instruments of destruction, into agents of healing.

Prayer Journal

_____

_____

_____

~ ~ ~ MAY 20 ~ ~ ~

"But know this, that in the last day perilous times will come: For men will be lovers of themselves, lovers of money, boasters, proud, blasphemers, disobedient to parents, unthankful, unholy, unloving, unforgiving, slanderers, without self-control, brutal, despisers of good, traitors, headstrong, lovers of pleasures rather than lovers of God, having a form of godliness but denying its power. And from such people turn away! ...But evil men and imposters will grow worse and worse, deceiving and being deceived" (II Timothy 3:1-5, 13).

Paul warned young Timothy about the perilous times that were fast encroaching into the hearts of men. Paul's words to Timothy were probably not very comforting, especially the part about the wickedness of men getting worse. What Paul had written to Timothy, we are reading as front-page headlines in newspapers; we are living in the perilous times of which Paul spoke.

Our Christian ethics and values are considered foolish and dangerous to our society. It is getting harder to live the Christian life in this generation without ridicule and persecution. Just when we think that things can't possibly get any worse, they do. If we are not careful to protect our hearts from becoming polluted with the sinful nature listed in Paul's warning to Timothy, everything we hold as sacred will slowly erode away and be lost forever.

Thought for Today

Be vigilant to guard your heart from any compromise resulting from rebellion and adhere to the Biblical boundaries of Christian conduct. Do not yield to the popular ethics and values of our deceived society, which are contrary to God's Word.

Prayer Journal

_____

_____

_____

~ ~ ~ MAY 21 ~ ~ ~

"For I am persuaded that neither death nor life, nor angels nor principalities nor powers, nor things present nor things to come, nor height nor depth, nor any other created thing, shall be able to separate us from the love of God which is in Christ Jesus our Lord" (Romans 8:38-39).

One of the great promises of God is found in this passage of Scripture. The Apostle Paul wanted to make sure that we knew just how secure we really are in the love and protection of God. Paul was not hoping that these things were true, for he was absolutely persuaded, and no one could dissuade him otherwise. Paul was convinced that death didn't have the power to separate us from the love of God, nor did anything else in life. The angels couldn't do it, and all of the combined powers of hell would not stand a chance of separating us from the love of God. Paul goes straight to the bottom line in the matter and states that there is absolutely nothing created that exists now, or ever will exist, that has the power to separate us from the love of God and His ability to protect us.

It is usually our sense of guilt over sin that tries to convince us that we have removed ourselves from the reach of God's love. Devils try to erode our confidence by telling us that what we have done has so angered God, that He has stopped loving us. Our failure grieves His heart, but never extinguishes His love.

Thought for Today

God's love is not based on our ability to perceive it or feel it. His love is an unchangeable fact. God's love is not based on how well we perform in His presence, nor is it diminished by our failures. God loves us, and that's that!

Prayer Journal

_____

_____

_____

~ ~ ~ MAY 22 ~ ~ ~

"For God has not given us a spirit of fear, but of power and of love and of a sound mind" (II Timothy 1:7).

One of the greatest differences between God and the devil is revealed in how each respond to people. The weapon most often used in the devil's arsenal is fear. He knows that fear strikes torment at the heart, and will bring confusion to the mind. Everything associated with the devil centers around the use of fear. The devil uses guilt and fear to gain control over peoples' minds, and ultimately their lives. Fear will always dismantle the sound thinking processes of the mind.

In contrast, God is a lover. He uses His eternal and unchanging love to draw us to Himself. It is our love for Him in return, that motivates us to walk uprightly before Him. God never uses guilt or fear of reprisal as a means of manipulating our hearts and behavior. When we fail Him, God forgives us and showers us with His love. Whenever we are tormented by fear, we can know with certainty that the fear did not come from God. Fear will bind us, but God's gift of power liberates us. God's gift of love forever establishes our self-worth and fulfills our deepest needs. Fear steals our ability to think soundly and will fog our minds with confusion. God's love dispels our confusion as He imparts His wisdom to our minds which will, in turn, help us make the right decisions.

Thought for Today

If you are confused and experiencing fear, you can rest assured it is not from God. Turn to God. Let His love and power banish the devils of confusion and fear away from you, and restore you to the *"sound mind"* that He intended for you to experience.

Prayer Journal

_____

_____

_____

~ ~ ~ MAY 23 ~ ~ ~

"No weapon formed against you shall prosper, and every tongue which rises against you in judgment you shall condemn. This is the heritage of the servants of the Lord, and their righteousness is from Me, says the Lord" (Isaiah 54:17).

If we lived in a perfect world, there wouldn't be a devil to deal with. There would be no problems, crime, sickness, pain, death, or heartaches. We would have perfect health and every relationship would be wholesome. Our bills would be paid on time and we would have money left over. Our thoughts would be pure and never harmful to anyone. Our ears would never hear an angry word, nor our eyes behold violence, and we would be treated fairly by everyone. Laughter would replace stress.

Sounds great, doesn't it? Actually, things will be just as described above, and so much more, when we get to our final destination—Heaven. There, in our Father's house, we will enjoy things that we do not have the capacity to understand from our earthly perspective. However, the stark reality is that we do not live in a perfect world. There is pain and suffering all around us and our resources are very limited. The devil is a real enemy who is seeking to steal, kill, and destroy everything that we hold precious. The pain and suffering in our world is a direct result of sin. Yet, God promised that no matter how difficult the circumstances might become, He will bring us through to victory.

Thought for Today

God never promised the devil wouldn't use his weapons against us, but He did promise that when they were used, they wouldn't succeed. We can trust God to bring us through to victory.

Prayer Journal

_____

_____

_____

~ ~ ~ MAY 24 ~ ~ ~

"Joseph said to them, 'Do not be afraid, for am I in the place of God? But as for you, you meant evil against me; but God meant it for good, in order to bring it about as it is this day, to save many people alive. Now therefore, do not be afraid; I will provide for you and your little ones.' And he comforted them and spoke kindly to them" (Genesis 50:19-21).

Jacob's pampering of his youngest son, Joseph, developed a root of jealousy and hatred in his brother's hearts. They devised an evil plan to get rid of him—once and for all. Sent to the fields to check on his brothers, Joseph soon found himself in the bottom of a deep pit. His brothers sold him to a caravan traveling to the distant land of Egypt. They assumed Joseph would live out his days in servitude within a foreign land. Jacob's heart broke when they told him that Joseph had been killed by a wild beast.

Joseph suffered a number of trials while in Egypt, but he never let go of his devotion to God, nor his faith that God would deliver him. A famine ravaged the land and Jacob sent his sons to the rulers of Egypt to beg for provisions. Jacob's sons soon learned that the brother, they had betrayed, was the one who would determine the answer to their request for provisions. They feared for their lives, but their fear was soon overcome through the forgiveness and compassion of Joseph.

Thought for Today

Joseph believed that regardless of what the devil had meant for harm, God would turn it for his good. What jealousy and hatred had tried to destroy—love and forgiveness had restored. What God did for Joseph, He will do for you. He cares—Trust Him.

Prayer Journal

_____

_____

_____

~ ~ ~ MAY 25 ~ ~ ~

"And we know that all things work together for good to those who love God, to those who are the called according to His purpose" (Romans 8:28).

Out of all the Scriptures in the Bible, this one is the most often misquoted. When someone gets into trouble, some well-meaning person slides an arm around their shoulders, and in an attempt to comfort them says, "Don't worry, all things work out for good." While they are to be commended for their sincere attempt to bring comfort to someone in pain, what they said was scripturally inaccurate. All things do not necessarily work out for good. One more time, read the verse—*"...all things work together for good to those who love God and are called..."*—which means fitting into His purpose for their lives. If we want all things to work for good, then the qualifier must be that we love God and are in the center of His will for our lives.

Loving God means much more than giving Him our lip-service. We would much rather that someone would demonstrate their love, than to tell us that they love us, and expect us to take their word for it. Love is an emotion of the heart and can only be validated by our actions. Our love for God is the same, in that our actions are the only source of validation to what we have declared to be true. We must surrender our will to His will as we daily discipline ourselves to seek His plan for our lives. We must come to the point that we do not insist on having our own way.

Thought for Today

The person who loves God, and has surrendered his will, can know that regardless of circumstances, something good is on the way.

Prayer Journal

_____

_____

_____

~ ~ ~ MAY 26 ~ ~ ~

"The righteous cry out, and the Lord hears, and delivers them out of all their troubles. The Lord is near to those who have a broken heart, and saves such as have a contrite spirit. Many are the afflictions of the righteous, but the Lord delivers him out of them all" (Psalms 34:17-19).

We have seen the scenario in a television show where the bad guy has captured the good guy and laughingly tells him, "Go ahead and scream; no one can hear you." The inference of the show's director is that the circumstances are so hopeless and the danger so perilous, that all hope of rescue is gone. While we get nervous about the plight of the good guy, we know that sooner or later, something will happen and he will be saved from the bad guy.

We can relate to this scenario. We have had those moments in our life when the attacks of the devil make our circumstances appear so overwhelming that we have little confidence in God. We start to question His ability to work things out. Actually, the devil loves to try to convince us that we are in so much trouble that even if we cry for help, God won't hear us. The Psalmist David knew differently. He knew that God's ears were ever open and fine-tuned to hear the cry of His people. David knew that God wouldn't run away at the first sign of trouble.

Thought for Today

The devil tries to bury you so deep in your problems that you don't feel like God can see you, much less hear your cry for help. Nothing could be further from the truth. God sees you, He hears your cry, and He will not fail to rescue you from the devil's hand. Walk in faith as you acknowledge God's ability to deliver you.

Prayer Journal

_____

_____

_____

~ ~ ~ MAY 27 ~ ~ ~

"But now, thus says the Lord, Who created you, O Jacob, and He who formed you, O Israel: 'Fear not, for I have redeemed you; I have called you by your name; you are Mine. When you pass through the waters, I will be with you; and through the rivers, they shall not overflow you. When you walk through the fire, you shall not be burned, nor shall the flame scorch you'" (Isaiah 43:1-2).

Each one of us has suffered at the hands of what we call, "fair-weather friends." You know who I am talking about—that person who claims to be your loyal friend through all of time and eternity; the person who has boasted on more than one occasion about their resolve to go the distance with you through the thick and thin of life; that person who at the first sign of trouble dumped you and disappeared from sight. We not only hurt over their abandoning us in our time of need, we are also angry that we invested so much time and energy in such "flakes."

While our friends may be tempted to bail on us when we get into trouble, our Father never will. God is not worried about whether or not our circumstances will work out. More importantly, God is not afraid of the devil's threats to do us greater harm. God has pre-determined to go the distance through every trial. God intends to bring us through the trial, not leave us in the midst of it.

Thought for Today

It doesn't matter what kind of trouble we are in, God promises to go through it with us. Notice that we are only going through the trouble…we are not staying in it? God has promised to be our constant companion. He will strengthen us daily and ultimately, He will deliver us.

Prayer Journal

_____

_____

_____

~ ~ ~ MAY 28 ~ ~ ~

"I thank my God upon every remembrance of you, always in every prayer of mine making request for you all with joy, for your fellowship in the gospel from the first day until now, being confident of this very thing, that He who has begun a good work in you will complete it until the day of Jesus Christ" (Philippians 1:3-6).

The Apostle Paul was deeply in love with the church at Philippi. It had started, much through the efforts of a handful of women willing to persevere in prayer. Paul's thoughts often drifted in their direction and in doing so, it brought him fond memories and fulfilling joy. Paul championed their willingness to embrace the gospel and to grow in its discipline. He wanted to encourage them to keep walking in faith and to work hard for the Gospel's sake. He knew that whatever stage of life and growth the church was currently in, it would be increased. He knew that God never makes a mistake. Whatever God starts, He completes.

Your journey was started by God—you didn't choose Him, He chose you. You didn't give God a break and decide to get saved—He gave you a break and opened the door of life to you. You never once looked His direction. He pursued you relentlessly, and drew you at every turn, until you surrendered your heart to Him. God sees something in you so exciting that He wanted to save you so that you can live with Him for eternity.

Thought for Today

God never makes a mistake! Everything He has started in you, He promises to bring to completion. No matter how difficult things may appear now, you must hold on to the promises of the Word. God is not finished with you!

Prayer Journal

_____

_____

_____

~ ~ ~ MAY 29 ~ ~ ~

"The thief does not come except to steal, and to kill, and to destroy. I have come that they may have life, and that they may have it more abundantly" (John 10:10).

One day a turtle was sunning himself on the river's bank and was approached by a scorpion. The scorpion asked the turtle to take him to the other side of the river by letting him ride on his back. The turtle declined the scorpion's request, citing that the scorpion might sting him and he would die. The scorpion assured him that he would not sting him and that he would be perfectly safe. Finally, against his better judgment, the turtle agreed to give the scorpion a ride across the river. Things started out fine—the turtle and the scorpion carried on a civil conversation and all seemed well. Then, just before reaching the other shore, the scorpion stung the back of the turtle's head. Incensed and dying, the turtle protested that he had promised not to sting him and that he had trusted him to keep his word. The scorpion replied, "I couldn't help it, for you see, it is in my nature to sting."

It may be a silly story, but there is a great truth within. Sometimes we are tempted to give into the enticements that the devil brings. Against our better judgment, we buy into his promises of how this will be all right for us to do and that no harm will come to us if we decide to participate. Like the turtle we discover, after it is too late, that it is the nature of the devil to steal, kill, and destroy.

Thought for Today

Don't make deals with the devil. He not only lies, but there is absolutely no truth in him to be found. It is impossible for him to circumvent his nature. He is a killer by nature.

Prayer Journal

_____

_____

_____

~ ~ ~ MAY 30 ~ ~ ~

"For what I am doing, I do not understand. For what I will to do, that I do not practice; but what I hate, that I do....For I know that in me (that is, in my flesh) nothing good dwells; for to will is present with me, but how to perform what is good I do not find. For the good that I will to do, I do not do; but the evil I will not to do, that I practice....For I delight in the law of God according to the inward man. But I see another law in my members, warring against the law of my mind, and bringing me into captivity to the law of sin which is in my members. O wretched man that I am! Who will deliver me from this body of death? I thank God—through Jesus Christ our Lord" (Romans 7:15, 18-10, 22-25)!

Paul is honest with us in this passage. He bears his soul concerning the struggle he was fighting between his carnal nature and his new spiritual nature. He lamented that he found himself doing the very things that he hated doing. He pointed out, that with his heart he wanted to serve God, but his flesh was not in agreement. You hear the torment of guilt in his words. He admits this battle rendered him miserable and that it lowered his opinion of himself to that of being a *"wretched man."*

Paul knew that his only hope of deliverance from his flesh was to be found in Jesus Christ. He knew that he couldn't just wish things were different and he also knew that ignoring them would not change them. He needed help, and his help was in Jesus.

Thought for Today

We can identify with Paul's struggle between his carnal nature and spiritual nature. Like Paul, our only hope of getting our act together spiritually, is in Jesus.

Prayer Journal

_____

_____

_____

~ ~ ~ MAY 31 ~ ~ ~

"When your son asks you in time to come, saying, 'What is the meaning of the testimonies, the statutes, and the judgments which the Lord our God has commanded you?' Then you shall say to your son: 'We were slaves of Pharaoh in Egypt, and the Lord brought us out of Egypt with a mighty hand; and the Lord showed signs and wonders before our eyes, great and severe, against Egypt, Pharaoh, and all his household. Then He brought us out from there, that He might bring us in, to give us the land of which He swore to our fathers'" (Deuteronomy 6:20-23).

Theologians have told us that God could have delivered the children of Israel out of Egypt, through the Red Sea, and into the Promised Land, in approximately eleven days. Camped at Kadesh, which was at the threshold of the Promised Land, the Israelites questioned God's ability to give them the land. They sent in the spies, and when they returned, they believed their negative reports. Because of their unbelief and refusal to go in and possess the land by faith, God punished them. They received a sentence of one year of wandering for every day that they had questioned God's integrity. The spies were in the land for forty days; which is in direct correlation to the fact the Israelites wandered for forty years until the generation of unbelievers died.

We are tempted to point a finger at the Israelites for their unbelief, especially after seeing all the powerful miracles on their behalf. Be careful in judging, for we are often guilty of the same unbelief.

Thought for Today

Many are wandering and dying in the wilderness of unbelief. While wandering, they stand at the threshold of God's promises.

Prayer Journal

_____

_____

_____

~ ~ ~ JUNE 1 ~ ~ ~

"Do not be deceived, my beloved brethren" (James 1:16).

We have all sat spell bound as a magician performed tricks that defy human logic and comprehension. While we know it is a trick, it still tickles our fancy just a little. Most of the fun is speculating on just how the trick was accomplished. The magician makes his living deceiving people with the slight of his hands, while using his powers of persuasion to distract the focus of the audience. Many people really enjoy this form of entertainment; however, when it comes to spiritual matters, getting tricked is not fun, it is disastrous.

The devil loves to trick people into believing the wrong things. He seeks to distract our focus from the truth of the Word and will convince us to focus on what he wants us to see instead. When a magician tricks us, it's just entertainment—when the devil tricks us, it's deadly. There is only one way to keep from getting tricked by the devil—you must be acquainted with the truth of the Word.

God lamented to Hosea, that His people were being deceived and destroyed because they didn't have knowledge of His Word, *"My people are destroyed for lack of knowledge"* (Hosea 4:6). It is only through our knowledge of the Word that we can discern between the devil's lies and the truth of God. II Timothy 2:15 says, *"Be diligent to present yourself approved to God, a worker who does not need to be ashamed, rightly dividing the word of truth."*

Thought for Today

To avoid being deceived by the devil's tricks, learn to discipline yourself to spend time studying the Word. What you think you see, must always be weighed against what you know to be true.

Prayer Journal

_____

_____

_____

~ ~ ~ JUNE 2 ~ ~ ~

"If anyone thinks himself to be a prophet or spiritual, let him acknowledge that the things which I write to you are the commandments of the Lord" (I Corinthians 14:37).

Do you consider yourself to be a spiritual person who is successfully accomplishing the perfect will of God for your life? Tragically, so many Christians do not perceive themselves as being spiritual, much less, accomplishing their God-given assignment.

Many live with the misconception that spirituality is determined by a person's outward appearance and behavior. While spirituality will have an affect on our appearance, speech, and conduct, our outward appearance is not the true indicator. We can take a man off of skid row, give him a bath, a shave and haircut, buy him a new suit, give him a Bible, teach him when to raise his hands and when to say "Amen,"—place him on the front row of most churches in America and his appearance and actions alone will cause most people to think that he is spiritual. The truth of the matter is that he is acting out the part of knowing God and has never been saved.

True spirituality is not determined by a man's outward appearance or conduct; it is solely determined by a relationship with Jesus Christ. God measures us by the attitudes of our hearts. God changes our lives from the inside out, not the outside in. When the condition of the heart changes so will the fruit of a man's life.

Thought for Today

The depth of your spirituality is not determined by your ability to adhere to a set of religious rules, but rather, by the reality of your relationship with Jesus Christ.

Prayer Journal

_____

_____

_____

~ ~ ~ JUNE 3 ~ ~ ~

"That in the ages to come He might show the exceeding riches of His grace in His kindness toward us in Christ Jesus. For by grace you have been saved through faith, and that not of yourselves; it is the gift of God" (Ephesians 2:7-8).

The custom of the first church I pastored was for the chairman of the deacon board to begin each service with a prayer. I cringed every time he stepped forward and gripped the side of the pulpit for he repeated the same prayer every Sunday. In his "holiest" voice he would proceed to tell God what a bunch of unworthy, rotten, no-good sinners we all were. He would say that not one of us deserved to be in His presence and we were unworthy to receive anything from Him. I must confess, if he had been speaking only for himself, I would have shouted "Amen," for I had suffered through many deacons' meetings with this man. However, when he decided to include me in his woeful prayer, and called me an unworthy, rotten, no-good sinner—it offended me. One Sunday, I couldn't take it anymore and in the middle of his prayer, I asked him to sit down. A deafening hush fell as the "Amen's" stopped and everyone's eyes opened in disbelief. I defended my actions by reminding them of the richness of God's grace which had been freely given to each of us when we asked. Furthermore, I reminded them that if we claim to be unworthy of the sacrifice of Christ, we are ignorant of His Word; therefore, we continually insult the precious gift of the Cross where Jesus died to make us worthy.

Thought for Today

We are all sinners; however, through the blood of Jesus, we are forgiven and robed in His righteousness. As sons, we are worthy to stand in His presence and receive the things He has for us.

Prayer Journal

~ ~ ~ JUNE 4 ~ ~ ~

"Confess your trespasses to one another, and pray for one another, that you may be healed. The effective, fervent prayer of a righteous man avails much" (James 5:16).

Many Christians have the misconception that the effectiveness of their prayer is measured by the number of manifested answers to prayer that they can see. We have all struggled at times with the feeling that we are not effective in prayer. Occasionally, we see a miracle answer to prayer; however, more often than not, what answers we see are very slow in arriving. Who among us can explain the frustration of praying for something and then the exact opposite of what we pray for happens. Someone approaches us and requests prayer; while our hearts agree when our prayer is offered, our mind is shouting that we need to give this person a break and send them to someone else who can effectively pray for their need!

Prayer is a command, not an option. The Scriptures teach us to pray about everything and not to stop praying. Prayer is God's invitation for us to communicate with Him and to invite His involvement into our circumstances. Jeremiah 33:3 tells us, *"Call to Me and I will answer you, and show you great and mighty things, which you do not know."* James tells us that the prayers of the righteous avail much. This means our prayers will prevail over every circumstance with great power. The responsibility to pray is ours, while the timing of the manifested answer belongs to God.

Thought for Today

Your effectiveness in prayer is determined by only one thing and one thing only—whether or not you pray. As a righteous man, your prayers will prevail with great power. Pray!

Prayer Journal

_____

_____

_____

~ ~ ~ JUNE 5 ~ ~ ~

"Then the serpent said to the woman, 'You will not surely die. For God knows that in the day you eat of it your eyes will be opened, and you will be like God, knowing good and evil'" (Genesis 3:4-5).

Satan approached Eve in the Garden of Eden with a question about the instructions that God had previously given to them. He asked Eve if God had told her that they couldn't eat the fruit of every tree in the Garden. Eve answered him by saying that only the fruit from the tree in the midst of the Garden was forbidden, and if eaten, they would die. Satan then countered by telling Eve that God lied—you won't die. God doesn't want you to eat the fruit of this tree because He knows that when you do, you will become like God. If you eat of the fruit, you can be the god of your own life.

Self-rule is one of the first issues that the devil entices us with so that we will transgress the commands of the Word. He continually seeks to convince us that God has lied to us, and that what we are forbidden to do would actually be good for us. God told Adam and Eve they could eat all they wanted from any of the trees in the Garden, except for one. Based on their choice to obey His command, they would enjoy life or experience death. God wanted to see if they would choose life over death, and if they would be governed by the love of self or the by their love for Him. That same choice is given to us. We must choose between being self-ruled or ruled by God. Life and death will hinge on the choice we make.

Thought for Today

Nothing has changed since Adam and Eve. We still want to be the ones to sit on the throne of our heart and be our own god. God or self—the choice is ours.

Prayer Journal

_____

_____

_____

~ ~ ~ JUNE 6 ~ ~ ~

"For those who live according to the flesh set their minds on the things of the flesh, but those who live according to the Spirit, the things of the Spirit. For to be carnally minded is death, but to be spiritually minded is life and peace" (Romans 8:5-6).

Many Christians live under the wrong assumption, in that they believe the devil to be their greatest enemy. While he is an enemy and a formidable foe, he is not our greatest enemy. Jesus defeated the devil at Calvary. Jesus, in turn, has given us His authority and power to use against the devil when he comes against us. Every attack of the devil can be turned to victory through our standing in Jesus' triumph over him. There is nothing that the devil can work against us that is greater than the power of the Cross. We must exercise the authority that Jesus gave us to overrule the plans the devil. His plans will ultimately destroy us.

The greatest enemy we have in life is not the devil it is our own carnal natures. Our carnal nature was not defeated at Calvary. We must choose to put our carnal nature to death every day if we are ever going to live in the fullness of God's promises to us. The Apostle Paul, in Romans, draws the contrast between a spiritual person and a carnal person. He describes the spiritual person as one who has set the focus of his thoughts and actions on the precepts of the Word and on those matters that are spiritual in nature. On the other hand, the carnal man is drawn away by the lusts of his flesh to pursue thoughts and actions that are fleshly, or carnal in nature.

Thought for Today

Spirituality or carnality—the choice is ours to make. It is a choice that we must make on a daily basis. Do not yield to carnality.

Prayer Journal

___

___

___

~ ~ ~ JUNE 7 ~ ~ ~

"Because the carnal mind is enmity against God; for it is not subject to the law of God, nor indeed can be. So then, those who are in the flesh cannot please God" (Romans 8:7-8).

Carnal Christians are self-ruled for they have placed self on the throne and have acted as a god unto themselves. Here are some indicators that will help you discover whether or not you are a self-ruled, carnal Christian; you seek self-promotion, you find justification for all of your actions, and you look for self-gratification. Furthermore, you are absorbed with yourself and are self-centered, you are full of pity for yourself, and you are self-willed, angry, unforgiving, and hateful to anyone who crosses you.

Paul tells us that to be carnally minded is to be at war with God. While you may attend church, you have made God, His Word, and His ways, your enemy. Instead of walking in obedience, you walk in opposition; and instead of embracing God's values, you make your own. You choose the portions of Scripture you deem to be relevant to your life, and to which portions you will adhere. You have determined that no one will tell you what you can or cannot do—not even God. Paul tells us that it is impossible for a carnally minded person to ever please God. Many Christians attempt to live life with a mix of spirituality and carnality. They delude themselves into believing, that even though they have problems with carnality, they are more spiritual than carnal and thus, acceptable to God.

Thought for Today

A carnal Christian is one who knows what is right, but chooses wrong. We must not allow our carnal nature to be anything other than dead to us, for the carnal man is at war with God.

Prayer Journal

_____

_____

_____

~ ~ ~ JUNE 8 ~ ~ ~

"I have been crucified with Christ; it is no longer I who live, but Christ lives in me; and the life which I now live in the flesh I live by faith in the Son of God, who loved me and gave Himself for me" (Galatians 2:20).

The Apostle Paul was well acquainted with the struggles of carnality. In his letter to his Christian family in Rome, he admitted to his struggle and declared his hope to be in Jesus Christ. Paul did not blame anyone but himself for his struggles. We must learn to do the same. As long as we blame someone, or something else, for our carnality, instead of admitting that our carnality is the result of the weakness of our flesh, we will continue to live in defeat. Paul knew that the secret of defeating his flesh was to choose to crucify it. The source of Paul's strength was derived through allowing the life and faith of Jesus to be the dominate force in his life.

We must understand that we cannot crucify our carnal natures. Crucifying self is a work of the Holy Spirit. As we allow the Spirit to bind our carnal natures to the Cross, we can then yield our flesh to the death that the Cross brings—thereby, we gain victory over our carnality. While on the Cross our carnal natures will make every attempt to escape the death of the Cross. The devil attempts to entice us with alternative plans so that he can have the power over our flesh. He will tolerate our attempts to discipline ourselves and dedicate ourselves to God, just as long as we do not crucify our carnal natures.

Thought for Today

When we are yielded and bound to the Cross, our fleshly, carnal nature cannot control us, and the devil cannot defeat us.

Prayer Journal

_____

_____

_____

~ ~ ~ JUNE 9 ~ ~ ~

"For you were once darkness, but now you are light in the Lord. Walk as children of light" (Ephesians 5:8).

When God created the heavens and the earth, the first creative word that He spoke was, *"Let there be light"* in Genesis 1:3. The first creative action that God took was to *"...divide the light from the darkness,"* as found in Genesis 1:4. The division of light from darkness is an eternal law of God which governs both the natural and the spiritual world. Naturally, and spiritually, light does not mix with darkness. Science tells us that light is a positive energy, while darkness is merely the absence of light. Light has the power to pierce the darkness, but the darkness has no power to penetrate the light. Without exception, light is always the dominate force. The darkness has no defense against the light's power to invade its domain, and has no offense to claim territory that is ruled by light.

Salvation is a sovereign act of God. Salvation lifts us out of the kingdom of darkness and delivers us safely into the Kingdom of His Son—the Kingdom of Light. As Christians, we are a threat to the devil and to his kingdom. We dwell in Jesus, the Light of the World; and the Light of the World, Jesus, dwells in us. Wherever we go, the light of Jesus will prevail over the darkness of hell's agenda. In Christ, we are not subject to the darkness of the devil's agenda; quite the contrary, for the devil's agenda of darkness is perpetually subject to the light of Jesus within us.

Thought for Today

As children of the Light, we are to advance the kingdom of Jesus, our Light, into the devil's kingdom of darkness. The Light within us will always drive back the darkness.

Prayer Journal

_____

_____

_____

~ ~ ~ JUNE 10 ~ ~ ~

"'For I,' says the Lord, 'will be a wall of fire all around her, and I will be the glory in her midst'" (Zechariah 2:5).

The Prophet Zechariah spoke of a day coming when the blessings of God would be so great upon the people of Jerusalem that they would run out of space within the walls that had been built for their protection. The number of people and livestock in Jerusalem would be so great that they would have to expand the city. The walls of a city served many purposes, but the primary purpose was for the protection of the inhabitants within. Zechariah promised that when the time came that the city walls could not serve as a protection for the people, that God, Himself, would become a wall of protection for them.

In the Scriptures, Jerusalem, of the Old Testament, is a picture of the Church in the New Testament. The prophecy of Zechariah spoke of Jerusalem's natural prosperity, but it also pointed to the coming spiritual Church of Jesus Christ. The Church is like a city with walls built for protection. God promises to be a "wall of fire" surrounding His glorious Church, protecting it against the powers of hell and from their intrusion. To gain access to the Church, the devil will have to go through God first. What a great sense of security this gives to every believer. We do not have to fear any enemy, for the Lord, Himself, will protect us from harm.

Thought for Today

We have the authority to cast out every devil which steps within the wall of God's protection surrounding our lives, and no devil has the power to drag us out from behind that protection. You can rest in knowing that God is watching over your life.

Prayer Journal

_____

_____

_____

~ ~ ~ JUNE 11 ~ ~ ~

"Do not be unequally yoked together with unbelievers. For what fellowship has righteousness with lawlessness? And what communion has light with darkness? And what accord has Christ with Belial? Or what part has a believer with an unbeliever? And what agreement has the temple of God with idols? For you are the temple of the living God. As God has said: 'I will dwell in them and walk among them. I will be their God, and they shall be My people. Therefore come out from among them and be separate,' says the Lord. 'Do not touch what is unclean, and I will receive you'" (II Corinthians 6:14-17).

Paul realized the importance of establishing healthy relationships that will enhance our spiritual well-being. The Bible warns us of relationships that are counter-productive and ultimately, destructive to our walk before the Lord. These relationships can be destructive as we do not share the same core values, ethics, or reverence for God. We must keep our relationships with unbelievers in a proper perspective or we will become unequally yoked. Paul is not telling us to isolate ourselves, for to do so would negate any opportunities to win them to Christ. However, he is warning us to remember we are called to live above the standards of our society which, for the most part, have been set by unbelievers. We are to live a separated life, thereby, becoming an example of a wholesome and righteous lifestyle. We are not to draw our counsel or values from any other source than from the Word.

Thought for Today

We need to see every relationship we have with unbelievers as a divine appointment to win them to Christ. We must be careful not to allow any relationship to erode our Christian values or character.

Prayer Journal

_____

_____

_____

~ ~ ~ JUNE 12 ~ ~ ~

"Therefore whoever hears these sayings of Mine, and does them, I will liken him to a wise man who built his house on the rock: and the rain descended, the floods came, and the winds blew and beat on that house; and it did not fall, for it was founded on the rock. Now everyone who hears these sayings of Mine, and does not do them, will be like a foolish man who built his house on the sand: and the rain descended, the floods came, and the winds blew and beat on that house; and it fell. And great was its fall" (Matthew 7:24-27).

Jesus told the parable of two builders who had each built a house. One builder built his house on the solid foundation of a rock, while the other builder built his house on the sand. When the storms began to rage, the house built on the rock withstood the assault of the storm, while the house that was built on the sand collapsed. The common denominator presented in this parable is that the storms came against what had been built and the outcome of the storm was determined by the foundation on which the builder chose to build.

In life, there are two types of storms. There is the storm that comes as the result of our disobedience to the Word and our disobedience will produce a harvest of pain and problems, as we find in the case of Jonah. Then there are the storms that are sent by the devil to steal, kill, and destroy those areas of lives that we hold precious. There is no way for us to avoid the storms of life, but there is a way to avoid the damage that those storms can cause.

Thought for Today

Building on the foundation of the Word assures us that regardless of how fierce the storm, we will still be standing when it is over.

Prayer Journal

_____

_____

_____

~ ~ ~ JUNE 13 ~ ~ ~

"...serving the Lord with all humility, with many tears and trials which happened to me by the plotting of the Jews" (Acts 20:19).

The Apostle Paul met with the elders of the church at Ephesus and spoke to them concerning the purity of his intent as he ministered to them. He also reminded them of the great suffering he had endured for the sake of the gospel. If anyone knew about trials, it was Paul. Trials are a fact of life on earth, and this is especially true for the Christian who has set his heart to serve the Lord.

The devil uses our trials to destroy our confidence in God and His Word. He knows that if we start doubting, our faith will dwindle and die. Without faith, we cannot withstand the attacks and lies of the devil. If we doubt God, we will not be able to hear His voice and receive His wisdom which will build our faith; thereby, enabling us to successfully come through our trial. If the devil cannot get us to worship him, he will use our trials to make us mad at God and thus, we will stop our worship. Satan knows that if we doubt God's integrity, and the validity of His Word, then we will stop lifting our hearts in worship and eventually, stop serving Him.

You may be in the greatest trial of your life right now, but child of God, do not quit. Your tears may be flowing like a river, but God sees them and He will not abandon you in your time of need. Hold tightly to the unseen hand of God.

Thought for Today

Regardless of how difficult your trial may be, how intense your pain, or how discouraged your heart has become; do not stop believing God. Press on, for there is victory ahead for you!

Prayer Journal

_____

_____

_____

~ ~ ~ JUNE 14 ~ ~ ~

"...nor give place to the devil" (Ephesians 4:27).

Tucked away in Paul's letter to the church at Ephesus, is this verse that tells us to literally close the door on the devil in our lives. In other words, we are to live in such a way that the devil does not have access to any area of our life. Just as a homeowner is wise to periodically check his house for unwanted openings that would give access to unwanted intruders, so it is wise for the Christian to conduct a similar search. The Psalmist David prayed a challenging prayer in Psalms 139:23-24, as he asked God to examine every nook and cranny of his life for anything that was offensive to God, *"Search me, O God, and know my heart; try me, and know my anxieties; And see if there is any wicked way in me, and lead me in the way everlasting."*

Ask the Lord to examine your heart and show you your attitudes, actions, and words that are offensive to Him and contrary to His Word. As He reveals them to you, do not defend yourself instead, humble yourself and repent. Ask God to cleanse your heart, not only from the offense, but from the desire as well. Paul told the Corinthian Christians to examine themselves to make sure that they were living within the ways prescribed by the Word. While it is the job of the Holy Spirit to convict us of sin, we are encouraged by the Word to examine ourselves and turn to God in repentance.

Thought for Today

Anything that we are participating in, or anything that we are tolerating, that is contrary to the Word, serves as an open door of access for the devil. We must repent before God and close the door on every destructive plan that the devil would use to destroy us.

Prayer Journal

_____

_____

_____

~ ~ ~ JUNE 15 ~ ~ ~

"Let not your heart be troubled; you believe in God, believe also in Me. In My Father's house are many mansions; if it were not so, I would have told you. I go to prepare a place for you. And if I go and prepare a place for you, I will come again and receive you to Myself; that where I am, there you may be also" (John 14:1-3).

It was a late autumn afternoon and the leaves on the trees were ablaze with colors of red, yellow, and orange. The air was crisp and the breeze seemed to dance lightly through the leaves on the ground—winter was coming. It wouldn't be long until the trees were barren and the ground would be covered with snow. They strolled slowly through the park, drinking in the beauty of the scene. Advanced in years, they knew in their hearts that there probably wouldn't be that many more fall seasons in their future. You could hear them laugh and talk softly; sometimes, only with their eyes. As the sun sank lower on the horizon, he gently took her hand into his and said, "Let's go home now." Off they went, hand in hand, to the home they had spent a lifetime preparing.

In preparing the disciples for His departure to heaven, Jesus told them not to let their hearts become heavy with sadness. He reminded them that He was going home and once there, He would be making preparations for their arrival. Jesus promised that He would return to earth to escort His people to their heavenly home.

Thought for Today

Each one of us will come to the time of our life where "winter" is just around the corner. One day Jesus will offer you His hand and say, "Let's go home now." Off you will go with your hand safely in His, to your eternal home He has prepared just for you.

Prayer Journal

_____

_____

_____

~ ~ ~ JUNE 16 ~ ~ ~

"For the word of God is living and powerful, and sharper than any two-edged sword, piercing even to the division of soul and spirit, and of joints and marrow, and is a discerner of the thoughts and intents of the heart" (Hebrews 4:12).

We live in a society today that debunks the validity, integrity, and relevance of the Word of God. The majority of people around the world live their lives as if the Word of God does not even exist. They have relegated it to being an historical document that is full of fables and ancient customs. For some, the Bible is nothing but a hoax and for others, it is considered a crutch for the weak and gullible. Anyone who chooses to build on its solid foundation is scoffed at and considered to be out of touch with reality.

The Bible declares of itself, that it is a *"living"* book. Its teachings are relevant to our past, our present, and will be relevant to our future. There is nothing in life that the Word does not address and lend its endless wisdom too. The Bible is also a *"powerful"* book, for it is alive with the power of God. The devil will do all within his power to steal the Word from your heart for he is convinced the Word has the power to deliver you. The Bible is a mighty weapon in the hand of the believer. It contains the secrets of spiritual warfare and when applied against an enemy, has never suffered defeat. The Word removes every pretense of falsehood and *"is a discerner of the thoughts and intents of the heart."*

Thought for Today

Build every facet of your life on the solid foundation of the Word of God. Daily, you must make a choice to order your steps by the precepts of the Word; thereby, you will find great success in life.

Prayer Journal

_____

_____

_____

~ ~ ~ JUNE 17 ~ ~ ~

"The entrance of Your words gives light; it gives understanding to the simple" (Psalms 119:130).

Unfortunately, there are times when we are not sure about a decision we need to make, or how to address a circumstance. We turn first to every source around us, except the Word. We ask our mates what we should do or we turn to our friends for their advice; when all the while, the answer to our question was tucked away in the Word of God. David tells us, that when the Word makes an entrance into our lives, it literally turns on the light of our understanding and we see things that we had never seen before. The wisdom of God is imparted to our minds and we begin to understand what the Lord wants us to do, and what decision He wants us to make regarding our circumstance.

When we do not turn to God and His Word for the answers to everything in our lives, we are very apt to make mistakes that will forever affect our future. How much time have you wasted seeking out the wisdom of others, that when applied, did not work. How much grief and anguish have you suffered because you thought you had the answer; however, your answer only made matters worse. God is like the commercial on television where the light bulb appears over the car, and the caption says that this particular manufacturer has a "better idea." The Word of God is the light turned on over our circumstances, that opens our understanding to agree with Him and therefore, it produces a—"better idea."

Thought for Today

The next time you don't know what to do turn to the Word first—not last. You will save yourself a great deal of time and heartache.

Prayer Journal

_____

_____

_____

~ ~ ~ JUNE 18 ~ ~ ~

"These all died in faith, not having received the promises, but having seen them afar off were assured of them, embraced them and confessed that they were strangers and pilgrims on the earth. For those who say such things declare plainly that they seek a homeland...But now they desire a better, that is, a heavenly country. Therefore God is not ashamed to be called their God, for He has prepared a city for them" (Hebrews 11:13-14, 16).

The story is told of the elderly missionary couple who were returning to the United States from their missionary assignment. They had invested their lives into that country and leaving was not an easy task. They had come home before, but they always knew that they would return to the field; this time, however, they had said goodbye knowing they would never return. The missionaries sent to replace them were already settled. When they arrived in New York harbor, their attention was turned to a ticker-tape parade in progress. They asked those standing close to them who the parade was for. They were astounded to learn that it was in honor of a rock star that had been on tour in Europe for one month. The husband's eyes filled with tears as he complained to his wife that he had given his life on the foreign fields, and there was no ticker-tape parade to mark their return. He reminded her that no one, except for their family, had even showed up to welcome them home. His wife lovingly responded, "But sweetheart, you're not home yet." Always remember, that we are but temporary citizens of this earth.

Thought for Today

When our assignments are completed on earth and we arrive at our eternal home in heaven, our ministries will be celebrated in that heavenly city. Always remember—you are not home yet!

Prayer Journal

_____

_____

_____

~ ~ ~ JUNE 19 ~ ~ ~

"Finally, brethren, whatever things are true, whatever things are noble, whatever things are just, whatever things are pure, whatever things are lovely, whatever things are of good report, if there is any virtue and if there is anything praiseworthy—meditate on these things" (Philippians 4:8).

It is far more important to guard our thought life than we realize. Whatever we allow to consume our thoughts will soon dominate us and will then manifest in our attitudes and actions.

The Apostle Paul sets forth a list of things by which to judge and qualify our thoughts. Our thoughts must be governed by that which is true; if it's not true, don't think about it. Our thoughts must be noble in nature; if there is not honor within our thoughts, we are to reject them. Our thoughts must be just in nature; if what we are thinking about does not lend itself to correcting a wrong motive, with a right motive, we must not meditate on such a thought. Our thoughts must be pure; we are constantly bombarded with impure thoughts that are designed to lead us astray. Our thoughts must be lovely; if our thoughts do not bring beauty, we are to release them. Our thoughts must be about things that give a good report and not an evil one. Our thoughts must be characterized by virtue. Our thoughts must be praiseworthy for we are to only meditate on those things that will be as praise to the Lord. Positive thoughts will yield positive attitudes and actions. Set the standard for your thoughts by the Word of God.

Thought for Today

What you dwell on will eventually manifest in your attitudes and actions—guard your mind. Ask the Spirit to qualify your thoughts.

Prayer Journal

_____

_____

_____

~ ~ ~ JUNE 20 ~ ~ ~

"By faith Noah, being divinely warned of things not yet seen, moved with Godly fear, prepared an ark for the saving of his household, by which he condemned the world and became heir of the righteousness which is according to faith" (Hebrews 11:7).

Noah was born at a critical time in history. His generation was the wickedest generation that had ever lived on the face of the earth. God, through Noah, had repeatedly warned this generation to repent, but sadly, they would not listen to the warnings. God then told Noah about a coming storm that would destroy all life from the face of the earth. Noah was the only righteous man left in this wicked generation; therefore, God gave him the plan that would redeem his family from the coming judgment.

Noah was a model father. He was married and had three grown and married sons; Shem, Ham, and Japheth. It is interesting to note, that even after his sons were grown and married, Noah continued to be a model father to them. On one hand, his responsibilities for daily provision had changed, but then on the other hand, his spiritual leadership still remained. The most important thing that Noah did was to hear God's voice. If Noah had not been listening, he would not have heard the instructions concerning the coming storm and the need to build the ark which would bring salvation for his family. As a father, Noah's discipline to hear God's voice, and his faith to obey God's instructions, saved his family from tragedy

Thought for Today

Parents, we need to hear God's voice in order to receive His instructions for the salvation of our families. Ask yourself if you have built a spiritual ark of safety for your family?

Prayer Journal

_____

_____

_____

~ ~ ~ JUNE 21 ~ ~ ~

"On the very same day Noah and Noah's sons, Shem, Ham, and Japheth, and Noah's wife and the three wives of his sons with them, entered the ark—So those that entered, male and female of all flesh, went in as God had commanded him; and the Lord shut him in" (Genesis 7:13, 16).

The ark was God's plan to provide Noah and his family a place of safety and deliverance from His judgment that was coming to the earth. Noah's assignment was to obey God's instructions when building the ark and then, to lead his family inside to safety. The promise to Noah was that after he had led his family into the Ark, the Lord would close and seal the door.

We also live in a very wicked generation. God's assignment to parents is to build a spiritual ark of safety for the salvation of their family. We are to be living examples, as we show our families what it means to live Godly, faithful, and righteous lives. We are to provide a spiritual climate within the home, through the removal of strife, bickering, anger, and unforgiveness, so that an atmosphere will develop which promotes spiritual growth. As parents, we must guard against anything that would seek to compromise the spiritual well-being of our families. Our mission in life is to first lead our families to a saving knowledge of Christ and then, teach them to be devoted followers of Jesus. Remember, you will never be able to teach your family something you do not faithfully walk in yourself.

Thought for Today

We have the same promise from God regarding our families as Noah had all those many years ago. If we will lead them in the ways of Christ, the Lord will then keep them in Christ.

Prayer Journal

_____

_____

_____

~ ~ ~ JUNE 22 ~ ~ ~

"This is the genealogy of Noah. Noah was a just man, perfect in his generations. Noah walked with God" (Genesis 6:9).

Noah was the spiritual leader of his family. He knew that one day he would have to give an account before God as to his spiritual leadership within the home. Noah took the full responsibility to lead his family into the ark, as well as, to lead them back out again after the flood waters subsided.

One reason that Noah was such an effective spiritual leader to his family was because he was determined to obey God's instructions. Noah would not alter any part of God's instructions to him, even if he didn't understand what each instruction meant. He didn't let the negative opinions and ridicule of others deter him from obeying God. In his heart, he knew that the well-being of his family totally depended on his obedience. Another reason that Noah was such an effective spiritual leader to his family was that he remained faithful to God, even though he lived amidst an unfaithful generation. He did not let the circumstances dictate his level of faithfulness to God. He refused to compromise even in the little things of his life.

Perhaps the greatest reason that Noah was such an effective spiritual leader was that he *"walked with God."* He was intimately acquainted with the Lord and His ways, and enjoyed his times of fellowship and communion. Noah was not content to just serve the Lord—he wanted to be the Lord's friend.

Thought for Today

Walking with God requires a daily interaction. Walking with God also demands quality times in His Word and His presence.

Prayer Journal

_____

_____

_____

~ ~ ~ JUNE 23 ~ ~ ~

"By the rivers of Babylon, there we sat down, yea, we wept when we remembered Zion. We hung our harps upon the willows in the midst of it. For there those who carried us away captive asked of us a song, and those who plundered us requested mirth, saying, 'Sing us one of the songs of Zion!' How shall we sing the Lord's song in a foreign land" (Psalms 137:1-4).

The Israelites had been led into captivity to Babylon. They wept when they remembered God's goodness and their unfaithfulness to Him. The sorrow of being enslaved was overwhelming, and they had lost their song. To make matters worse, their captors mocked them saying, "Let us hear you sing your victory songs. Go ahead and sing now." Their mockery drove the Israelites into despair.

When the devil brings an attack against our lives, he will often challenge us to demonstrate our faith, hope, and victory. He will continually mock us saying; "I want to hear you sing 'Victory in Jesus' now. Now that I have touched your health, your finances, your family, your children, your church . . . go ahead, sing to me about the lovingkindness of the Lord . . . come on, sing and shout your praise now!" Listen, child of God, the devil cannot defeat you as long as you still have your song. Your song is evidence that you still have your joy; and your joy is the indicator that you still draw your strength from the Author and Finisher of your faith—Jesus.

Thought for Today

"The joy of the Lord is your strength!" No matter what, do not allow your song to be stolen. You may have to sing through your pain and tears—but sing. Do not allow your mind to overrule what your heart knows to be true—do not stop singing!

Prayer Journal

_____

_____

_____

~ ~ ~ JUNE 24 ~ ~ ~

"With goodwill doing service, as to the Lord, and not to men, knowing that whatever good anyone does, he will receive the same from the Lord, whether he is a slave or free" (Ephesians 6:7-8).

The heart of everyone who has ever lived on earth, except Jesus, has been infected with the non-medical disease known as "ME-itus." The symptoms of "ME-itus" are easy to detect. If you have ever been self-centered or self-absorbed, you have "ME-itus." If you have ever insisted that you be the center of attention and that everything revolves around you, you have "ME-itus." If you believe that everyone is against you and that your problems are worse than anyone else's, you have "ME-itus." You must not despair, for "ME-itus" can be easily cured.

The Bible teaches, that as the family of God, we are to care for one another, bear one another's burdens, pray for one another, encourage one another, stir one another up to love and good works, share our resources with one another, and finally, speak the truth to one another in love. We are to help each other get back up when we stumble and fall. When you consider this list of responsibilities, there really isn't enough time to live with "ME-itus." The fastest way out of your own trouble is to help someone else get out of theirs; *"Pray one for another, that you may be healed"* (James 5:16). How you treat others sets a standard for how the Lord will treat you.

Thought for Today

The resolution to your problem is linked to the investment of yourself into the problems of others. The investment of yourself into the lives of others will cure your "ME-itus."

Prayer Journal

_____

_____

_____

~ ~ ~ JUNE 25 ~ ~ ~

"I will extol You, O Lord, for You have lifted me up, and have not let my foes rejoice over me. O Lord my God, I cried out to You, and You healed me" (Psalms 30:1-2).

Many years ago I was driving down a country road in Louisiana when I noticed something unusual on the side of the road. There, perched on top of a fence post, was a turtle. Louisiana is famous for its swamps, and it is not unusual to see various animals cross the road, especially turtles. Stopping the car, I got out and took a closer look at this turtle on the fence. Speaking to the turtle in my most reassuring tone, I said, "Hey little fellow, how in the world did you get up there? I didn't know you could get up there by yourself." It was obvious that someone was playing a cruel joke. The turtle needed help, so I gently placed him on the ground and he bolted (as fast as a turtle can bolt) for the safety of the nearby swamp.

As I drove away, I thought of the plight of the turtle. Obviously, he did not get to where he was by himself. I thought of how God had blessed my life over the years and I realized that, like the turtle, I had not gotten where I was by myself. The Lord had faithfully lifted me up and had preserved me from my enemies. It was the Lord, Who had touched and healed my sin-sick life. We must take the time to begin each day and recount the Lord's goodness, lovingkindness, and blessings on our lives. When we take the time to reflect, it will make a difference in how we approach the day.

Thought for Today

Your list of successes may be long and impressive but remember, you didn't get to where you are by yourself. The Lord's hand lifted you to where you are.

Prayer Journal

_____

_____

_____

~ ~ ~ JUNE 26 ~ ~ ~

"And being in Bethany at the house of Simon the leper, as He sat at the table, a woman came having an alabaster flask of very costly oil of spikenard. Then she broke the flask and poured it on His head" (Mark 14:3).

Jesus was invited to dinner at Simon, the leper's, house. Simon used to be a leper before he met Jesus, and he would never forget what Jesus had done. Fingers and toes were missing, and his facial features were distorted due to this dreaded illness. His infected back was covered with oozing sores that soaked through the layers of tattered rags he had draped over his wretched body. However, his physical pain couldn't compare to the pain of his heart. Against his will, he was an outcast and was quarantined from his family and friends. No one wanted him and everyone misunderstood his need to be loved and accepted. Then he met Jesus, and everything changed. Simon was healed in his body and restored to his life and loved ones.

The dinner party Simon hosted was for "wanted men." Jesus and Lazarus dined at the table of Simon, and the Pharisees wanted to put both of them to death. Simon knew what it was like to be alone, misunderstood, and facing death. The dinner party at Simon's home was Simon's "someday." After Jesus healed him, no doubt Simon said in his heart, "Someday I'll try to repay his kindness to me."

Thought for Today

Like Simon, we can never repay the Lord for saving us. However, we have promised the Lord that "someday" we would use our gifts in service for Him. What is your "someday?" When will your, "someday" be "today?"

Prayer Journal

_____

_____

_____

~ ~ ~ JUNE 27 ~ ~ ~

"Then Mary took a pound of very costly oil of spikenard, anointed the feet of Jesus, and wiped His feet with her hair. And the house was filled with the fragrance of the oil" (John 12:3).

One evening, Simon, the leper, hosted a dinner party for Jesus and Lazarus at his home. Mary, Lazarus' sister, was also in attendance. At some point in the evening's activities, Mary slipped up behind Jesus and poured costly perfumed oil over His head and shoulders. The house was filled with the fragrance of this act of kindness and worship. One of the disciples rebuked Mary for the wasteful act, and he reminded her of the poor. Jesus in turn rebuked the disciple and commended Mary's action of love. Jesus told the disciples in so many words, that Mary was the only one who believed Him when He spoke of His death—and believe Him, she did. You see, Mary could not forget what Jesus had done for her. Her act was not an act of logic, nor was it practical; but then, logic and practicality were not responsible for raising her brother Lazarus from the dead.

Mary had heard Jesus talking of His impending death. Perhaps Jesus remembered the soothing affect of Mary's perfume when He was draped over the Roman stump awaiting the next lashing of the whip. There was a silent statement in Mary's act that no one else in the room seemed to grasp; "Wherever You go, and whatever happens to You, remember the sweet aroma of the perfume and be reminded that there is one who believes in You and loves You."

Thought for Today

What is the greatest thing that God has ever done for you? What would your life be like if He had not taken care of you? How are you showing Him your appreciation?

Prayer Journal

_____

_____

_____

~ ~ ~ JUNE 28 ~ ~ ~

"Then the Angel of the Lord answered and said, 'O Lord of hosts, how long will You not have mercy on Jerusalem and on the cities of Judah, against which You were angry these seventy years?' And the Lord answered the angel who talked to me, with good and comforting words. So the angel who spoke with me said to me, 'Proclaim,' saying, 'Thus says the Lord of hosts: I am zealous for Jerusalem and for Zion with great zeal...Therefore thus says the Lord: I am returning to Jerusalem with mercy; my house shall be built in it, says the Lord of hosts, And a surveyor's line shall be stretched out over Jerusalem'" (Zechariah 1:12-14, 16).

While Israel was being held captive in Babylon, Zechariah prophesied that in the rebuilding of Jerusalem, the rebuilding of the Temple would take priority. Zerubbabel was raised up by God to be responsible to rebuild the Temple. Through a series of events that granted favor to the Israelites, Zerubbabel led 50,000 people back to Jerusalem to begin the rebuilding process. God instructed them to rebuild the Temple first because God wanted Israel to re-establish their worship of Him as the center of every activity.

At times, our lives are left in shambles because we have made bad decisions and therefore, we suffer terrible consequences. God is interested in our deliverance and restoration. Just as with the return of the Israelites to Jerusalem, the first step in our restoration is to re-establish our daily worship of God as our first priority.

Thought for Today

When the worship of God is established as the center of our lives, we gain a proper perspective on all the other issues of our life and we are then able to properly prioritize them.

Prayer Journal

_____

_____

_____

~ ~ ~ JUNE 29 ~ ~ ~

"So he answered and said to me: 'This is the word of the Lord to Zerubbabel: Not by might nor by power, but by My Spirit,' says the Lord of hosts. 'Who are you, O great mountain? Before Zerubbabel you shall become a plain! And he shall bring forth the capstone with shouts of 'Grace, grace to it'" (Zechariah 4:6-7)!

Zerubbabel was in charge of rebuilding the Temple. The people rallied behind his leadership and the project began with great enthusiasm. However, the process of assembling the Temple was very slow and the work itself was extremely difficult. Weariness set in as the people were confronted with their own lack of skill for such a project. The Samaritans heckled the Israelites and did all within their power to hinder their work. Under these discouraging conditions, the work soon came to a stop. Zerubbabel felt like a failure as a leader; he felt embarrassed, frustrated, and angry. God sent Zechariah to give a word of encouragement to Zerubbabel. The prophet told him that in spite of what he was now seeing and feeling, the project would be completed. However, the completion of the project would not be by the strength of men, but it would be by the mighty working of the Holy Spirit.

We all have areas that need to be brought to completion. We have worked hard, but things still are not finished; leaving us embarrassed, frustrated, and even angry. Do not despair, for the Holy Spirit has not abandoned the project that He started in us.

Thought for Today

The purposes of God are brought to completion through the work of the Holy Spirit in our lives. We need to let the Holy Spirit do His perfect work in us. What God has started—He will finish.

Prayer Journal

_____

_____

_____

~ ~ ~ JUNE 30 ~ ~ ~

"Who are you, O, great mountain? Before Zerubbabel you shall become a plain! And he shall bring forth the capstone with shouts of 'Grace, grace to it!'...The hands of Zerubbabel have laid the foundation of this temple; his hands shall finish it. Then you will know that the Lord of hosts has sent Me to you" (Zechariah 4:7, 9).

Zerubbabel had tried with all of his heart and strength to be a good leader and finish his assignment of rebuilding the Temple. The people finally became so weary, that they abandoned the work and their leader. Zerubbabel's eyes brimmed with tears of anger and discouragement as he stared at the mountain of stone waiting to be put into place. It was as though the stones were silently mocking him and reminding him of his failure to complete the work at hand.

The Prophet Zechariah's word to him was encouraging; yet confusing at the same time. He had been told the work would be completed upon his obedience to shout, *"Grace, grace,"* at the headstone. This specific instruction defied all of his logic. How could shouting *"Grace, grace"* to a stone, move the building project to completion? To Zerubbabel's credit, he chose to obey the instructions of the prophet and the Holy Spirit completed the project in time. God had promised Him that what his hands had started they would finish, if he did it God's way. God's promise to Zerubbabel in the Old Testament is still God's promise to us.

Thought for Today

God wanted Zerubbabel to realize that it was not in the strength of men, nor in a mere formula, that would bring His divine purposes to completion. Rather, it was in the simple act of obedience, wrapped in faith that would release the Holy Spirit to do His work.

Prayer Journal

_____

_____

_____

~ ~ ~ JULY 1 ~ ~ ~

"Then news of these things came to the ears of the church in Jerusalem, and they sent out Barnabas to go as far as Antioch. When he came and had seen the grace of God, he was glad, and encouraged them all that with purpose of heart they should continue with the Lord" (Acts 11:22-23).

There were rumors of a revival among the Gentiles. The Jerusalem church leaders sent Barnabas to Antioch to see what was happening and then report his findings. The Bible tells us, that when Barnabas saw *"the grace of God, he was glad."* The Holy Spirit was bringing many to salvation and then filling their lives with His presence.

The word "grace" has a dual meaning in Scripture. It means to receive something you do not deserve, or unmerited favor. It also means there is a work of the Holy Spirit bringing the purposes of God to completion. Seventeen, out of twenty-one epistles in the New Testament, begin with the greeting, *"Grace and peace be unto you."* What was being said in this greeting was more than just, "Let there be unmerited favor towards you." Certainly, anything that we receive from the Lord's grace is unmerited favor, but this greeting cries out something else as well. The greeting is saying in essence, "Let there be a work of the Holy Spirit among you, and may you be comforted in the peace of knowing that He is at work, bringing to completion the purposes of God in your lives."

Thought for Today

We are saved by the grace of God and not through any effort of our own—and that is unmerited favor. We are kept by the grace of God—and that is the working of the Holy Spirit. The Holy Spirit will faithfully bring to completion the purposes of God in our lives.

Prayer Journal

_____

_____

_____

~ ~ ~ JULY 2 ~ ~ ~

"If My people who are called by My name will humble themselves, and pray and seek My face, and turn from their wicked ways, then I will hear from heaven, and will forgive their sin and heal their land" (II Chronicles 7:14).

Within this verse of Scripture, there are three promises from God to us. First, God promises that when we pray, He will listen. Through the Prophet Jeremiah, God issues His people a challenge in Jeremiah 33:3, *"Call to me and I will answer you and show you great and mighty things which you do not know."* He promises if we will turn to Him and pray, He will hear us and answer our prayers.

The next promise from God, involves His willingness to forgive our sins when we repent. In His Word, God promises to forgive our sins, and then remove them as far as the East is removed from the West. He promises that He will not hold them against us in the future. The devil may try to beat us up over them, but God will never bring up failures that He has forgiven.

The third promise from God, speaks of His desire to heal our land. Land within a Scriptural context can represent the purposes of God for our lives. However, it can also represent a literal piece of property such as the Promised Land of Canaan. Our great nation is in need of God's healing touch. As a people, we have strayed from His purposes and from the precepts of His Word.

Thought for Today

God promises that if we will pray and seek His forgiveness, He will hear our prayers, forgive our sins, and heal our land.

Prayer Journal

_____

_____

_____

~ ~ ~ JULY 3 ~ ~ ~

"If My people who are called by My name will humble themselves, and pray and seek My face, and turn from their wicked ways, then I will hear from heaven, and will forgive their sin and heal their land. Now My eyes will be open and My ears attentive to prayer made in this place. For now I have chosen and sanctified this house, that My name may be there forever; and My eyes and My heart will be there perpetually" (II Chronicles 7:14-16).

God clearly states His desire to hear our prayers, forgive our sins, and heal our land. However, the promises of God are all preceded by a condition that must be met. The first condition requires that God's people wake up to their responsibility and turn to God. God is not asking for unbelievers to pray, just His own people.

The second condition involves God's people being willing to humble themselves before Him. Instead of trying to solve our problems, which we can't do, God wants us to humble ourselves and admit that our problems are bigger than our ability to solve them. We must remove all pride and all attempts to justify our sins.

The third condition requires us to seek God's face in prayer. We are to re-examine our priorities to make sure that our pursuit of God is the number one priority. The final condition demands that we make radical changes in our attitudes and in our behavior. We must turn from everything that is in violation of God's Word and ways.

Thought for Today

God is waiting for us to meet His conditions. He does not answer our prayers out of a sense of duty. He answers our prayers out of a desire that springs forth from a faithful and loving heart.

Prayer Journal

_____

_____

_____

~ ~ ~ JULY 4 ~ ~ ~

"Blessed is the nation whose God is the Lord, the people He has chosen as His own inheritance" (Psalms 33:12).

While everyone from our legislators to our educators do their best to deny the spiritual heritage that our nation was founded upon, the facts of our written history do not lie. Almost every one of our forefathers believed strongly in the Lord and His teachings, as was evidenced in their personal writings. They were students of the Old and New Testaments and their way of life was profoundly influenced by the life and teachings of Jesus Christ. Our forefathers used the Holy Scriptures as the primer from which to teach their children to read. The laws that governed their lives were drawn from the eternal laws of God's Word. Leaders, from the president down, consulted with God before decisions were made that would impact our nation. So deeply entrenched in their beliefs were our forefathers, that many of them sacrificed their wealth, their health, and even their lives, to protect the spiritual heritage of our nation.

The one fear that loomed in the hearts of our forefathers was what our nation would become if we strayed from the Godly principles on which our nation was founded. The fears of our forefathers are being realized in our generation. Our spiritual heritage has been abandoned, and our nation suffers the consequences. Our nation will only be blessed if we return to the God of our fathers.

Thought for Today

We have abandoned our spiritual roots and allowed laws to be passed that have removed God from the White House and from the school house. If we do not wake up soon, God will be outlawed within His own house, the church. Pray for our nation!

Prayer Journal

_____

_____

_____

~ ~ ~ JULY 5 ~ ~ ~

"So Satan answered the Lord and said, 'Does Job fear God for nothing? Have You not made a hedge around him, around his household, and around all that he has on every side? You have blessed the work of his hands, and his possessions have increased in the land. But now, stretch out Your hand and touch all that he has, and he will surely curse You to Your face'" (Job 1:9-11).

Satan accused Job of being righteous and faithful to God only because God had so abundantly blessed him. Satan then proceeded to challenge God by telling Him that if He were to remove His hedge of protection from around Job's life and stop blessing him, Job would turn on God and curse Him to His face. However, God was convinced that this would not be true of Job. He allowed Satan to touch Job in three vital areas of Job's life. All of heaven watched as the prince of hell descended on Job and all that he held dear. In the span of one day, Job lost his wealth, his family, and his health.

Devastated, Job sought answers for his trials from his friends. They told him that he was reaping the harvest for his sins, but Job knew in his heart that he hadn't sinned and that God wasn't the author of his misery. Job then turned to his wife for answers. She blamed God, so she encouraged him to curse God and die. Job then looked within his own heart and lamented that he didn't die at his birth. Job rejected the errant counsel he had received and refused to blame God. Instead, he humbled himself and worshiped the Lord.

Thought for Today

Like Job, the devil is convinced that you only choose to serve God because you have been blessed. In the midst of every trial, prove the devil wrong and worship the Lord.

Prayer Journal

_____

_____

_____

~ ~ ~ JULY 6 ~ ~ ~

"Though He slay me, yet will I trust Him" (Job 13:15).

Job had suffered a great loss at the hands of the devil. Before the sun could set on the horizon, Job would lose his family, his wealth, and his health. He was emotionally devastated from the loss of everything that he held close to his heart. He was also physically tormented from the pain of the boils that covered his entire body. His friends had accused him of secret sin, while His wife wanted him to die and put an end to his misery, as well as, to hers.

Job was about to discover God's faithfulness to bring him through difficult times. Job was as committed to God as was humanly possible. He trusted God to the point, that even if God chose to kill him, he would not stop trusting in Him as his Redeemer. He was content in knowing that he would someday see Him face to face.

Job was so committed to God, that he asked God to never lift His hand from his life. The greatest indicator of his commitment and trust in the Lord, is perhaps found in Job 19:25-27, *"For I know that my Redeemer lives, and He shall stand at last on the earth; And after my skin is destroyed, this I know, that in my flesh I shall see God, Whom I shall see for myself, and my eyes shall behold, and not another. How my heart yearns within me!"* Job was convinced that God would deliver him from all of his trials.

Thought for Today

What level of commitment have you made to the Lord and how much of that commitment are you walking in? How much trust do you place in Him to deliver you? If God answers in a way you had not planned on, is that all right with you?

Prayer Journal

_____

_____

_____

~ ~ ~ JULY 7 ~ ~ ~

"And the Lord restored Job's losses when he prayed for his friends. Indeed the Lord gave Job twice as much as he had before...After this Job lived one hundred and forty years, and saw his children and grandchildren for four generations. So Job died, old and full of days" (Job 42:10, 16-17).

The story of Job is one that takes you from tragedy to triumph. Job was miserable and had suffered from his losses; however, God rewarded Job's faithfulness. God restored Job with twice as much as what he had lost and blessed him with a long and satisfying life.

There are two treasures that come from the story of Job. Job was tested, and yet, He emerged with character. Paul tells us of the value of our trials in Romans 5:3-5, *"And not only that, but we also glory in tribulations, knowing that tribulation produces perseverance; and perseverance, character; and character, hope. Now hope does not disappoint, because the love of God has been poured out in our hearts by the Holy Spirit who was given to us."* If we allow the Holy Spirit to do His perfect work in us, our tribulation will produce within us perseverance, which will build our character and therefore, will yield hope. Because of God's love for us, we will not be disappointed when we trust Him. God found a trophy of grace in Job. The grace of God is able to bring us triumphantly through every trial. Consider Paul's own testimony in II Corinthians 12:9, *"And He said to me, 'My grace is sufficient for you, for My strength is made perfect in weakness.'"*

Thought for Today

God will bring you through your trial in great triumph. He will faithfully restore you and abundantly bless your life.

Prayer Journal

_____

_____

_____

~ ~ ~ JULY 8 ~ ~ ~

"Indeed we count them blessed who endure. You have heard of the perseverance of Job and seen the end intended by the Lord—that the Lord is very compassionate and merciful" (James 5:11).

One of the themes in the Book of Job is "learning to hear God's voice." Job's trials hit in such a rapid succession that he didn't have time to recover from one trial before the next one struck. Job desperately wanted to know why these things were happening.

Not able to find a satisfactory answer in his wife or his friends, Job turned to God. Job pleaded with God to speak with Him face to face. However, God chose to speak to Job first through his four friends, and then, from out of the midst of the whirlwind. God was not playing hard to get with Job. He wanted Job to learn to hear His voice through whatever channel He chose to speak.

Job wanted to come and speak to God, but God wanted Job to discover and learn that He was right there with him all of the time. In Hebrews 13:5, we are reminded, *"For He Himself has said, 'I will never leave you nor forsake you.'"* God wanted Job to know that He was Job's ever-present help in the time of trouble. God also wanted to make Job aware of the fact that He would forever be with him and He was there to stay. God used Satan's attack on Job's life to enlarge Job's concepts of God and His faithfulness.

Thought for Today

God allowed Satan to remove things that Job and his friends used as a measurement of Divine approval. God wanted Job to know that his trials did not lessen His love. Like Job, as our concepts of God increase, our worship will reach new levels of adoration.

Prayer Journal

_____

_____

_____

~ ~ ~ JULY 9 ~ ~ ~

"I will bring the one-third through the fire, will refine them as silver is refined, and test them as gold is tested. They will call on My name, and I will answer them. I will say, 'This is My people,' and each one will say, 'The Lord is my God'" (Zechariah 13:9).

No one in Job's life saw him as God saw him: His wife deemed him to be a loser, not fit to live: His friends saw him as a sinner that God was punishing; and His community saw him as a fallen leader. However, God saw Job as a righteous man and He boasted of such to satan. When God allowed satan to touch Job's life, He did so in order to perfect in Job what He had declared him to be.

God sees our end from our beginning, and He is committed to complete every work in us that He initiates. Paul tells us in Philippians 1:6, *"Being confident of this very thing, that He who has begun a good work in you will complete it until the day of Jesus Christ."* What God sees in us today is not what we will ultimately become, for God said that He will transform us into the image of Jesus. God uses our trials to enlarge us, as well as, bring us to spiritual completion. Trials refine our lives in the same manner that silver and gold is refined. Refining by fire always causes the impurities to float to the top and therefore, enables the smelter to skim them off. One day, a visitor at a silver refining plant asked the smelter, "How do you know when the silver is pure?" The smelter replied, "When I can see my face in it without any distortion."

Thought for Today

God allows us to go through His refining fire so that all of the impurities in our lives will be removed. When the impurities are gone, His image can then be seen in us without distortion.

Prayer Journal

~ ~ ~ JULY 10 ~ ~ ~

"Although You know that I am not wicked, and there is no one who can deliver from Your hand? Your hands have made me and fashioned me, an intricate unity; yet You would destroy me" (Job 10:7-8).

In his heart, Job knew better, but he still got so mad at God over his trials, that he actually accused God of trying to destroy him. Job's trials caused him to start complaining. It was not long until his complaining turned to anger, and his anger produced a deep-seated bitterness, *"My soul loathes my life; I will give free course to my complaint, I will speak in the bitterness of my soul"* (Job 10:1). Job allowed himself to become so angry and bitter at his circumstances that he literally began to hate his very existence. Job's bitterness caused him to become angry with God and he proceeded to blame Him for being unjust. Job says in Job 19:6-7, *"Know then that God has wronged me, and has surrounded me with His net. If I cry out concerning wrong, I am not heard. If I cry aloud, there is no justice."*

We may be tempted to point a finger at Job and say, "Shame on you for getting mad at God." However, before we do something this foolish, we need to remember the times we felt the same way Job did. We all have had misplaced anger as we mistakenly blamed God for our problems. We know that God is not the source of our trouble, but we blame Him anyway. Complaining may be a vent for anger, but it will also make you captive to bitterness.

Thought for Today

Quit complaining and blaming God for your problem; instead, praise God for His faithful deliverance—He hasn't abandoned you.

Prayer Journal

_____

_____

_____

~ ~ ~ JULY 11 ~ ~ ~

"My soul loathes my life; I will give free course to my complaint, I will speak in the bitterness of my soul" (Job 10:1).

Job was mad—and he was mad at God, *"Know then that God has wronged me, and has surrounded me with His net"* (Job 19:6). Among his complaints, Job brought three accusations against God that we can identify with. First, Job accused God of not listening to, or answering his prayers. Job 30:20 says, *"I cry out to You, but You do not answer me."* We lodge this same complaint when we do not see the answers to our prayers on our time schedule, or according to our dictates. However, Psalms 34:17 says, *"The righteous cry out, and the Lord hears, and delivers them out of all their trouble."*

The second accusation that Job made was that God was punishing him. Job 7:19-20 says, *"How long? Will You not look away from me, and let me alone till I swallow my saliva? Have I sinned? What have I done to You, O watcher of men? Why have You set me as Your target, so that I am a burden to myself?"* God disciplines us, but He never seeks to destroy us.

The third accusation of Job was that God was blessing the ungodly and punishing the righteous, *"Why do the wicked live and become old, yes, become mighty in power"* (Job 21:7)? We accuse God of not being fair when we see the ungodly prosper in their wickedness, while the Godly suffer and are told to call it a blessing.

Thought for Today

Refuse to let the devil use your circumstances to cause you to change your beliefs in God and in the integrity of His Word. Hold fast to what you know to be true.

Prayer Journal

~ ~ ~ JULY 12 ~ ~ ~

"Now prepare yourself like a man; I will question you, and you shall answer Me. 'Where were you when I laid the foundations of the earth? Tell Me, if you have understanding. Who determined its measurements? Surely you know! Or who stretched the line upon it? To what were its foundations fastened? Or who laid its cornerstone'" (Job 38:3-6)?

Job's story reveals how longsuffering God really is, even when we wrongly accuse Him. Job was mad at God and accused God of being unfair, unavailable, uncaring, unable, and in general, trying to destroy him. God in His infinite love and mercy allowed Job to vent his anger for a season—then enough was enough. God tells Job *"prepare yourself like a man."* God confronts Job with some questions since Job has made such serious accusations against Him.

God grills Job concerning the contrast of God's infinite wisdom and power, versus Job's ignorance and weakness (Job 38-41). This encounter was so humiliating, that Job pleaded with God to accept his apology and stop pointing out his lack of knowledge and understanding. God wasn't rubbing Job's nose in his ignorance, but was sending Job a message. He wanted Job to know He knew more about Job's circumstances than Job was giving Him credit for. God contrasted His knowledge, wisdom, and power, against Job's ignorance and weakness. He wanted Job to realize that he didn't know as much about his situation as he thought he did.

Thought for Today

God knows that our knowledge and understanding of our circumstances is extremely limited. He is aware of everything that concerns us and promises that He will bring us through safely.

Prayer Journal

_____

_____

_____

~ ~ ~ JULY 13 ~ ~ ~

"Can you draw out Leviathan with a hook, or snare his tongue with a line which you lower? Can you put a reed through his nose, or pierce his jaw with a hook? Will he make many supplications to you? Will he speak softly to you? Will he make a covenant with you? Will you take him as a servant forever? Will you play with him as with a bird, or will you leash him for your maidens? Lay your hand on him; remember the battle—never do it again" (Job 41:1-5, 8)!

God continued Job's schooling by contrasting His knowledge, wisdom, and power, to that of Job's. God asked Job if he could control the uncontrollable creature known as Leviathan. As best as we can determine, God's reference to Leviathan is the creature we know as the alligator and by all human means, Leviathan was uncontrollable, as well as, deadly. Yet, God told Job that He could do as He wished with this creature and the creature would respond to Him as would a domesticated pet.

God was not boasting to belittle Job; He wanted Job to discover something about Him that would release Job from his anger and unbelief. God wanted Job to know that He was able to control the most uncontrollable of circumstances. What was out of the realm of Job's ability to control was not out of God's. He wanted Job to know, that no matter what the circumstances, He was in control.

Thought for Today

Your circumstances may be spinning out of control and you realize that you do not have the ability to take back the control to master them. You can take comfort in knowing that God is still in control. Remember that our God is in control of the uncontrollable.

Prayer Journal

_____

_____

_____

~ ~ ~ JULY 14 ~ ~ ~

"For the eyes of the Lord are on the righteous, and His ears are open to their prayers; but the face of the Lord is against those who do evil" (I Peter 3:12).

In the midst of his pain and suffering, Job discovered three deep-seated beliefs that enabled him to persevere during his problems. The first discovery was that Job knew God was his source of supply; *"Naked I came from my mother's womb, and naked shall I return there. The Lord gave, and the Lord has taken away; blessed be the name of the Lord"* (Job 1:21). Job reaffirmed his belief that God was the only source from which everything had come.

The second discovery came when Job stated his belief that no matter what was happening, and how much it hurt, his God would outlast his season of suffering. In Job 19:25-26, he declared, *"For I know that my Redeemer lives, and He shall stand at last on the earth. And after my skin is destroyed, this I know, that in my flesh I shall see God."* Job was convinced that God would eventually deliver him from his trials. He was convinced his eyes would behold his God, even if his trials resulted in his death.

The third discovery came in realizing that even if his eyes could not see God, God could see him. Job proclaims in Job 23:9-10, *"When He works on the left hand, I cannot behold Him; when He turns to the right hand, I cannot see Him. But He knows the way that I take; when He has tested me, I shall come forth as gold."*

Thought for Today

Reaffirm your belief that God is your source and that He will outlast any trial. Even when you can't see Him, He can see you.

Prayer Journal

_____

_____

_____

~ ~ ~ JULY 15 ~ ~ ~

"Continue earnestly in prayer, being vigilant in it with thanksgiving" (Colossians 4:2).

Prayer is a command, not an option. There is great power in prayer, and we must come to the realization that prayer is one of the most powerful weapons we possess as a Christian. The Bible teaches us that we are to make prayer a vital part of our daily routine. Through prayer, we invite our mighty God to become involved in our circumstances. Through prayer, we have the ability to bind the forces of hell and release the powers of heaven. Prayer is the key which will open doors that were previously locked to us.

The principle for prayer is simple, yet profound. The Scriptures teach us to pray to our Father in heaven, in the name of Jesus. We are to pray with the power of the Holy Spirit, and in harmony with the Word. When we pray, adhering to this principle, nothing can stop our prayers from reaching the throne room of God; and there is nothing that can prevent God's purposes from coming to pass.

Through prayer, we find answers to the questions that plague us. We read God's promise to answer prayer in Jeremiah 33:3, *"Call to Me, and I will answer you."* Through prayer, Jesus promises to lift our burdens from us and He promises to give us rest as we bring our problems to Him, *"Come to Me, all you who labor and are heavy laden, and I will give you rest"* (Matthew 11:28).

Thought for Today

There is power in prayer—but only if you pray. God promises to answer—but only if you ask. Devils will tremble—but only if you bow your hearts and lift your voice to God. Prayer works—pray!

Prayer Journal

_____

_____

_____

~ ~ ~ JULY 16 ~ ~ ~

"Even when I cry and shout, He shuts out my prayer" (Lamentations 3:8).

We must learn to be honest with ourselves. While God promises to answer our prayers, we are often guilty of building roadblocks to His answers. There are many things that can be responsible for building a roadblock to answered prayer. One such roadblock, is praying with wrong motives. James 4:3 warns us, *"You ask and do not receive, because you ask amiss, that you may spend it on your pleasures."* When our motives are selfish and could damage us or those around us, God will not answer. I John 3:21-22 reminds us that it is the attitude of our heart that will reveal the confidence we can have in prayer and in the purity of our motives, *"Beloved, if our heart does not condemn us, we have confidence toward God. And whatever we ask we receive from Him, because we keep His commandments and do those things that are pleasing in His sight."*

Another road block to answered prayer is sin that we have not yet confessed. When we refuse to confess our sin, God refuses to hear our prayers. We must come into agreement with God regarding our iniquity. In Psalms 66:18 we read, *"If I regard iniquity in my heart, the Lord will not hear."* Isaiah 59:2 tells us, *"But your iniquities have separated you from your God; and your sins have hidden His face from you, so that He will not hear."*

Thought for Today

That prayer is powerful—is undeniable. That we are commanded to pray daily—is not debatable. That we can move the heart of God through prayer—is unfathomable. That we do not take advantage of this gift of communion with God every day—is unbelievable.

Prayer Journal

_____

_____

_____

~ ~ ~ JULY 17 ~ ~ ~

"Husbands, likewise, dwell with them with understanding, giving honor to the wife, as to the weaker vessel, and as being heirs together of the grace of life, that your prayers may not be hindered...For the eyes of the Lord are on the righteous, and His ears are open to their prayers" (I Peter 3:7, 12).

Peter encouraged husbands and wives to live within God's prescribed order for marriage—showing honor towards one another. When honor is not given, or loving submission to another is violated, your prayers will be hindered.

Another hindrance to answered prayer is having idols. An idol is anything we pursue that takes a higher priority than our pursuit of God and His Word. We are warned in Ezekiel 14:3 that if we have idols, God will not even let us inquire of Him: *"Son of man, these men have set up their idols in their hearts, and put before them that which causes them to stumble into iniquity. Should I let Myself be inquired of at all by them?"*

Another hindrance to answered prayer is the way we treat the poor and needy, *"Whoever shuts his ears to the cry of the poor will also cry himself and not be heard"* (Proverbs 21:13). If we refuse to help the poor, God refuses to hear us when we cry out for His help. God promises to answer our prayers, but our responsibility is to guard against any attitude or action that would prohibit Him from doing so.

Thought for Today

We must have our hearts clean from sin and our motives pure when we approach God in prayer. Anything less will hinder our prayers.

Prayer Journal

_____

_____

_____

~ ~ ~ JULY 18 ~ ~ ~

"Let the wicked forsake his way, and the unrighteous man his thoughts; let him return to the Lord, and He will have mercy on him; and to our God, for He will abundantly pardon" (Isaiah 55:7).

I had been invited to conduct a revival for a church in a small town in northern Louisiana. Driving in the late afternoon, just outside of town, I noticed a crude, homemade sign nailed to a tree along the road. The words on the sign said, "Johnny, please come home. Everything is going to be all right. I love you, Dad." I pulled off to the side of the road and stared at the sign for quite a while. As I pondered the words of this sign, I pictured a family that had been torn apart. I could only imagine that Johnny must have made a serious mistake and perhaps, he and his father had bitterly argued about it. Whatever had transpired, Johnny had left home. Whether Johnny was afraid to return home or not wasn't known, but what was known, was that Johnny and his father were separated. The sign attested to the fact that the father loved Johnny, had forgiven him, and wanted him to come home again.

In contemplating this sign, I couldn't help but think of another sign, nailed to the side of a tree, on a hillside called Calvary. Mistakes had been made, and a Father's family was separated and torn apart. Love's eternal message from the sign on Calvary's tree pleads with those separated from the Father—come home.

Thought for Today

If you are estranged from your heavenly Father today, look to Calvary and read the sign on the tree. It will remind you that you have been forgiven, that you are loved, and that the Father wants you to come home. Come home—He is waiting for you.

Prayer Journal

~ ~ ~ JULY 19 ~ ~ ~

"Then the king said to me, 'What do you request?' So I prayed to the God of heaven. And I said to the king. 'If it pleases the king, and if your servant has found favor in your sight, I ask that you send me to Judah, to the city of my fathers' tombs, that I may rebuild it'" (Nehemiah 2:4-5).

The Israelites were in captivity in Babylon and Jerusalem lay in ruins. The walls had been broken down, the gates and the city had been burned, and the Temple had been destroyed. The remnant that remained in the city, were oppressed by evil rulers. Nehemiah, a type of the Holy Spirit, is sent by God to rebuild the city. God is committed to rebuild and restore what the devil has torn down.

Nehemiah was the cupbearer to King Artaxerxes in Babylon. They were well acquainted and the king noticed that the countenance of Nehemiah had fallen, so he asked why. Nehemiah explained that he was grieving over the plight of his beloved hometown and his people who were being oppressed. The king granted Nehemiah's request to return to Jerusalem to rebuild the city. To make sure that Nehemiah was able to accomplish his assignment, the king gave him a letter of authority. Nehemiah would be able to show this letter to anyone who would oppose him, for this letter would give him the authorization to do the work. Next, the king granted Nehemiah all of the supplies necessary to rebuild the city, and he sent armed troops to make sure it all happened.

Thought for Today

What the devil has destroyed, the Lord wants to restore. He has given us His Word, and the resources of heaven are ours. God has assigned angels to help us. Restoration is assured as we trust God.

Prayer Journal

_____

_____

_____

~ ~ ~ JULY 20 ~ ~ ~

"So we built the wall, and the entire wall was joined together up to half its height, for the people had a mind to work" (Nehemiah 4:6).

Nehemiah had left the captivity of Babylon to return to Jerusalem. He would be responsible to lead the remnant of people as they rebuilt the city. The first project to be addressed was the rebuilding of the wall. Since the wall had been torn down, the enemy could go and come at will. However, as the gaps in the wall were repaired, the enemies of the people became very angry and tried to stop the work. They not only physically attacked the workers, but they verbally harassed them, and tried to confuse them by planting doubt in their minds as to their capacity to finish the task. In spite of the assaults of their enemies, the Israelites completed the rebuilding of the wall. They accomplished this, not because of their skills as craftsmen, nor because of their ability to ignore the taunting of their enemies, but they finished their task because they had a mind to work. They weren't casual in their interest of rebuilding the wall; they were obsessed with getting it done.

We need people like this for the work of ministry today. We need people who have a mind to work—people who are obsessed with their assignments and will not let anything or anyone break their focus. We need people with a mind to work, who do not need someone to constantly encourage them or stir them up in order for them to be productive.

Thought for Today

The people who have a mind to work have learned to encourage themselves and to stir their own hearts so they will continue their assigned work. They will work even if everyone else stops.

Prayer Journal

_____

_____

_____

~ ~ ~ JULY 21 ~ ~ ~

"Nevertheless we made our prayer to our God, and because of them we set a watch against them day and night" (Nehemiah 4:9).

The work of rebuilding the wall was progressing rapidly and under Nehemiah's leadership, the people were slowly gaining confidence in their ability to finish the task. As the gaps in the wall began to close, the attacks of the enemy grew more intense. Nehemiah encouraged the people not to listen to their threats, instead he encouraged them to pray and ask God for help. The people worked in shifts, which allowed the work to continue around the clock. For safety's sake and for the sake of the work itself, they set watchmen around the clock to warn of any encroachment from the enemy.

When I was a young boy my brother and I, and our two cousins, went camping with our grandfather. As the sun set and the temperatures began to drop, my grandfather built a campfire to keep us warm. As the oldest, my assignment was to make sure that there was wood on the fire to keep it going. At some point, I got busy playing and forgot the fire. The fire was almost out when my grandfather called for me to put more wood on it. I will never forget what he said, "Michael keep the fire going. Don't let the fire go out, or we'll all get cold." I've often thought about his statement in relation to prayer. I've prayed so many prayers that have been void of any fiery passion. Without a Godly passion in our prayers, our hearts are subject to spiritual coldness.

Thought for Today

When we pray, we need to put some fire into it. We cannot afford to let the fire of faith die out of our prayers, for if we do, all around us will get cold. You are responsible to keep the fire going.

Prayer Journal

~ ~ ~ JULY 22 ~ ~ ~

"And our adversaries said, 'They will neither know nor see anything, till we come into their midst and kill them and cause the work to cease....Therefore I positioned men behind the lower parts of the wall, at the openings; and I set the people according to their families, with their swords, their spears, and their bows'" (Nehemiah 4:11, 13).

The taunting of the enemy grew increasingly worse as the Israelites attempted to complete the Jerusalem wall. Their enemies mocked them, claiming that they could attack and there was nothing the Israelites could do to stop them. Nehemiah positioned men in strategic places to turn the enemy back, if and when they attacked.

There is a tremendous clue to successful spiritual warfare hidden in this verse. Each of them had a position to fill and they filled it and, in doing so, they successfully turned the enemy back. We need to realize that each of us have a position to fill in the church. We have been uniquely gifted by God to bring a special contribution to the life-flow of the church and thus, to the promotion of the Kingdom of God in the earth. Our assignment in life and our gifts are to be discovered and developed. We are to fulfill our responsibilities to the ministry of the church with great faithfulness. If someone is out of place, we are exposed to the attack of the enemy within the place they were to fill. It doesn't matter how important you deem your gift to be: Remember, there is no gift that is unimportant, and no person insignificant to the ministry they have been assigned.

Thought for Today

Are you fulfilling your position and contributing your God-given gift to the life of the church to which you have been assigned?

Prayer Journal

_____

_____

_____

~ ~ ~ JULY 23 ~ ~ ~

"And I looked, and arose and said to the nobles, to the leaders, and to the rest of the people, 'Do not be afraid of them. Remember the Lord, great and awesome, and fight for your brethren, your sons, your daughters, your wives, and your houses'" (Nehemiah 4:14).

The Israelites were growing increasingly concerned about the threats of their enemies. Their enemies had not only threatened to stop the rebuilding of the wall, but they had threatened to kill them as well. Nehemiah gathered the people together and pleaded with them not to be afraid of the threats of the enemy. He wanted them to remember that God was on their side and that He had promised to protect them. Nehemiah also wanted them to realize what was at stake if they gave into their fears and did not continue to turn the enemy back. The building of the wall at Jerusalem was one thing, but the well-being of their families was quite another. Nehemiah wanted them to overcome their fear and fight for the well-being of their families.

Like the Israelites, we have a mortal enemy that threatens to not only to stop our work for God, but to steal, kill, and destroy everything we hold precious. We cannot afford to become afraid and fearful of the enemy's sneering threats. We must realize what is at stake and what we stand to lose if we do not consistently fight and turn the enemy back. Our children, our families, our marriages, our finances, our futures, and our ministries are on the line.

Thought for Today

You will only fight for something as long as it has a place of value to you. What matters enough to you that will consistently cause you to fight the good fight of faith on its behalf?

Prayer Journal

_____

_____

_____

~ ~ ~ JULY 24 ~ ~ ~

"And it happened, when our enemies heard that it was known to us, and that God had brought their plot to nothing, that all of us returned to the wall, everyone to his work...Those who built on the wall, and those who carried burdens, loaded themselves so that with one hand they worked at construction, and with the other held a weapon...So we labored in the work, and half of the men held the spears from daybreak until the stars appeared" (Nehemiah 4:15, 17, 21).

God had revealed the plot of the enemy to Nehemiah—the enemy planned to come among the people and stop the rebuilding of the wall. The people returned to their work on the wall with a tool in one hand, and a weapon in the other hand to fight the enemy. They were prepared to work and also, prepared to fight for the work they were doing. Though the work was hard and the progress slow, the people were committed to the work in spite of the enemy's threats.

The progress of your work may be going slow and the results may be hard to see—but do not stop working. The enemy may be harassing you without mercy—but do not stop working. The temptation to quit may be overwhelming—but do not stop working. Be committed to see the work you have started, finished. Let the words of a once popular song encourage you; "Keep on walking for you don't know how far you've come. Keep on walking, for all you know it might be done, and the Father might be standing up right now, to give the call, that will end it all. Keep on walking."

Thought for Today

Don't quit, anybody can do that. Become a champion committed to completing your assignment—you don't know how close you are.

Prayer Journal

_____

_____

_____

~ ~ ~ JULY 25 ~ ~ ~

"So it was, from that time on, that half of my servants worked at construction, while the other half held the spears, the shields, the bows, and wore armor; and the leaders were behind all the house of Judah....So we labored in the work, and half of the men held the spears from daybreak until the stars appeared. At the same time I also said to the people, 'Let each man and his servant stay at night in Jerusalem, that they may be our guard by night and a working party by day'" (Nehemiah 4:16, 21-22).

Unity among the people was crucial to completing the work. If there was ever a time that they needed one another, it was now. The threats of the enemies' attack were taking a tremendous toll on their nerves, but not on their resolve to complete the project. Nehemiah devised a plan that would allow the work to continue safely around the clock. He divided the people into two groups; while one group worked, the other stood guard against the enemies.

We live in a self-centered society and everyone is so focused on their survival and success, they often do not see or care about the needs of others. In the family of God, we should be as committed to each other's success as we are to our own, for we need to realize that we are in this together. Victory will be realized when we commit to help each other complete our individual assignments, and when we are committed to protect each other from the enemies attacks. We are to encourage and protect one another.

Thought for Today

When was the last time that you entered into the fray of someone else's battle? When was the last time you stood shoulder-to-shoulder with someone to fight the good fight of faith?

Prayer Journal

_____

_____

_____

~ ~ ~ JULY 26 ~ ~ ~

"Every one of the builders had his sword girded at his side as he built. And the one who sounded the trumpet was beside me. Then I said to the nobles, the rulers, and the rest of the people, 'The work is great and extensive, and we are separated far from one another on the wall. Wherever you hear the sound of the trumpet, rally to us there. Our God will fight for us'" (Nehemiah 4:18-20).

The rebuilding of the wall around Jerusalem was an extensive project. Sections of the wall were intact while other sections were torn down. Repairing each torn down section required the workers to divide up into teams, and in so doing, the workers were often spread far apart. This separation made the workers even that much more vulnerable to the attacks of the enemy. Nehemiah instituted a plan by which each team was to listen for the sound of the trumpet, and when heard, rally to that place and help fight the enemy.

God has given us a similar plan to fight the enemy whenever he attacks an area of our lives. Resident within us is the person of the Holy Spirit. When the enemy comes against us in any area of our lives, where we have exposure or where we are vulnerable, the Holy Spirit will sound the alarm and we are to fight the enemy at that point. It is crucial that we learn to listen for the Holy Spirit's voice, for only when we learn to hear the sound of His alarm can we successfully defeat the enemy. To ignore the warning sounds of the Holy Spirit will always bring defeat to our circumstances.

Thought for Today

The Holy Spirit will always sound the alarm when we need to come to the aid of another and help them fight the attack of the enemy on their lives. However, we must listen for the voice of the Spirit.

Prayer Journal

_____

_____

_____

~ ~ ~ JULY 27 ~ ~ ~

"So neither I, my brethren, my servants, nor the men of the guard who followed me took off our clothes, except that everyone took them off for washing" (Nehemiah 4:23).

The rebuilding of the Jerusalem wall was extensive in scope, and the enemies' opposition to its completion was intensive. Nehemiah divided the workers into teams and established a strategy to give them protection. He instituted a plan to rally the people in the event of an attack. Everyone was so busy working, and standing guard, that they only took their clothes off for one reason—to bathe.

As small a detail as it may appear to be, staying clean spiritually is an important factor in waging spiritual warfare. We cannot afford to allow ourselves to compromise in any area of our lives, for to do so, gives the enemy an open door to attack us. The Bible clearly warns us not to give the enemy an opening where he can breach our defenses and successfully wound us. In Ephesians 4:27 we read, *"nor give place to the devil."* Sin that is not confessed in our lives will hinder our prayers from getting answered and this is especially dangerous when it comes to fighting the attacks of the enemy. We read the following warning in Isaiah 59:2, *"But your iniquities have separated you from your God; and your sins have hidden His face from you, so that He will not hear."* The Bible tells us how we can stay clean before the Lord in Psalms 119:9, *"How can a young man cleanse his way? By taking heed according to Your Word."*

Thought for Today

Daily spend time in the Word and allow it to wash your heart and mind. Stay clean. Ask the Holy Spirit to reveal anything He sees that makes you live compromised.

Prayer Journal

_____

_____

_____

~ ~ ~ JULY 28 ~ ~ ~

"For there stood by me this night an angel of the God to whom I belong and whom I serve, saying, 'Do not be afraid, Paul; you must be brought before Caesar; and indeed God has granted you all those who sail with you.' Therefore take heart, men, for I believe God that it will be just as it was told me" (Acts 27:23-25).

God revealed to Paul that he was to give his testimony concerning Jesus in Rome. After being arrested and enduring a series of trials before various magistrates, Paul was sent to Rome to stand trial before Caesar. Paul, along with his guards, started their journey to Rome. As they sailed, Paul warned them that sailing at this time of year was dangerous and that if they didn't hold up in port, they would suffer great loss. The guards ignored Paul's warning and continued sailing. Then, just as Paul had warned, a storm struck with such force that their ship went off course and they were shipwrecked. God spoke to Paul reassuring him that no one would die from the shipwreck and that he would safely arrive in Rome. Paul told his guards, that in spite of what they were seeing and perceiving, that he believed what God had said.

In the storms of life, we are tempted to believe the wrong voices. Our eyes tell us to believe what we can see. Our bodies tell us to believe what we can feel. Our minds tell us to believe what we can comprehend. However, our spirits tell us to believe God and stand on His Word—no matter what the circumstances.

Thought for Today

Determine which voice you are going to listen too. Choosing to believe God's voice, over all of the other voices, will assure your survival through any storm you may encounter.

Prayer Journal

_____

_____

_____

~ ~ ~ JULY 29 ~ ~ ~

"You are of your father the devil, and the desires of your father you want to do. He was a murderer from the beginning, and does not stand in the truth, because there is no truth in him. When he speaks a lie, he speaks from his own resources, for he is a liar and the father of it. But because I tell the truth, you do not believe Me" (John 8:44-45).

The Jews and their religious leaders were constantly debating with Jesus. They sought to trap Him by asking difficult questions about matters of the Law. It didn't matter how Jesus responded to them or what He said, they simply chose not to believe Him. Jesus told them that the reason they couldn't believe the things He was telling them is because they had chosen to believe the lies of their father, the devil. Jesus taught that the devil is a murderer and a liar, and that there is absolutely no truth found in him. Whenever the devil speaks it is a lie, and whatever lie he tells has been drawn from the resources of his own wickedness. On the other hand, Jesus told them that whatever He spoke was the absolute truth of God.

The devil tells us that we will never see our families saved, that we will never be healed, that we will never be free from a habit, that we will never find love, that we will never know financial freedom, and a myriad of other lies. It is a sad commentary of many, for they have chosen to believe the lies of the devil about their circumstances, instead of believing what the Lord has said.

Thought for Today

Tragically, instead of believing the liberating truth of God's Word about our lives, there are many who have chosen to believe the devil. You cannot ever believe what a liar says—believe God.

Prayer Journal

_____

_____

_____

~ ~ ~ JULY 30 ~ ~ ~

"Now concerning things offered to idols: We know that we all have knowledge. Knowledge puffs up, but love edifies" (I Corinthians 8:1).

What code of ethics should govern a Christian's lifestyle? As Christians, how do we successfully deal with the areas of life where the Scripture does not give us a specific instruction as to our conduct or attitude? Paul faced these ethical questions in the church at Corinth. It was a routine practice to purchase and eat meat that had been previously offered to idols. The Christians at Corinth wanted Paul to settle a dispute that had risen among them. Some of them believed it was all right to eat such meat, while others thought it was wrong. They argued about whether or not it really mattered if the meat was eaten, and if so, whether or not it should be eaten in private, or was it permissible to eat it in public. Both groups supported their positions with their belief of what they felt the Scriptures taught, and they each insisted their position was right. Paul rebukes them for their disagreement. Both groups had become arrogant in their attitudes towards the other group, deeming themselves to be superior in their knowledge of the Word. Paul reminds them that knowledge alone will promote spiritual pride, but love, always seeks the edification of another.

As you consider your personal code of ethics, based on what you believe the Word teaches, guard your heart from becoming puffed up with spiritual pride. You must respect the position of another.

Thought for Today

Avoid the temptation to assume your convictions are superior to those held by others who may, with sincerity, not agree with you.

Prayer Journal

_____

_____

_____

~ ~ ~ JULY 31 ~ ~ ~

"Let us not judge one another anymore, but rather resolve this, not to put a stumbling block or a cause to fall in our brother's way...Therefore let us pursue the things which make for peace and the things by which one may edify another. Do not destroy the work of God for the sake of food" (Romans 14:13, 19-20).

Love for one another must be the first consideration as we establish our convictions and the code of ethics that will govern our lives as followers of Christ. Paul warns us that we should not be so bent on exercising our liberties in Christ, that we cause someone else to stumble and thus, destroy the work of God.

We must answer the following questions as we review the personal liberties we have established, as well as, ones we are considering establishing. Will this be good for my life? Will this be positive and aid me in spiritual growth, or will it be negative and tear me down spiritually? Will this control me and lessen the control of Christ over my life? As God's property, can I justify this activity and reconcile it with the Word? As a representative of Christ, is this a befitting activity? Could my actions negatively influence my friends or cause them to stumble in their discovery of God? Will my actions keep anyone from receiving Christ as their Savior? How will my testimony be affected by this? After participating in this activity, can I thank God for what I have participated in?

Thought for Today

Be willing to ask yourself difficult questions. Am I willing to limit the freedoms I have in Christ so that others will see Jesus in me? As I make decisions concerning my actions and where I will go, will I consider the well-being of others?

Prayer Journal

_____

_____

_____

~ ~ ~ AUGUST 1 ~ ~ ~

"Now it came to pass, as He was praying in a certain place, when He ceased, that one of His disciples said to Him, 'Lord, teach us to pray, as John also taught his disciples'" (Luke 11:1).

The disciples came to Jesus and asked Him to teach them how to pray. It wasn't that they were ignorant about prayer; rather, it was when Jesus prayed, things happened. The disciples were regular attendees at the Synagogue and no doubt had repeated the ritual prayers that were part of the worship services led by the priests. They had grown accustomed to hearing and watching others pray, but never had they heard or seen anyone pray like Jesus.

When Jesus prayed, it was as though God was standing right by His side and listening to every word. The prayers of Jesus were void of mere religious ritual for His prayers were intimate in nature. Jesus really seemed to enjoy praying instead of enduring it, as had been their experience. The greatest draw to learn how to pray like Jesus was that when Jesus prayed, His prayers were answered and answered in a big way: the blind received their sight, the lame walked again, the dead were raised, and even nature obeyed Him.

Prayer is one of the most difficult disciplines to master, and one of the most rewarding ones when we do. Like the disciples, we would do well to ask the Lord to teach us to pray as He prayed. Jesus wants us to know that through prayer, we can touch heaven with our needs and move earth with His power.

Thought for Today

There is power in learning to pray as Jesus prayed. Ask Him to teach you how to pray with the same power with which He prayed.

Prayer Journal

_____

_____

_____

~ ~ ~ AUGUST 2 ~ ~ ~

"Coming out, He went to the Mount of Olives, as He was accustomed, and His disciples also followed Him. When He came to the place, He said to them, 'Pray that you may not enter into temptation.' And He was withdrawn from them about a stone's throw, and He knelt down and prayed" (Luke 22:39-41).

Jesus set the example of a prayer life for throughout His earthly ministry, He moved from one place of prayer to another. Through prayer, the power of Jesus for ministry was constantly refueled.

There are three ingredients necessary to establish a successful prayer life. The first ingredient is a desire for prayer which is born out of our desire for God. We must allow the Holy Spirit to give birth to the desire to pray and this desire will be evidenced by a hunger for God. The stronger your desire to spend intimate time with the Lord, the stronger your desire to pray will be.

The second ingredient is discipline. The outgrowth of our discipline is our commitment to achieve a desired result. Our discipline is directly proportionate to our desire to achieve our goal. The proof of our desire is evidenced by the discipline of our pursuit.

The third ingredient is delight. The end result of our desire and our discipline will be our delight in prayer. Prayer will no longer be a mere religious ritual, or a duty to be performed; rather, it will become the delight of our hearts.

Thought for Today

As the Holy Spirit gives birth to the desire to pray, discipline yourself to pray. Discipline will yield the delight of His presence.

Prayer Journal

_____

_____

_____

~ ~ ~ AUGUST 3 ~ ~ ~

"Give ear to my words, O Lord, consider my meditation. Give heed to the voice of my cry, my King and my God, for to You I will pray. My voice You shall hear in the morning, O Lord; in the morning I will direct it to You, and I will look up" (Psalms 5:1-3).

No subject brings more conviction and yet, no obedience has a greater reward than does prayer. Scripture declares that prayer is a command, not an option. The words, "pray, prayer, prayers and praying," occur 530 times throughout the Scriptures. Prayer, in its purest form, is communion with God and is a verbal exchange with God that will enhance our companionship with Him. Communion with God goes far beyond our petitioning Him and centers on enjoying His presence. Just as God judges a man by his heart, so also, God weighs the heart of the one praying to determine the sincerity of the heart. Jeremiah 29:13 tells us, *"And you will seek Me and find Me, when you search for Me with all of your heart."* You haven't prayed until your heart prays.

It is through prayer that we are ushered into the presence of God, and there in His presence, we are granted the desires of our hearts. The Psalmist said in Psalms 145:18-19, *"The Lord is near to all who call upon Him, to all who call upon Him in truth. He will fulfill the desire of those who fear Him; He also will hear their cry and save them."* The sweetest reward a person who is committed to prayer will ever know is the awareness of God's presence; for it is only in His presence that our joy is made complete.

Thought for Today

Step away from the busy schedule you have set and spend time with Him. Give Him your hearts' devotion and your deepest cares.

Prayer Journal

_____

_____

_____

~ ~ ~ AUGUST 4 ~ ~ ~

"Behold, I stand at the door and knock. If anyone hears My voice and opens the door, I will come in to him and dine with him, and he with Me" (Revelation 3:20).

We have all seen the artist's portrayal of Jesus standing and knocking at the door. Over the years, we have interpreted this to mean that Jesus stands at the door to the sinner's heart as He pleads to gain an entrance; for surely it is the desire of Jesus to gain entrance into every sinner's heart. However, this verse references that it is actually at the door of the Christian's heart that He patiently stands as a gentleman, and awaits our invitation to enter.

What a great picture of the Lord's desire to fellowship with His children. Unfortunately, many have shut this door of fellowship. Jesus' desire to fellowship with us is so great, that He knocks on the door of our heart and then patiently awaits our acknowledgment of His knocking. Jesus is a gentleman, and will never force His way into our schedules—He awaits our invitation. Once given, He promises to come in and stay with us. His desire is to sit with you and to hear what is on your heart and mind and He is not in a hurry to move on. Jesus wants to come in and enjoy your presence—as much as He hopes you will enjoy His. Tragically, we are the ones in a hurry. We rapidly rattle off our complaints and our petitions; then, if we remember, we breathe a half-hearted "thank you."

Thought for Today

It is amazing, the One Who holds the universe in His hands, wants to spend time with you. He wants to hear your stories and tell you some of His own. All He asks for is a little of your time. Decide at this very moment to set time aside for fellowship with Him.

Prayer Journal

_____

_____

_____

~ ~ ~ AUGUST 5 ~ ~ ~

"Seeing then that we have a great High Priest who has passed through the heavens, Jesus the Son of God, let us hold fast our confession. For we do not have a High Priest who cannot sympathize with our weaknesses, but was in all points tempted as we are, yet without sin. Let us therefore come boldly to the throne of grace, that we may obtain mercy and find grace to help in time of need" (Hebrews 4:14-16).

We have in Jesus, someone Who completely understands our every need. Jesus has been where we are…He has walked in our shoes…He has felt what we are feeling. There is nothing that touches our lives that has not touched His. He knows what we are going through and it matters that we come through safely. We are invited to come with boldness and approach His throne in prayer. Boldness is not arrogance, but it is the absolute confidence that God is Who He claims to be and will do what He promised to do. We read in Hebrews 11:6, *"But without faith it is impossible to please Him, for he who comes to God must believe that He is, and that He is a rewarder of those who diligently seek Him."*

When we pray, we have the desire for our prayers to be answered. Yet, we need to understand just how great God's desire is toward us. We see His desire in that, even before we pray, the answer is on the way. Isaiah 65:24 says, *"It shall come to pass that before they call, I will answer; and while they are still speaking, I will hear."*

Thought for Today

God is aware of every need we have now, and will have in the future. He is more anxious to answer the cry of our heart through prayer, than we are to have our prayers answered.

Prayer Journal

_____

_____

_____

~ ~ ~ AUGUST 6 ~ ~ ~

"Who can understand his errors? Cleanse me from secret faults. Keep back Your servant also from presumptuous sins; let them not have dominion over me. Then I shall be blameless, and I shall be innocent of great transgression. Let the words of my mouth and the meditation of my heart be acceptable in Your sight, O Lord, my strength and my Redeemer" (Psalms 19:12-14).

When we look into the perfect law of the Lord, we clearly see the errors and faults that are resident within us. When we recognize these faults, we must humble ourselves before the Lord and confess our faults to Him and seek His forgiveness. The wise disciple will request the search light of the Holy Spirit to seek out anything in his life that may be offensive to the Lord so that they can be cleansed from his life. The Holy Spirit is faithful to remind us of those areas that need to be dealt with as He brings His conviction to every one of our thoughts, every word, and to every action we take.

One of the greatest desires that we should have, is that the words we speak might be acceptable to the Lord. The acceptability of our words in the sight of God, is determined by, and dependent upon, their being lined up with the truth of what we actually believe about God and His Word. God wants to hear what we truly believe in our heart. If our mouth and actions contradict our heart, our speech is invalid and unacceptable in the sight of the Lord.

Thought for Today

With our heart, we believe, resulting in righteousness; and with our mouth, we declare what our heart believes. We need to discipline ourselves to reconcile the belief of our heart with the absolute truth of the Word of God.

Prayer Journal

_____

_____

_____

~ ~ ~ AUGUST 7 ~ ~ ~

"Likewise the Spirit also helps in our weaknesses. For we do not know what we should pray for as we ought, but the Spirit Himself makes intercession for us with groanings which cannot be uttered. Now He who searches the hearts knows what the mind of the Spirit is, because He makes intercession for the saints according to the will of God" (Romans 8:26-27).

Prayer is a conversation in which we speak to God and God, in turn, speaks to us. God promises to answer our prayers, if we are faithful to pray. It is through prayer that we are able to release our cares and problems; as well as, our negative emotions such as fear, unbelief, worry, anxiety, and anger. We are admonished to give all of our cares to the Lord and let Him carry them, *"Casting all your care upon Him, for He cares for you."* (I Peter 5:7). No one will ever love us like God loves us and no one will ever care for us as He does. Our burdens are welcomed on His shoulders.

There are times when we simply do not know how to pray for a situation or person. There are other times, when our hearts are so heavy with sorrow or concern that we cannot find the right words to say in prayer. It is in these times, that we can turn to the Holy Spirit and allow Him to intercede in prayer through us. He will help us in our weakness, as He comes along beside us and lifts the heavy end of our load. When we allow the Holy Spirit access, He will help us release our burdens into the capable hands of our God.

Thought for Today

Once you are willing to release your burdens to the Lord, do not be guilty of taking them back and trying to deal with them on your own—leave them in His faithful and competent hands.

Prayer Journal

_____

_____

_____

~ ~ ~ AUGUST 8 ~ ~ ~

"Confess your trespasses to one another, and pray for one another, that you may be healed. The effective, fervent prayer of a righteous man avails much" (James 5:16).

God cares about those who are sick and He desires that they be healed. Jesus purchased our healing through the stripes that were laid upon His back. In I Peter 2:24 we are promised *"Who Himself bore our sins in His own body on the tree, that we, having died to sins, might live for righteousness—by whose stripes you were healed."* Everywhere that Jesus went, He healed the sick. Hurting people touched His heart and He touched them with His healing hand. In Matthew 9:35-36, we see the heart of Jesus, *"Then Jesus went about all the cities and villages, teaching in their synagogues, preaching the gospel of the kingdom, and healing every sickness and every disease among the people. But when He saw the multitudes, He was moved with compassion for them, because they were weary and scattered, like sheep having no shepherd."*

Before Jesus ascended into heaven, He commissioned us to continue His ministry and to spread it to the ends of the earth. We are to lay hands on the sick and pray for their healing. The Word teaches us that the *"fervent prayer of a righteous man avails much."* The word avail means, "to prevail with great power." We have the power through prayer to overrule the power of the enemy and to bring God's healing touch to hurting people.

Thought for Today

The next time you see someone who is sick and hurting, ask yourself, "what would Jesus do and how would He pray concerning their circumstance?" Then, in faith, follow His example of caring.

Prayer Journal

_____

_____

_____

~ ~ ~ AUGUST 9 ~ ~ ~

"So I say to you, ask, and it will be given to you; seek, and you will find; knock, and it will be opened to you. For everyone who asks receives, and he who seeks finds, and to him who knocks it will be opened" (Luke 11:9-10).

Perhaps as a child, you played the game called "Hide and Seek." The ones hiding would do everything possible to stay concealed, while the one trying to find them, would exhaust every possibility in locating their hiding place. This game can be fun for children, but it looses its appeal when you think that you are playing it with God. Sometimes, when we pray, we get the feeling that God is playing "Hide and Seek" with us. We think He's the one hiding and we are trying to find Him—nothing could be further from the truth.

God promises us that as we are persistent in prayer that: whatever we ask will be granted, whatever we seek we will find, and whatever has been closed to us will be opened. Jesus told us in Matthew 21:22, *"And whatever things you ask in prayer, believing, you will receive."* God wants to release His abundant supply into our lives and He takes no delight when we suffer lack. His answer to our prayers will exceed our requests and our expectations. Paul tells us in Ephesians 3:20, *"Now to Him who is able to do exceedingly abundantly above all that we ask or think, according to the power that works in us."* Do not allow a perceived silence from God bring the assumption that God is hiding His face from you.

Thought for Today

Every promise in the Word of God is preceded by a condition that must be met. If we are faithful to meet the condition, God is more than faithful to fulfill His end of the bargain and keep His promises.

Prayer Journal

_____

_____

_____

~ ~ ~ AUGUST 10 ~ ~ ~

"Beloved, if our heart does not condemn us, we have confidence toward God. And whatever we ask we receive from Him, because we keep His commandments and do those things that are pleasing in His sight" (I John 3:21-22).

One of the indicators that we are praying the will of God, and not according to the lusts of our flesh, is how our heart responds to our prayer. If our heart is at peace and not accusing us, we can be confident we have prayed in accordance with the Word and in agreement with the Holy Spirit. When our confidence is high, so is our faith; and when doubt is destroyed, peace is released in our hearts. Then we know that our prayers have been heard by God.

There is another indicator that gives us assurance in prayer, and that is our keeping the commandments of God's Word. When we make our attitudes and conduct conform to the principles and precepts of the Word, we can know with certainty that our prayers are being heard by that Father and will be answered. However, we run into problems when we attempt to live with a mixture of obedience to the Word. We cannot live in obedience to areas that are comfortable, and live in disobedience to areas that are not comfortable. Assurance will never be found if we treat the principles and precepts of the Word as optional. Actually, having confidence in our prayers being answered is dependent on our choice to live in harmony with the precepts of God's Word.

Thought for Today

You can have the absolute assurance that when you pray, your prayers are being heard and answered in the throne room of heaven. We must set our hearts to faithfully obey the Word of God.

Prayer Journal

_____

_____

_____

~ ~ ~ AUGUST 11 ~ ~ ~

"Again I say to you that if two of you agree on earth concerning anything that they ask, it will be done for them by My Father in heaven. For where two or three are gathered together in My name, I am there in the midst of them" (Matthew 18:19-20).

Jesus promised that when two people come into agreement on a matter in prayer, that their Father in heaven will grant them their petition. We understand that this doesn't mean we can pray in agreement with someone according to the lustful desires of our flesh. Just because we find someone to agree, we should not be led to believe that God is obligated to answer such an errant prayer. The Scriptures teach us in I John 5:14-15, that our prayers must line up with the will of God in His Word, *"Now this is the confidence that we have in Him, that if we ask anything according to His will, He hears us. And if we know that He hears us, whatever we ask, we know that we have the petitions that we have asked of Him."* If we are not sure how to pray, we need to turn to God's Word and discover His will in the matter, and then pray accordingly.

When we as believers gather together in agreement, and we pray over a request, something tremendous takes place; Jesus comes and enters into agreement with us. Whenever Jesus gets into the midst of any circumstance, things are guaranteed to change. Jesus has granted us "power of attorney" to use His name when we pray.

Thought for Today

We must pray in the name of Jesus according to the will of God as is expressed in the Word of God. When we do so, and we come into agreement with others, we can know beyond a shadow of a doubt that our prayers are going to be answered.

Prayer Journal

_____

_____

_____

~ ~ ~ AUGUST 12 ~ ~ ~

"Then Jesus went into the temple of God and drove out all those who bought and sold in the temple, and overturned the tables of the money changers and the seats of those who sold doves. And He said to them, 'It is written, My house shall be called a house of prayer, but you have made it a den of thieves'" (Matthew 21:12-13).

Jesus drove the money changers out of the Temple and declared the Temple to be *"a house of prayer."* Individually, we are the temple of God and He expects us to be a house of prayer. For this to happen, just as Jesus cleansed the Temple from the money changers, so we must cleanse our hearts from any compromise and sin. We will never be *"a house of prayer"* if we do not establish a daily habit of spending time with the Lord in prayer. To become a house of prayer, we will have to make a choice.

When our temples are cleansed from sin and we have developed a habit of prayer, we can then expect the power of God to be made manifest through us. This was also true in the Temple after Jesus cleansed it and re-established its purpose. In Matthew 21:14 we read, *"Then the blind and the lame came to Him in the Temple, and He healed them."* The miracles did not just happen on their own, they happened because Jesus was resident in the Temple. Make your temple a house of prayer, where Jesus is resident in all of His power.

Thought for Today

We must discipline ourselves to become *"a house of prayer"* by cleansing our hearts and praying. Only then, will the presence of Jesus be made manifest through answers to prayer, and we will see miracles happening in every arena of our life.

Prayer Journal

_____

_____

_____

~ ~ ~ AUGUST 13 ~ ~ ~

"Praying always with all prayer and supplication in the Spirit, being watchful to this end with all perseverance and supplication for all the saints—" (Ephesians 6:18).

Paul concludes his instructions, regarding our putting on the whole armor of God, with an admonition to continue praying all kinds of prayer with perseverance. There are many types of prayer in Paul's list of *"all prayer."* Prayer forms include: confession, petition, fellowship, communication, intercession, thanksgiving, praise, and adoration. We are exhorted by Paul to persevere in *"all prayer"* as we stand in the armor of God and wage war against the enemy.

Perseverance means "steadfastness, constancy, and continuing in much-at-a-time prayer." Many people have the wrong concept of what perseverance means and how we actually incorporate it into our prayer lives. Many have mistakenly thought that to persevere in prayer means that we have to groan and grovel before the Lord, as if we are trying to gain God's approval; or worse yet, seeing if we can arouse His interest. Others have adopted a "grit your teeth and hang tough until God finally decides to hear and answer your prayer" attitude. To embrace either of these misguided approaches is to assume that answers to prayers have to be earned through persistent badgering and bullying of God. If answers are to be earned from God, then prayer becomes a work of our flesh instead of a work of God's grace.

Thought for Today

Our perseverance in prayer is the manifestation of our discipline to not become discouraged by what we do not see. We must remain consistent in prayer until we have an answer.

Prayer Journal

_____

_____

_____

~ ~ ~ AUGUST 14 ~ ~ ~

"And He said to them, 'Which of you shall have a friend, and go to him at midnight and say to him, 'Friend, lend me three loaves; for a friend of mine has come to me on his journey, and I have nothing to set before him;' and he will answer from within and say, 'Do not trouble me; the door is now shut, and my children are with me in bed; I cannot rise and give to you?' I say to you, though he will not rise and give to him because he is his friend, yet because of his persistence he will rise and give him as many as he needs" (Luke 11:5-8).

This parable has been misinterpreted over the years to mean that you must literally beat on the door of heaven until you get what you want from God. In other words, you have to persistently beg God until He decides to give in to your complaints and blesses you. Jesus was not teaching us that we have to weary God with our begging before He will answer our prayers. Rather, Jesus was teaching us to pray with boldness as He drew the contrast between an earthly friend, and God, our heavenly friend.

Jesus wanted us to know that a friend can approach a friend at any time. He wanted us to know that no request goes unanswered, and that regardless of how big or small our request may be He desires that we ask Him for help. The one asking in this parable didn't get his request answered because he repeatedly beat on the door, but because of his boldness to ask his friend for help.

Thought for Today

We have in God, a friend in heaven; therefore, we can be bold in asking for our every need to be met. Don't be afraid to petition God—He will not mind! He is your very best friend!

Prayer Journal

_____

_____

_____

~ ~ ~ AUGUST 15 ~ ~ ~

"There was in a certain city a judge who did not fear God nor regard man. Now there was a widow in that city; and she came to him, saying, 'Get justice for me from my adversary.' And he would not for a while; but afterward he said within himself, 'Though I do not fear God nor regard man, yet because this widow troubles me I will avenge her, lest by her continual coming she weary me.' Then the Lord said, 'Hear what the unjust judge said. And shall God not avenge His own elect who cry out day and night to Him, though He bears long with them? I tell you that He will avenge them speedily'" (Luke 18:2-8).

Jesus used this parable to teach perseverance in prayer. The corrupt judge did not care about God or about man. He also was not concerned about justice, for he only helped the widow because he grew weary of her continually bothering him with her request. Well-meaning people have used this parable to teach that we are to persevere in our complaints until we wear down God's resistance and thus, prove we are sincere and worthy of His response. Jesus was portraying the need for our assurance in prayer by drawing a contrast between an "unjust judge" and God, Who is a "just judge."

This parable does not reveal reluctance on God's part to answer us; instead, Jesus is encouraging us to ask with boldness, and be assured that God will hear our prayer and act quickly. Our perseverance in prayer recognizes that there is never a situation to which we need to surrender.

Thought for Today

In God, we have a just and faithful judge handling our case. We can be assured that He will act quickly, and in our best interests.

Prayer Journal

_____

_____

_____

~ ~ ~ AUGUST 16 ~ ~ ~

"For His anger is but for a moment, His favor is for life; weeping may endure for a night, but joy comes in the morning" (Psalms 30:5).

We all want God to manifest His answer to our prayers immediately after we offer them, for none of us are comfortable with delays. We want the answer now, as waiting frustrates us and challenges our faith to keep on believing God for His answer. Our tenacity to persevere in prayer will largely hinge upon our understanding that delays do not denote disinterest on God's part.

Sometimes what we have requested will require the passage of time, much like the maturation process required in childbirth. We have God's promise, even though our eyes may not see anything happening. Just as our eyes cannot see the baby being formed and matured in the womb of its mother, so our eyes cannot always see God at work behind the scenes, developing the birth of a miracle in response to our prayers. It is your responsibility to persevere in prayer, and it is God's responsibility to give birth to the miracle.

We may not see progress, so we are tempted to feel like God will never answer our prayers. We are to stand on the promises of God's Word by faith, until it is done. What our eyes currently see, doesn't tell the whole story. Don't be moved by your current circumstance. God is faithful to keep His Word, when we pray in faith.

Thought for Today

Hold on, and keep praying in faith, as you continue to believe God for your miracle. Your labor of tears may continue through the night, but your joy will come with the morning.

Prayer Journal

_____

_____

_____

~ ~ ~ AUGUST 17 ~ ~ ~

"In this manner, therefore, pray: our Father in heaven, hallowed be Your name" (Matthew 6:9).

The disciples asked Jesus to teach them how to pray like He prayed, for it was evident that when He prayed that there was a tremendous difference in the Father's response. Jesus begins His teaching on prayer by placing an emphasis on our relationship with God as our heavenly Father. He established the grounds for our confidence in prayer, by introducing the strength of the father/child relationship. This was a radical thing for the disciples to hear, as their only reference was that He was the God of their forefathers; the God of Abraham, Isaac, and Jacob. The disciples had never considered God to be in a parental role; the role of a father.

Nothing is more crippling to effective prayer than lacking confidence in our relationship with God. When our confidence with God is intact, then our faith reaches out to Him unimpeded. In I John 5:14-15, we read, *"Now this is the confidence that we have in Him, that if we ask anything according to His will, He hears us. And if we know that He hears us, whatever we ask, we know that we have the petitions that we have asked of Him."* When Jesus referenced God as One to be addressed in prayer as *"Father,"* He was revealing the relationship that we are intended to have with God. Tragically, for many, the concept of *"father"* has been marred by painful memories stemming from earthly relationships. Whether our memories are good or bad, God is not like our earthly fathers.

Thought for Today

Jesus reveals God to be a *"Father"* Who transcends even the finest of earthly fathers. Establish a confidence in your Heavenly Father.

Prayer Journal

_____

_____

_____

~ ~ ~ AUGUST 18 ~ ~ ~

"And he arose and came to his father. But when he was still a great way off, his father saw him and had compassion, and ran and fell on his neck and kissed him" (Luke 15:20).

The parable of the prodigal son is a story of a young man who had wasted everything he had been given; he wasted his inheritance, his opportunities, and his father's trust. Jesus uses this story to reveal the heart of God and to establish our confidence in our relationship with God as "our Father." The son came to his senses and decided to return home to see if his father would take him back—even if it was only as a servant. Jesus said that the father saw the son while he was yet a great distance away. This reveals to us that the heart of the father was yearning and watching for the return of his wayward son. Overwhelmed with guilt and feeling unworthy of forgiveness, the closer the young man got to home, the more he doubted his father's acceptance. Jesus tells us that the father was so moved with love for his returning son, that he ran out to meet him and fell upon his neck in a loving embrace. He repeatedly kissed his son, as he expressed his joy over their renewed fellowship.

This should give us great confidence for no matter where we have been, or what we have done, or for that matter where we are now, our Heavenly Father has not stopped loving us. He is anxiously awaiting our return.

Thought for Today

Our confidence in our relationship with God will be strengthened when we come face-to-face with His incredible love for us. He demonstrated it with the Cross. He is a loving Father, and no matter what happens, God loves YOU!

Prayer Journal

_____

_____

_____

~ ~ ~ AUGUST 19 ~ ~ ~

"And the son said to him, 'Father, I have sinned against heaven and in your sight, and am no longer worthy to be called your son.' But the father said to his servants, 'Bring out the best robe and put it on him, and put a ring on his hand and sandals on his feet'" (Luke 15:21-22).

Jesus told the parable of the prodigal son to illustrate what God intends our relationship with Him to be like. When the son returned home, he stated to his father that he no longer felt worthy to be his son. The father responded by ordering one of the servants to bring a new robe and put it on his son, for in that day and culture, robes were reserved for those who held positions of honor. In placing a robe on his son, the father was saying that he was being restored to his former position as an heir, complete with privileges and rights belonging to an heir. When we fail, our Father in Heaven is willing to forgive and restore us from the loss our sin may have caused.

In placing a jeweled ring on his son's finger, he was restoring his son to full partnership in the family business. The ring gave the son the right to exercise his authority to use the family name in matters pertaining to the family business. Placing the sandals on his son's feet was symbolically saying that the time for mourning had passed and the time of celebration had arrived. We also can walk with confidence knowing that God has restored to us the right to use the family name of Jesus, and He celebrates our restoration.

Thought for Today

Our confidence in prayer is based on the forgiveness and restoration we have received from God. He is a loving Father, Who is patiently waiting for us to return to Him and walk uprightly.

Prayer Journal

_____

_____

_____

~ ~ ~ AUGUST 20 ~ ~ ~

"In this manner, therefore, pray: 'Our Father in heaven, hallowed be Your name'" (Matthew 6:9).

The first thing that Jesus wanted His disciples to understand, as He taught them how to pray, was that their confidence in prayer was derived from the father/child relationship that they had with God, Who was their heavenly Father. Jesus taught them, that as they fellowshipped with their Father, they would experience the transforming power of God. Jesus said to pray, *"hallowed be Your name"* and as the disciples approached their heavenly Father in prayer, they were to offer Him their hearts in worship.

When we worship, we are to do so at an actual place. I am not talking about a country, city, or even a church building; I am talking about worshiping at the throne of God. We don't just offer expressions "out there somewhere," but we are to offer our worship at His throne, for it is through our worship that we provide an "earthly place" for God to be enthroned. Psalms 22:3 says, *"But You are holy, enthroned in the praises of Israel."* As our praise and worship begins to ascend to God, His presence begins to descend into our midst. Worship is God's prescribed way to bring His presence and power into the midst of our circumstances. The most powerful "life changing" action we can take is to spend time in the transforming presence of God, through praise and worship. The more time we spend in worship, the greater the transformation.

Thought for Today

Our worship releases the transforming presence and power of God into our hearts and lives. The areas that are unholy within us will be impacted by His Holiness as we worship Him.

Prayer Journal

_____

_____

_____

~ ~ ~ AUGUST 21 ~ ~ ~

"As obedient children, not conforming yourselves to the former lusts, as in your ignorance; but as He who called you is holy, you also be holy in all your conduct, because it is written, 'Be holy, for I am holy'" (I Peter 1:14-16).

When Jesus taught His disciples to pray, "Hallowed be Your name," He was actually saying, "holy be Your name." Holiness is a term that is often associated with the expression of worship, and yet it is rarely understood. Many Christians have the misconception that holiness constitutes the incorporation of external characteristics. When such a view is held, many are left feeling very intimidated and unqualified, especially when they compare themselves to the holiness of God. Others maintain the misconception that holiness is a forbidding trait of God's nature—sort of an attitudinal barrier created by His perfection, which is continually weighed against our imperfection.

The truth of the matter is that holiness relates to God's completeness. God is complete, in that there is nothing lacking in His person. There is absolutely nothing that needs to be added to make Him "enough" and this holds great promise for us. God is holy (complete) and it is His nature to give; and He makes His holiness (completeness) available to "complete" us. Through our worship, we invite God to reside in us and to complete those areas that are unholy (incomplete), as a result of sin.

Thought for Today

Holiness is not a demand, but rather, holiness is a guaranteed promise that God's resident presence and power will transform and complete us as we extol Him in worship.

Prayer Journal

_____

_____

_____

~ ~ ~ AUGUST 22 ~ ~ ~

"Your kingdom come. Your will be done on earth as it is in heaven" (Matthew 6:10).

Many Christians continue to live under the misconception that man is nothing more than a mere pawn on the chessboard of life. They have been deceived to believe that God will do with them as He pleases, regardless of the needs and wants of the individual. This misconception reduces man to being a hopeless and helpless victim of circumstances. This "mind set" is contrary to the hope of victory; for this hope comes through prayer that is offered in faith. Jesus taught His disciples to discharge their responsibility through prayer. They were to ask God for His kingdom and His will to be done on the earth, just as it is done in heaven.

God gave man dominion over His creation; thereby, man is responsible. The plethora of problems and sickness that exist in the world is the result of man's failure to execute the responsibility of rulership that God gave him. Adam's sin not only cost him his relationship with God, but it also had a profound affect on his ability to rule under God. Adam's sin placed the authority to rule the earth into the hands of satan. I John 5:19 says, *"We know that we are of God, and the whole world lies under the sway of the wicked one."* Mankind's failure in sin, coupled with satan's quest to destroy God's creation, has had a devastating effect on mankind.

Thought for Today

We must exercise our responsibility to pray, *"Your kingdom come, Your will be done on earth as it is in heaven."* This prayer invites the intervention of God's presence and power to work on our behalf, reversing the agenda's of hell.

Prayer Journal

_____

_____

_____

~ ~ ~ AUGUST 23 ~ ~ ~

"From that time Jesus began to preach and to say, 'Repent, for the kingdom of heaven is at hand'" (Matthew 4:17).

The first message that Jesus preached was that men should repent for the kingdom of God was present among them. Even with His trust in man betrayed, God provided man with hope for restoration to the purposes of God's kingdom through Jesus. Jesus declared that the "rule of God" was once again available to mankind and that no one would need to remain a victim to the sin of Adam. Throughout His ministry, Jesus demonstrated every aspect of kingdom rule that He was offering, and this kingdom rule would be restored to mankind. In meeting the needs of the people, Jesus put into action the power of God's rule that is now available to us.

Jesus had a war-like opposition to the invisible powers of hell that had seduced man into relinquishing his relationship with God and therefore, his rulership under God. While on the Cross, Jesus redeemed man's relationship with God and restored his rulership under God. He destroyed the power of hell to enslave anyone who would decide to come to Jesus for salvation. In Colossians 2:15 we read, *"Having disarmed principalities and powers, He made a public spectacle of them, triumphing over them in it."* The Cross of Christ restores man's authority to overrule any of hell's powers that we may encounter. Every believer must decide whether or not he will draw upon the resources of Christ's triumph on the Cross.

Thought for Today

Our new birth initiates our entrance into God's kingdom. After our new birth, we are commissioned to advance the kingdom of God into every arena of life through prayer.

Prayer Journal

_____

_____

_____

~ ~ ~ AUGUST 24 ~ ~ ~

"Give us this day our daily bread" (Matthew 6:11).

Jesus taught His disciples the necessity of requesting the provision for their daily needs from their Father in heaven through their faithfulness in prayer. There is far more in this portion of the prayer than merely asking that provision for food and physical needs be granted. This portion of the prayer extends an invitation to daily come before our Father in heaven for refreshing, renewal, and nourishment, for both our souls and our bodies. It is also a specific command for us to recognize our dependency on the Lord for all of our provision. We need to acknowledge that this daily provision from our Father will only continue to flow as we discipline ourselves in daily prayer.

In James 4:2 we read, *"You lust and do not have. You murder and covet and cannot obtain. You fight and war. Yet you do not have because you do not ask."* This passage reveals the Lord's readiness to release His promises; however, it does not release us from the responsibility to ask. Through an act of our will, we must stop relying on our own strength and declare our dependency on God. Our dependency will be evidenced by our asking in prayer. Our dependence on prayer is not desperate prayer; for we shouldn't turn to God only as a last resort in times of crisis. Dependent prayer is not demeaning, for God will never demand that we beg Him for His provision.

Thought for Today

Dependent prayer is the way to gain a realization of the unchanging love and commitment of God. Dependent prayer will show us how we can participate in requesting the provision of God for our lives.

Prayer Journal

_____

_____

_____

~ ~ ~ AUGUST 25 ~ ~ ~

"So teach us to number our days, that we may gain a heart of wisdom" (Psalms 90:12).

The psalmist requested wisdom from God to recognize how few days we have been given; therefore, He wanted God's wisdom to embrace each day. In praying Matthew 6:11, *"Give us this day our daily bread,"* we are requesting that our needs be met spiritually, as well as, physically. We are declaring our dependency on God to meet those needs out of His abundant supply.

When we pray this portion of the prayer, we are learning to be accountable for every day, every hour, and every event of the day. Committing the details of the day to God will deliver us from wasted time and pointless pursuits that will cost us valuable time. Placing ourselves in God's hands will deliver us from the enemy of self, such as procrastination and weakness; however, we will also be delivered from hell's demonic conspiracies. In Psalms 31:15 we read, *"My times are in Your hand; deliver me from the hand of my enemies, and from those who persecute me."*

When we declare our dependency in prayer, the Lord will deliver us from anything, or anyone, that seeks to wrench us from God's purposes for our lives. Our declared dependency through prayer fulfills the promises of God's Word to release the Holy Spirit to work in our lives.

Thought for Today

Declaring our dependency on the Lord through prayer releases the Lord's strength in us. Our prayer will release His provision in the proportion that is required to provide for the needs of the day.

Prayer Journal

_____

_____

_____

~ ~ ~ AUGUST 26 ~ ~ ~

"And forgive us our debts (trespasses), as we forgive our debtors" (Matthew 6:12).

Some translators translated this passage using the word *"debts"* and others translated it *"trespasses."* Actually, both are correct and needful as they show the two sides of human disobedience. In asking to be forgiven of our trespasses, we are speaking of our need to be forgiven for stepping over the established boundaries of the Word. These trespasses are considered to be sins of commission. The Word establishes territorial boundaries which protect us from destruction and are posted with "no trespassing" signs.

In asking to be forgiven for our debts, we are speaking of our need to be forgiven for our failure to do the right thing in any given situation. Our failure to do the right thing renders us to be debtors; and is considered to be a sin of omission. This portion of the prayer, when prayed, will release us from the shame of guilt that comes to us through our trespasses and from the pain of neglect that is inflicted on our hearts when we become debtors. Jesus knew of our need to be taught to pray for forgiveness, for it is an inherited tendency in all of us to sin, and then avoid admitting to the sin. This portion of the prayer also reminds us of the grace that is freely given to us, and raises our sensitivity to the ability of sin to stunt our spiritual growth. Whether it is sins of commission or sins of omission, God is always willing to forgive us—but we must ask.

Thought for Today

Praying to be forgiven of our *"debts (trespasses)"* holds for us the promise of the willingness of God to forgive. The only requirement is that we must confess our sins and acknowledge we are wrong.

Prayer Journal

_____

_____

_____

~ ~ ~ AUGUST 27 ~ ~ ~

"And be kind to one another, tenderhearted, forgiving one another, even as God in Christ forgave you" (Ephesians 4:32).

Jesus taught His disciples that their request, to be forgiven for their trespasses and debts, was conditionally linked to their willingness to forgive others their trespasses and debts. Our willingness to forgive and release others sets the standard that God uses to forgive and release us. The Word of God establishes the perfect standard of forgiveness of others—Forgive as Christ forgave you.

The hardest words to say are, "I'm sorry, please forgive me." However, equally as hard to say is, "I forgive you." The Scriptures teach us that we are obligated to forgive, whether or not the offender apologizes. We sometimes say, "I'd forgive if they would admit they were wrong." Most of the time what we mean is, "I'd consider forgiving them if they would crawl to me on broken glass and bleed profusely." We are to forgive regardless of what they have done and how many times they have done it—no exceptions.

There is a very high price tag on our failure to forgive others. First, it will cost us our own forgiveness, for our unforgiveness will require our sins to remain on record. Secondly, it will cost us our being released from anger, guilt, and bitterness. Thirdly, it will cost us the flow of God's miracles into our lives. And fourthly, it will cost us God's acceptance of our worship.

Thought for Today

Considering how Jesus has forgiven us, and counting the cost of not forgiving others—we must forgive. The grudges you may be carrying are not worth the price exacted because of unforgiveness.

Prayer Journal

_____

_____

_____

~ ~ ~ AUGUST 28 ~ ~ ~

"And do not lead us into temptation, but deliver us from the evil one" (Matthew 6:13).

In considering this portion of the prayer that Jesus taught His disciples, it would appear that He was teaching them to ask God not to tempt them. However, James 1:13 clearly tells us, *"Let no one say when he is tempted, 'I am tempted by God'; for God cannot be tempted by evil, nor does He Himself tempt anyone."* Jesus was not teaching us to ask God not to trick us, for God never tempts anyone to sin. God does not lead us into temptation that will result in sin, but He does allow trials that develop our faith.

Immediately after Jesus was baptized, the Spirit led Him into the wilderness to face the devil. The word *"temptation"* as used in Scripture, carries a dual meaning. The first meaning has to do with the desire of an adversary to test and break through our spiritual defenses. The second meaning deals with strength that is gained as we are victorious over an adversary's test. The result of the wilderness temptation was that Jesus gained victory and dominion over the devil: thus, He can promise this same victory to us, *"I will no longer talk much with you, for the ruler of this world is coming, and he has nothing in Me"* (John 14:30). Jesus declared the devil to be defeated; therefore, he couldn't claim to have any part of Jesus' life or testimony. Jesus promises us that we can stand in His victory over the devil, and then His testimony will become ours.

Thought for Today

Praying this portion of the prayer, *"And do not lead us into temptation,"* does not constitute a plea for relief; however, it does hold a great promise for guaranteed victory over the devil.

Prayer Journal

_____

_____

_____

~ ~ ~ AUGUST 29 ~ ~ ~

"No temptation has overtaken you except such as is common to man; but God is faithful, Who will not allow you to be tempted beyond what you are able, but with the temptation will also make the way of escape, that you may be able to bear it" (I Corinthians 10:13).

Jesus taught His disciples to pray in Matthew 6:13, *"And do not lead us into temptation, but deliver us from the evil one."* In this passage He was teaching them to rise up with obedient faith and confront the reality of their vulnerability to temptation. This portion of the prayer teaches us of our need to establish our steps in advance of any given situation. It also teaches us to commit ourselves to receive His deliverance—instead of becoming ensnared in the trap of temptation. Jesus reveals that the nature and desire of God is for us to be successfully delivered from every trap that the devil has set for us.

When we pray and ask our Father to deliver us from temptation, we establish our commitment to stand in Christ's victory over the devil and the traps that have been prepared for our destruction. Praying this portion of the prayer will not remove temptation's challenge, but it reminds us of God's promise to provide a way out. II Timothy 4:18 says, *"And the Lord will deliver me from every evil work and preserve me for His heavenly kingdom."* II Peter 2:9 says *"The Lord knows how to deliver the Godly out of temptations."* God makes a way of escape—all we have to do is take it.

Thought for Today

Jesus taught us to walk in triumph and dominion over things that seek to conquer us. God promises to deliver us, if we will ask.

Prayer Journal

_____

_____

_____

~ ~ ~ AUGUST 30 ~ ~ ~

"For Yours is the kingdom and the power and the glory forever. Amen" (Matthew 6:13).

The closing portion of the model prayer that Jesus taught His disciples reveals a heart that has found assurance of triumph in God and has accepted His timing. After the resurrection, the disciples asked Jesus if the time had come for Him to establish the kingdom. In their opinion, the circumstances were right for the Messianic Kingdom to be established and for Israel to be delivered from the tyranny of Rome. Jesus responded that it was not for them to know the times or the seasons which God had set into order. He told them that the Holy Spirit would empower them to deal with every circumstance, and would also empower them to accomplish their assignment of spreading the gospel to the ends of the earth. In Acts 1:8 we read, *"But you shall receive power when the Holy Spirit has come upon you; and you shall be witnesses to Me in Jerusalem, and in all Judea and Samaria, and to the end of the earth."*

Jesus was not avoiding the question of the disciples; He just redirected their focus. This portion of prayer teaches us the pathway by which we trust God. The timing with which anything is answered is in the Lord's hands, and the Holy Spirit is present to assist in matters of concern. We can trust God even when we do not see what we consider to be timely answers. God's purposes will not be lost as the Holy Spirit impacts our circumstances.

Thought for Today

Our acknowledgment that the kingdom belongs to God reveals our willingness to submit to the rule of God. We must be committed to His timing for the answers to our prayers of faith.

Prayer Journal

_____

_____

_____

~ ~ ~ AUGUST 31 ~ ~ ~

"Give unto the Lord the glory due to His name; worship the Lord in the beauty of holiness" (Psalms 29:2).

The first step in developing trusting faith is to acknowledge that all rule, power, and glory, belongs to the Lord. God allows us to share His authority, but only He is Lord of all. God gives us His power, but only He is all-powerful. God teaches us His knowledge, but only He is all-knowing. Trusting faith will rise up and present a challenge to the status quo: where evil reigns, where pain and sickness prevail, and where hatred and human failure breed confusion. Trusting faith will always rise up and present a faith challenge. We need to develop a militant attitude against the devil's intrusion into the affairs of our lives. Under the rule of the Holy Spirit, we can boldly confront any opposition to that rule.

A legitimate question is, "What about the times that we do not see any visible results to the prayers we have prayed?" There are two things that rise out of praying with trusting faith. First, we know that the ultimate triumph of God's power will come in His perfect time. Second, we are assured that until that time arrives, the Holy Spirit will enable us to carry out our assignment in life and help us gain the victory over the attacks of the devil. When we continue to pray with trusting faith, we know that even if we do not see immediate victory over our circumstances, we haven not been abandoned, for the Holy Spirit is our ever present Helper.

Thought for Today

Trusting faith stands firm regardless of the circumstances. We can rest in the fact that God, in His perfect timing, will cause us to triumph in matters that concern us.

Prayer Journal

___

___

___

~ ~ ~ SEPTEMBER 1 ~ ~ ~

"In the Lord I put my trust; how can you say to my soul, 'Flee as a bird to your mountain?' For look! The wicked bend their bow, they make ready their arrow on the string, that they may shoot secretly at the upright in heart. If the foundations are destroyed, what can the righteous do" (Psalms 11:1-3)?

Every construction project begins with laying a foundation. The more elaborate the structure, the more critical a proper foundation becomes. The foundation is critical as it supports the building's weight and establishes its strength. Without it, the building would be at risk of collapse due to the fact it is not anchored to anything.

Just as a proper foundation is crucial for a construction project, it is even more imperative in a spiritual sense. Tragically, far too many attempt to build their spiritual lives without first laying the proper foundation in the Word. The end result is often the collapse of their belief system, which leaves them confused and discouraged.

Jesus spent a great deal of time teaching His disciples, and those who followed Him, the fundamental truths of Christianity. In doing so, He laid the foundation upon which the early church was built. In the writings of the Apostle Paul, he continually reminded the churches of the need to adhere to the fundamental principles of Christianity as taught by Jesus.

Thought for Today

When we discipline ourselves to study the Word, we can lay a foundation for our beliefs. When we faithfully study the Word we will eliminate misconceptions and doubts that we have been exposed to through the opinions of others.

Prayer Journal

_____

_____

_____

~ ~ ~ SEPTEMBER 2 ~ ~ ~

"But sanctify the Lord God in your hearts, and always be ready to give a defense to everyone who asks you a reason for the hope that is in you, with meekness and fear" (I Peter 3:15).

Every believer needs to know what they believe and why they believe it. For many, what they believe is a product of how they were raised. Such as, "My parents and grandparents believed it this way and if it is good enough for them, it is good enough for me." Tragically, they have taken the word of their family, their pastor, or their denomination, to be the truth. They have never made the effort to search the Scriptures for themselves. While the traditions and beliefs of our family, friends, and church are important, everyone should know what they believe and why they believe it, based solely on the Word of God. The beliefs and traditions of all the other voices around us should be seen as only a support to what the Holy Spirit has personally has taught us.

The Scriptures teach us that we should be able to give a sound answer to anyone that may ask of us what we believe and why we believe what we do. Hosea, the Old Testament prophet, warned that men would literally perish without the knowledge of God's will as revealed in His Word, *"My people are destroyed for lack of knowledge. Because you have rejected knowledge, I also will reject you from being priest for Me; because you have forgotten the law of your God, I also will forget your children"* (Hosea 4:6).

Thought for Today

Most Christians generally know what they believe, but would be hard pressed to point to the verses to substantiate their beliefs. Study the Word, know what you believe, and stand on it!

Prayer Journal

_____

_____

_____

~ ~ ~ SEPTEMBER 3 ~ ~ ~

"That we should no longer be children, tossed to and fro and carried about with every wind of doctrine, by the trickery of men, in the cunning craftiness of deceitful plotting" (Ephesians 4:14).

Jesus rebuked the religious leaders of His day because they spoke their opinions as though they were the Word of God. Their lack of knowledge and understanding of the Scriptures caused them to live and minister under deception and misconceptions. Jesus indicted the religious leaders with being powerless in their ministries, due to their lack of understanding of the Scriptures in Matthew 22:29, *"Jesus answered and said to them, 'You are mistaken, not knowing the Scriptures nor the power of God.'"*

The power of God is directly tied to His Word. When the Word of God becomes the foundation on which we build our beliefs, our walk with God will become strong. When we are confronted by strange or different doctrines we will not be swayed, but rather, we will remain rooted and grounded on the authority of the Scriptures. A proper foundation in the Word will also give us an anchor in the trials of life. When the enemy attacks us, we can turn to the Word and find a place of refuge. Our knowledge of the Word will become a line of defense against the attack of the enemy, as well as, the Word will be a powerful weapon that will bring us deliverance and victory. Without a proper foundation in the Word, there is little hope of withstanding the enemy's attacks against us.

Thought for Today

Our knowledge and understanding of the Word of God releases the power of God into our lives. It is through the power of the Word that our enemy is defeated and turned back.

Prayer Journal

_____

_____

_____

~ ~ ~ SEPTEMBER 4 ~ ~ ~

"Therefore if there is any consolation in Christ, if any comfort of love, if any fellowship of the Spirit, if any affection and mercy, fulfill my joy by being like-minded, having the same love, being of one accord, of one mind" (Philippians 2:1-2).

The Apostle Paul was deeply concerned about Christians living in unity and harmony. He knew that wherever there was division, the devil had an opportunity to work against the cause of Christ. A proper foundation in the Word of God will promote unity and establish a common platform from which we can bridge the gaps in our differences and therefore, unite our hearts in the love of God. While we may not all agree on every aspect of interpretation and application of the Scriptures, we can find common ground in the fundamental principles of Christianity. This common ground will enable us to unite in reaching our world with the glorious gospel of Jesus Christ.

Psalms 119:89, tells us, *"Forever, O Lord, your word is settled in heaven."* God is never going to change His mind about His Word. Therefore, we can build our lives on His Word with the assurance of its truth, and without fear of its failure. Jesus, in His priestly prayer, prayed that God would set us apart from the world, its values and its ways, by establishing us in His Word, *"They are not of the world, just as I am not of the world. Sanctify them by Your truth. Your Word is truth"* (John 17:16-17).

Thought for Today

As you allow the writings and opinions of men to enhance your understanding, always remember to base your beliefs on the Word so you will not be tossed to and fro by every wind of doctrine.

Prayer Journal

_____

_____

~ ~ ~ SEPTEMBER 5 ~ ~ ~

"But without faith it is impossible to please Him, for he who comes to God must believe that He is, and that He is a rewarder of those who diligently seek Him" (Hebrews 11:6).

Our faith in God depends on our belief that God exists and that He is Who He claims to be. Hebrews 11:6 makes it clear that simply believing that there is a God is not enough to please Him. We must believe that He is everything that He claims to be; and that He will do all that He promises to do if we ask in faith, believing.

God makes many claims concerning Himself throughout Scripture, and for lack of space and time we will consider only a few of them. God claims to be our healer in Exodus 15:26, *"If you diligently heed the voice of the Lord your God and do what is right in His sight, give ear to His commandments and keep all His statutes, I will put none of the diseases on you which I have brought on the Egyptians. For I am the Lord who heals you."* God claims to be our provider in Genesis 22:14, *"And Abraham called the name of the place, The-Lord-Will-Provide; as it is said to this day, 'In the Mount of The Lord it shall be provided.'"* God claims to be our peace in Judges 6:24, *"So Gideon built an altar to the Lord there and called it The Lord is Peace."* God claims to be our shepherd in Psalms 23:1, *"The Lord is my shepherd, I shall not want."* Just these few claims should build our faith to believe that God is Who He says He is and that He wants us to live a life of faith.

Thought for Today

Tragically, many Christians don't enjoy the benefits of relationship with God. They don't believe He is all that He claims to be and therefore, they don't believe He will do what He claims He will do.

Prayer Journal

_____

_____

_____

~ ~ ~ SEPTEMBER 6 ~ ~ ~

"Thus says the Lord, the King of Israel, and his Redeemer, the Lord of hosts: 'I am the First and I am the Last; besides Me there is no God'" (Isaiah 44:6).

Suppose that someone asked you, "What is God like?" How would you answer? The Bible doesn't try to prove the existence of God, it just declares it as found in Genesis 1:1, *"In the beginning God created the heavens and the earth."* The Word tells us that God is eternal—He had no beginning, He has no end, and He has no equal.

John 4:24 reveals to us that God is Spirit, *"God is Spirit, and those who worship Him must worship in spirit and truth."* Essentially, God is a spiritual being, rather than a physical one. We also find in I John 1:5 that God is light, *"This is the message which we have heard from Him and declare to you, that God is light and in Him is no darkness at all."* Light is a reference to the majestic glory of God. The light of God is pure and is impossible to defile.

In I John 4:16, we discover that God is love, *"And we have known and believed the love that God has for us. God is love, and he who abides in love abides in God, and God in him."* Love is not what God does, love is what God IS. One of the most reassuring things to know is that God is immutable—God never changes. Malachi 3:6 says, *"For I am the Lord, I do not change."* He is eternally the same in His character and being and He desires to touch our lives.

Thought for Today

We can know with certainty that we can approach God with a request for Him to fulfill His promises. We can be assured that He won't change His mind about what His promises—for God IS love.

Prayer Journal

_____

_____

_____

~ ~ ~ SEPTEMBER 7 ~ ~ ~

"For as the Father has life in Himself, so He has granted the Son to have life in Himself" (John 5:26).

One of the most difficult questions to answer is, "Where did God come from?" Everyone has a beginning and an end….everyone that is—except God. The Word says God is eternal, never having a beginning, and never having an end. *"Before the mountains were brought forth, or ever You had formed the earth and the world, even from everlasting to everlasting, You are God"* (Psalms 90:2). There's never been a time God didn't exist.

The great preacher S. M. Lockridge, in his famous sermon, "Jesus Is Lord," answered the question as to where God came from: "God came from nowhere! The reason that God came from nowhere, is that there was nowhere for God to come from. Coming from nowhere, He stood on nothing, for there was nothing for Him to stand on. Standing on nothing, He reached out where there was nowhere to reach, and caught something when there was nothing to catch. He then hung something on nothing and told it to stay there. He took the hammer of His will and struck the anvil of His Omnipotence, and sparks flew there from. He caught the sparks on the tips of His fingers and flung them out into space and thus, bedecked the heavens with stars. Nobody said a word. The reason nobody said a word, was because there was nobody to say a word, so God said, 'That's good!'"

Thought for Today

When you consider the greatness of God, in that He is has no beginning point and there is no end to His existence, it is amazing that we doubt Him and His ability to do what He said He would do.

Prayer Journal

_____

_____

_____

~ ~ ~ SEPTEMBER 8 ~ ~ ~

"Every good gift and every perfect gift is from above, and comes down from the Father of lights, with whom there is no variation or shadow of turning" (James 1:17).

God is a good God all of the time and we see His goodness expressed in everything He does. James tells us that in God there is no *"shadow of turning."* In the natural world, when the sun is at it's apex in the sky, no shadow is cast. When we consider this we realize that God never changes and He never a casts a shadow; therefore, God is always at the apex of His power, His love, His knowledge, His forgiveness, and mercy. Revelation 19:6 declares God to be omnipotent, *"Alleluia! For the Lord God Omnipotent reigns!"* God is sovereign and governs as it pleases Him. He is all-powerful; therefore, nothing is impossible.

Psalms 147:5 says, *"Great is our Lord, and mighty in power; His understanding is infinite."* God is all-knowing and has perfect knowledge—past, present, and future. The omniscience of God makes Him infallible; thus, incapable of error in judgment. Omniscience involves perfect knowledge, which is the accurate possession of facts. It involves perfect understanding, which is the perception and interpretation of facts. It also involves perfect wisdom, which is proper application of facts. Jeremiah 23:24 says, *"'Can anyone hide himself in secret places, so I shall not see him?' says the Lord; 'Do I not fill heaven and earth?' says the Lord."* God is not limited to time or space and is present at all times.

Thought for Today

God is with you wherever you go. There isn't anything He doesn't know or that He cannot do.

Prayer Journal

_____

_____

_____

~ ~ ~ SEPTEMBER 9 ~ ~ ~

"And when He had sent them away, He departed to the mountain to pray. Now when evening came, the boat was in the middle of the sea; and He was alone on the land. Then He saw them straining at rowing, for the wind was against them" (Mark 6:46-48).

The disciples had just returned from an evangelistic tour and were physically exhausted. Upon their return, their emotions were impacted when they were greeted with the news that John the Baptist had been beheaded. Then to top the day off, Jesus was holding an all day teaching convention and they were expected to act as hosts—serving and cleaning up after the people. When the day was over and the last of the people had left, the disciples were glad as they wanted some time to rest and grieve over John's death. Jesus told them to get into the boat and cross to the other side of the lake. The disciples loved and respected Jesus, but they didn't want to go: Jesus convinced them and they started their journey into the night. Suddenly, a storm arose threatening their safety.

Notice, the disciples were obedient and they still found themselves in the midst of a storm. The storm's opposition did not invalidate them, nor indict them, as to being out of God's will. You and I can be in the absolute center of God's will and still find ourselves in the midst of a raging storm. Like the disciples, the storm does not suggest we have a secret sin in our lives and therefore, God has decided to punish us. Nor, does the storm invalidate our claims to love and serve God with all of our hearts.

Thought for Today

When a storm is present in your life, it is not a sign that you are out of God's will. Rest in His Word and His instructions to you.

Prayer Journal

_____

_____

_____

~ ~ ~ SEPTEMBER 10 ~ ~ ~

"Then He saw them straining at rowing, for the wind was against them. Now about the fourth watch of the night He came to them, walking on the sea, and would have passed them by...Then He went up into the boat to them, and the wind ceased. And they were greatly amazed in themselves beyond measure, and marveled" (Mark 6:48, 51).

The disciples were trying to make their way across to the other side of the lake, when a storm arose. As the intensity of the storm grew, the disciples feared for their lives. These were seasoned sailors and they had been in many a storm upon the lake before: they knew exactly what to do to get safely through it. However, everything they knew to do was failing. The storm was bigger than their ability to deal with it. Jesus was on the mountain praying and He saw them struggling. He came to them and He stilled the storm.

This story reveals to us that Jesus can see us through the darkness of the storms that we face. There is never a circumstance so dark that He cannot see us. Neither is there a circumstance so severe that it can keep Jesus from coming to our aid. Just as Jesus walked through the storm to get to the disciples, so He walks through our adversity to get to us. Jesus never intended for the disciples to get into the middle of the lake and die there. He intended for them to go through the storm to reach the other side safely. It is God's will for us to come through our storms and reach heaven's shore safely.

Thought for Today

Just as God brought Noah through the flood, parted the Red Sea for Moses, and preserved Daniel in the lion's den, even so, He will bring you through your storm. Do not fear.

Prayer Journal

_____

_____

_____

~ ~ ~ SEPTEMBER 11 ~ ~ ~

"For I looked, and there was no man; I looked among them, but there was no counselor, who, when I asked of them, could answer a word. Indeed they are all worthless; their works are nothing; their molded images are wind and confusion" (Isaiah 41:28-29).

We are the Lord's mouthpiece as we speak the truth of His Word into the hearts of hurting people. Yet, for the most part, many Christians have lost their focus as to what their purpose on earth really is—that being, to continue the ministry of Jesus. Jesus came to seek and save the lost, to reveal the Father, to destroy the works of the devil, and to restore the kingdom of God.

A quick examination of each of these categories will help us understand our personal assignment for ministry. First, we should be concerned about people who are lost. Peoples' eternal destinies mattered to Jesus and the same must matter to us. Secondly, we are to be living revelations of the Father. We are to live in such a manner that people around us will come to know and understand what God is really like. Thirdly, we are to use our faith to destroy the works of the devil in peoples' lives. Jesus has given us power over all the power of the enemy and we can use His name to drive back the works of hell over a person's life. Finally, we are to live under the rule of the Holy Spirit so that the purposes of God for our lives, and the lives of others, can be restored.

Thought for Today

Be honest, does the plight of the lost really matter to you? Are you living in such a way that people will want to know your God? Are you opposing the works of the devil, or are you contributing to them? Does the Holy Spirit have complete rule in your life?

Prayer Journal

_____

_____

_____

~ ~ ~ SEPTEMBER 12 ~ ~ ~

"Behold! My Servant whom I uphold, my Elect One in whom My soul delights! I have put My Spirit upon Him; he will bring forth justice to the Gentiles. He will not cry out, nor raise His voice, nor cause His voice to be heard in the street. A bruised reed He will not break, and smoking flax He will not quench; He will bring forth justice for truth. He will not fail nor be discouraged, till He has established justice in the earth; and the coastlands shall wait for His law" (Isaiah 42:1-4).

Jesus is our example in all matters of life, including what characteristics we need to develop to be used by God in ministry. We are to be servants; therefore, we must be obedient to every instruction of the Lord and be cognizant of the fact that we are here to serve the Lord and others, not ourselves. We need to realize that the Lord has chosen us to be His servants. We must understand that we have been hand selected by God for ministry to our generation.

We must live under the influence of the Holy Spirit. It is the Holy Spirit Who empowers us for ministry, as well as, for daily living. We must not be complainers as we guard the words of our mouths so that we do not give the devil an opportunity to work against us.

We must be ministers of reconciliation. Those who have made mistakes need help to take what is left and rebuild their lives. We must never give in to the temptation to quit. We must be tenacious about our assignment and refuse to give up until it is completed.

Thought for Today

We must not give in to our feelings and let our circumstances dictate to us our level of service or devotion to God our Father.

Prayer Journal

_____

_____

_____

~ ~ ~ SEPTEMBER 13 ~ ~ ~

"Ahaz was twenty years old when he became king, and he reigned sixteen years in Jerusalem; and he did not do what was right in the sight of the Lord, as his father David had done" (II Chronicles 28:1).

God's summary of the life of King Ahaz is recorded forever in the Word of God, *"and he did not do what was right in the sight of the Lord."* Ahaz abandoned God and turned his attention towards the worship of idols. He lived and acted like a pagan. He not only participated in idol worship, but he promoted it as well. He was responsible for the moral decline of the entire nation. Ahaz had stolen the treasures from the Lord's house and used them for himself. Because of his rebellious heart towards God, Ahaz was defeated by the King of Syria and his people taken captive.

We need to be aware of a pattern of unfaithfulness in order to avoid falling into its deadly trap. God's place in our hearts must be our number one priority of pursuit and we must refuse to make idols of anything. Tragically, many Christians are so worldly, that you can't tell the difference from an unbeliever. Many are guilty of stealing what belongs to God, such as our time, talents, and tithes, and using it for themselves. Unfaithfulness can bring a moral decline in your life. What you once abhorred, you begin to tolerate. What you tolerate, you eventually embrace as acceptable. What you deem acceptable, you allow, and it becomes a lifestyle.

Thought for Today

When your life is over and you stand before God, what will be His summary evaluation of your life? Will He be able to say to you, *"Well done, thou good and faithful servant?"*

Prayer Journal

_____

_____

_____

~ ~ ~ SEPTEMBER 14 ~ ~ ~

"Hezekiah became king when he was twenty-five years old, and he reigned twenty-nine years in Jerusalem. His mother's name was Abijah the daughter of Zechariah. And he did what was right in the sight of the Lord, according to all that his father David had done" (II Chronicles 29:1-2).

When Ahaz died, his son, Hezekiah became king. God's summary of the life of Hezekiah was not like his father's, *"and he did what was right in the sight of the Lord."* Hezekiah knew firsthand the steps his father had taken in his unfaithfulness to the Lord. In II Chronicles 29:7 we read, *"They have also shut up the doors of the vestibule, put out the lamps, and have not burned incense or offered burnt offerings in the holy place to the God of Israel."*

The first mistake that Ahaz made was to shut the doors to the Temple. He had shut God out of his life and his idols had taken God's place in his heart. The second mistake was to put out the lamps within the Temple. He stopped listening to the voice of God and turned away from God's Word. The third mistake was that he stopped burning incense at the altar. Literally, this meant he stopped praying and communing with the Lord. The fourth mistake that Ahaz made was to stop offering sacrifices to the Lord as an act of worship. When he stopped his worship of God he also stopped his service to God. However, Hezekiah re-established the priesthood and restored the Temple as the house of God.

Thought for Today

Do not give God's place in your heart to idols. Do not shut God out of your life, and do not turn off the light that His Word brings to your life. Worship and serve the Lord daily.

Prayer Journal

_____

_____

_____

~ ~ ~ SEPTEMBER 15 ~ ~ ~

"They soon forgot His works; they did not wait for His counsel...They made a calf in Horeb, and worshiped the molded image. Thus they changed their glory into the image of an ox that eats grass. They forgot God their Savior, who had done great things in Egypt" (Psalms 106:13, 19-21).

It is amazing how quickly the nation of Israel stopped trusting God. While in slavery to the Egyptians, the Israelites cried out to God for deliverance and God answered them with demonstrations of great power. Delivered from the hand of Pharaoh, they witnessed miracle after miracle of the manifest presence of God and His consistent and faithful provision for their families. Yet, with all that God had done, they turned away in indifference. They soon forgot the great things He had done for them. They sought the counsel of everyone except God. They gave the affection of their hearts to an idol, and in doing so they traded the glory of God's presence for a cold, lifeless image of an ox. Simply put, they forgot about God

Before we cast too many stones at the Israelites we need to examine our own hearts, as we have often been guilty of doing the same thing. We know what it is like to start out totally depending on the Lord, and then over time, slip back into taking the controlling position of our lives. We seem to easily forget the great demonstrations of His love and power towards us. Instead of seeking His counsel, we start trusting our own counsel; without His counsel we end up giving our affection to things, instead of to God.

Thought for Today

Place your trust in the Lord and keep it there. Do not yield to the temptation to take the leadership of your life back from God.

Prayer Journal

_____

_____

_____

~ ~ ~ SEPTEMBER 16 ~ ~ ~

"O foolish Galatians! Who has bewitched you that you should not obey the truth, before whose eyes Jesus Christ was clearly portrayed among you as crucified? This only I want to learn from you: Did you receive the Spirit by the works of the law, or by the hearing of faith? Are you so foolish? Having begun in the Spirit, are you now being made perfect by the flesh" (Galatians 3:1-3)?

The Apostle Paul rebuked the Christians at Galatia for starting out dependent upon the Holy Spirit and then reverting to trusting their flesh. They had reverted back to living by the Law of Moses, rather than living by the grace of Jesus Christ.

Spiritual maturity subjects us to two things. First, we develop a false sense of arrival and end up with an unteachable spirit. Somewhere along the line, we gather just enough information about spiritual matters to assume that we have arrived at a point that we do not need to be taught anything more about the Word. This is a gross mistake, in that we will never arrive spiritually on this side of heaven. A wise Christian will seek the instruction of the Holy Spirit as to the secrets of the Word and their application to daily living. Secondly, we succumb to the temptation to place the full weight of our trust in our natural resources. We don't pray, or read the Bible as much, again assuming that we have enough knowledge to deal effectively with the situation at hand. We lean on our logic and use our influence in an attempt to solve our problems.

Thought for Today

When we first came to Christ, He was the center of our attention, the object of our thoughts, and the consideration for our every action. Let us go back to our first love and remain there.

Prayer Journal

_____

_____

_____

~ ~ ~ SEPTEMBER 17 ~ ~ ~

"And at that time Hanani the seer came to Asa king of Judah, and said to him: 'Because you have relied on the king of Syria, and have not relied on the Lord your God, therefore the army of the king of Syria has escaped from your hand...And in the thirty-ninth year of his reign, Asa became diseased in his feet, and his malady was severe; yet in his disease he did not seek the Lord, but the physicians. So Asa rested with his fathers; he died in the forty-first year of his reign" (II Chronicles 16:7, 12-13).

The story of Asa, the King of Judah, has a great beginning and a tragic ending. At the beginning of his reign, Asa was faced with a tremendous challenge. Two nations had gathered in battle against him. The enemy army numbered just over a million soldiers, while Asa's army was only half that size. Yet, Asa called upon the Lord for His help and Asa was victorious over his enemies.

Years later, Asa was again faced with an enemy. This enemy was much smaller than the enemy in his first battle, so Asa decided he could handle them without God's help. Instead of calling upon the Lord for help, Asa went and allied himself to the King of Syria. As a result of this alliance, Asa lost the battle. Not long afterward, Asa contracted a disease in his feet and again, instead of calling upon the Lord for help, Asa placed his full trust in the skills of his doctors. This time, his turning away from God cost him his life.

Thought for Today

Unfortunately, there is a little of King Asa in all of us. We turn to God for help with the big problems and then we think it is okay to try and solve the smaller ones ourselves. God desires that we give Him all of our cares, not just the ones that we classify as big ones.

Prayer Journal

_____

_____

_____

~ ~ ~ SEPTEMBER 18 ~ ~ ~

"For I am already being poured out as a drink offering, and the time of my departure is at hand. I have fought the good fight, I have finished the race, I have kept the faith" (II Timothy 4:6-7).

The Apostle Paul likened the Christian life to that of one running a race. We read his words in I Corinthians 9:24, *"Do you not know that those who run in a race all run, but one receives the prize? Run in such a way that you may obtain it."* Paul knew first-hand of the hardships that accompany the running of such a race; yet, his one goal was to finish the race. Paul did not take the time to consider what the race might cost him personally.

Derek Redmond of Great Britain was determined to finish the 400 meter race in the 1992 Olympics in Barcelona, Spain. Crippled by a torn hamstring near the half-way point, Redmond hopped the rest of the way with the help of his father Jim, who rushed from the stands to aid his son. Another great example of determination to finish a race was seen in Tanzania's, John Stephen Akhwari. In the 1968 Olympics, held in Mexico City, with his right leg bloody and bandaged, he staggered into the stadium more than an hour behind the winner of the marathon. When interviewed as to why he didn't quit the race because of his injuries, he replied, "My country didn't send me to Mexico City to start the race, they sent me to finish the race." Redmond and Akhwari were both focused upon finishing the race that they had started, in spite of their pain.

Thought for Today

Often we are confronted with problems that seem to tear at our hearts. Whatever you do, do not stop running. Press through your pain and finish the race that is set before you.

Prayer Journal

_____

_____

_____

~ ~ ~ SEPTEMBER 19 ~ ~ ~

"'And often he has thrown him both into the fire and into the water to destroy him. But if You can do anything, have compassion on us and help us.' Jesus said to him, 'If you can believe, all things are possible to him who believes.' Immediately the father of the child cried out and said with tears, 'Lord, I believe; help my unbelief'" (Mark 9:22-24)!

In this story we meet a dad with an epileptic son who is a deaf mute and in desperate need of a miracle. He was also possessed by a demon, who on numerous occasions tried to kill him by throwing him into the fire and into the water to drown him. Imagine for a moment this father's pain. While the other fathers watched their kids mature, he watched his son suffer. While other fathers were busy teaching their sons a trade, he was trying to keep his son alive. He could never leave his son alone, for he never knew when the next attack would take place.

Jesus was on the mountain praying when the father brought his son for help. He had turned to the disciples, and they were no help at all. By the time Jesus arrived, the father's faith was almost gone. His request for Jesus to help him was timid and full of doubt. His saying, *"If You can do anything...,"* was the same as saying, "This one may be out of your league, but if You can help my son—please do." His prayer was not impressive, but at least he was honest. "My faith is almost gone. Please help me," and Jesus did.

Thought for Today

Sometimes our faith is such that we are hesitant to even pray. However, even when our faith is weak, God hears our prayer. The power is not in the words, the power resides in the One Who hears.

Prayer Journal

_____

_____

_____

~ ~ ~ SEPTEMBER 20 ~ ~ ~

"However, when He, the Spirit of truth, has come, He will guide you into all truth; for He will not speak on His own authority, but whatever He hears He will speak; and He will tell you things to come" (John 16:13).

Jesus called the Holy Spirit *"the Spirit of truth."* He revealed that one of the assignments of the Holy Spirit would be to *"guide you (us) into all truth."* In calling the Holy Spirit *"the Spirit of truth,"* Jesus was telling us that the Holy Spirit could be trusted to say what is true. The Father talks to the Holy Spirit about us and reveals His plan, His will, and His blessings that are scheduled for us. He then assigns the Holy Spirit to guide us into all that the Father has purposed. The Holy Spirit accomplishes His assignment by giving us a series of instructions that He receives from the Father, that when obeyed, will produce the desired results.

The secret of moving into the purposes of God for our lives will hinge upon our ability to obey one instruction; that being, the last instruction the Holy Spirit gave us. The Holy Spirit's instructions are not given to be applauded, but they are given so that we will obey them. His instructions are not necessarily to be understood, but they are to be embraced and obeyed by faith. His instructions are not optional suggestions, they are windows of opportunity. If we will be obedient to these instructions, we will discover that the purposes of God will be unlocked within our lives.

Thought for Today

The Holy Spirit is not waiting for our approval concerning His last instruction—He is waiting for our obedience. He will not give you a new instruction, until you obey the last one He gave you.

Prayer Journal

_____

_____

_____

~ ~ ~ SEPTEMBER 21 ~ ~ ~

"For your obedience has become known to all. Therefore I am glad on your behalf; but I want you to be wise in what is good, and simple concerning evil" (Romans 16:19).

The Apostle Paul championed the level of obedience that some of the Christians in Rome were exhibiting. The Holy Spirit daily seeks to guide us into the intended purposes of God for our lives. He does this by giving us instructions, that when obeyed, will unlock God's purposes. Whether or not we live in the fullness of the purposes of God, is determined by our willingness to be obedient and fulfill every instruction that the Holy Spirit gives us. Our disobedience to one instruction will stop the flow of His anointing and will open us up to the enemy's attacks. As with the story of Jonah, our disobedience opens us up to God-appointed storms that are sent to break our self-will. Disobedience will break our focus from fulfilling the purposes of God for our lives.

Consider a few examples of the damage that disobedience brings. Our disobedience in not forgiving others forfeits our forgiveness from God and imprisons us in anger, hatred, and bitterness. Our disobedience in paying our tithes closes the windows of heaven over our lives, places us under a self-imposed financial curse, and opens the door for the devil to hinder our financial well-being. Our disobedience in daily putting to death the lusts of our carnal natures will cause us to live in rebellion, compromise, and self-rule.

Thought for Today

What instructions of the Holy Spirit have you not yet obeyed. Realize that the price of your disobedience is too great for you to pay—purpose to obey His every instruction.

Prayer Journal

_____

_____

_____

~ ~ ~ SEPTEMBER 22 ~ ~ ~

"He went with them. And when they came to the Jordan, they cut down trees. But as one was cutting down a tree, the iron ax head fell into the water; and he cried out and said, 'Alas, master! For it was borrowed.' So the man of God said, 'Where did it fall?' And he showed him the place. So he cut off a stick, and threw it in there; and he made the iron float. Therefore he said, 'Pick it up for yourself.' So he reached out his hand and took it" (II Kings 6:4-7).

Elisha, the prophet, was mentoring several proteges that were living with him; however, his house was too small, so they decided to build larger quarters in which to live. As they were cutting down trees, one of the servant's ax head fell off into the river. Without the ax head, the servant couldn't complete his assignment of cutting down the tree. He turned to Elisha for help and Elisha asked him to take him to the place where it had fallen off into the river. Arriving at the place where it had been lost, Elisha restored the ax head to the servant.

Tragically, our disobedience causes us to be lost to the incredible purposes of God for our lives. However, what has been lost through our disobedience can again be found by our returning to the place, or that point, where we chose to be disobedient. We must be willing to accept full responsibility for our actions, or for the lack of action. The Lord will always take us back to the point where we failed and give us the opportunity to repent and be restored, as we are obedient to His Word and to His ways.

Thought for Today

Your next instruction from the Holy Spirit is waiting for you—on the completed side of His last instruction to you.

Prayer Journal

~ ~ ~ SEPTEMBER 23 ~ ~ ~

"The sacrifices of God are a broken spirit, a broken and a contrite heart—-these, O God, You will not despise" (Psalms 51:17).

One of the dangers of living in sin is that our hearts will become hardened to God's voice. There is a tremendous difference between being remorseful and being repentant of our sins. Remorse is an expression of sorrow, but only because we got caught and therefore, has nothing to do with repentance. Repentance means that the hardness of our hearts has been broken with a Godly sorrow that will cause us to repent and seek the Lord's forgiveness. Repentance releases a sense of shame over our sin. In Ezra 9:6, we read, *"O my God: I am too ashamed and humiliated to lift up my face to You, my God; for our iniquities have risen higher than our heads, and our guilt has grown up to the heavens."*

Repentance will be evidenced when we acknowledge our responsibility for our sin. If we admit that we were wrong but then proceed to give the reasons why it really was not our fault, then we have not yet repented. We must be willing to call sin, sin. We cannot blame it on a lifestyle, a habit, or a family trait. We must acknowledge that what we have done is a sin against God as David did in his repentant cry in Psalms 51:3-4, *"For I acknowledge my transgressions, and my sin is always before me. Against You, You only, have I sinned, and done this evil in Your sight—that You may be found just when You speak, and blameless when You judge."*

Thought for Today

Repentance always involves changing your mind about your sin. Until you learn to hate the sin, you will constantly be tempted to return to its invitation.

Prayer Journal

_____

_____

_____

~ ~ ~ SEPTEMBER 24 ~ ~ ~

"And you shall love the Lord your God with all your heart, with all your soul, with all your mind, and with all your strength. This is the first commandment" (Mark 12:30).

When it comes to the definition of worship, there is not a single verse, or even a passage of Scripture, that clearly spells out what worship is. Our understanding of worship must be derived from the various verbs that are used in conjunction with the Biblical examples of worship. Worship involves a commitment of the heart, in which we respond to the love that God has so lavishly poured out on us. Our worship should never be allowed to become stagnant, as it is to flow out of our relationship with the Lord. Actually, as our relationship grows more intimate, so should the intimacy of our worship. The depth and warmth of our worship is proportionate to the depth and warmth of our relationship with God.

Worship is an inter-personal action between an individual and God. Based on this fact, worship cannot transpire outside of God's presence. We may exact the rituals of worship, but we can never worship Him in spirit and truth without His manifest presence. Worship occurs in our embrace of His presence as we, through the aid of the Holy Spirit, release our heartfelt emotions and attitudes to Him. The end result of true worship will always be a renewed commitment to love and serve the Lord. We have not worshiped until we have offered unto the Lord all of our heart's love, our soul's adoration, our mind's admiration, and our body's strength.

Thought for Today

Worship involves the pursuit of God for Who He is, rather than just for the works of His hands.

Prayer Journal

_____

_____

_____

~ ~ ~ SEPTEMBER 25 ~ ~ ~

"The Lord is near to those who have a broken heart, and saves such as have a contrite spirit" (Psalms 34:18).

Our worship of God is to be characterized by our brokenness before Him. When we come into God's presence through our worship, we will immediately recognize our imperfections in the light of His holy perfection. This stark contrast should result in our becoming broken before Him. In Psalms 51:17 we are reminded, *"The sacrifices of God are a broken spirit, a broken and a contrite heart—these, O God, You will not despise."* Worship always lays bare our motives, our integrity, our purity, and our priorities. When in the Lord's presence, we cannot pretend to be something that we are not. Worship will reveal the status of our relationship with the Lord. Exposure to His presence should convict us of our inconsistencies and bring us to a Godly repentance. If we are complacent with the condition of our hearts and spiritual lives, we will not be able to truly worship the Lord.

Our worship is also characterized by our humility. Humility in worship is the ability to worship freely without thought or concern about our reputations where other people are concerned. When we approach the Lord in humility, we approach Him from the position of His grace, rather than our own self-righteousness. Humility demands the absence of pride, for pride repels the very presence of God. Pride makes us more concerned about other's opinions, than we are about God's opinion.

Thought for Today

Pride keeps us from freely expressing our praise and worship—pride makes us self-conscience instead of being God-conscience.

Prayer Journal

_____

_____

_____

~ ~ ~ SEPTEMBER 26 ~ ~ ~

"Having disarmed principalities and powers, He made a public spectacle of them, triumphing over them in it" (Colossians 2:15).

Jesus completely defeated satan through His death on the Cross and through His resurrection from the dead. When satan attacks us, we can stand in the victory Christ has won over him. Jesus destroyed the power of the devil over us, as well as, destroyed the works of the devil against us. The word "destroyed" means to make of no affect, to render powerless. Whatever the devil attempts to do against us, it will be powerless if we stand in Christ's victory and exercise the power He gave us over the devil. In Luke 10:19, we read, *"Behold, I give you the authority to trample on serpents and scorpions, and over all the power of the enemy: and nothing shall by any means hurt you."*

In order to stand in Christ's victory over the devil, we must not give place to the devil in any area of our lives. We open the door to the devil and his agenda through our disobedience to God and His Word. Willful disobedience to God's Word will always result in sin, and sin will give the devil access to us. Furthermore, any involvement with the occult will open the door for the devil to gain access. Some of the things we must avoid are; New Age music, literature and crystals; fortune tellers and psychics; horoscopes and astrological signs; literature, computer games, television shows, movies, and music in which there is satanic involvement.

Thought for Today

Jesus Christ has delivered us from satan's kingdom and his power over us; therefore, he has no right to us. Regardless of how strong the devil's attack may appear to be, Jesus within us is greater.

Prayer Journal

~ ~ ~ SEPTEMBER 27 ~ ~ ~

"Whose voice then shook the earth; but now He has promised, saying, 'Yet once more I shake not only the earth, but also heaven.' Now this, 'Yet once more,' indicates the removal of those things that are being shaken, as of things that are made, that the things which cannot be shaken may remain. Therefore, since we are receiving a kingdom which cannot be shaken, let us have grace, by which we may serve God acceptably with reverence and Godly fear" (Hebrews 12:26-28).

Over the last several years, the Lord has allowed the church of Jesus Christ to be shaken. Leaders have compromised their lives and have been removed from their ministries in front of the eyes of the world. Individual church members have been called to task for their compromised lifestyles. There is a two-fold purpose for God shaking His church. First, He is going to shake everything not of God out of the Body of Christ. In many instances, the church has become far more carnal than sacred. God must remove everything worldly from His church; and thus, the reason for His shaking.

Secondly, the Lord is shaking His church in order to establish the spiritual kingdom of God within the heart of every believer. The kingdom of God is established by allowing the Holy Spirit to take charge and rule every facet of our lives. The kingdom that the Lord is establishing in us cannot be shaken by anything, or anyone.

Thought for Today

God may be shaking your life, but remember, it is for your good. He is shaking everything that is not of Him out of you. He wants to establish a kingdom within you that will hide you in the time of trouble and will not crumble around you.

Prayer Journal

_____

_____

_____

~ ~ ~ SEPTEMBER 28 ~ ~ ~

"And I also say to you that you are Peter, and on this rock I will build My church, and the gates of Hades shall not prevail against it. And I will give you the keys of the kingdom of heaven, and whatever you bind on earth will be bound in heaven, and whatever you loose on earth will be loosed in heaven" (Matthew 16:18-19).

The church belongs to Jesus and He carefully builds it according to His blueprint. The church the Lord is building is built on the Word. Any church that is being built on the opinions and traditions of men is not a church being built by the Lord. Ephesians 2:19-22 says, *"Now, therefore, you are no longer strangers and foreigners, but fellow citizens with the saints and members of the household of God, having been built on the foundation of the apostles and prophets, Jesus Christ Himself being the chief corner stone, in whom the whole building, being joined together, grows into a holy temple in the Lord, in whom you also are being built together for a dwelling place of God in the Spirit."* This reminds us that Jesus has promised to build in us a permanent residence for His presence.

The church that Jesus is building is not weak, but rather, it is full of the mighty power of God and therefore, is unstoppable. All of the combined powers of hell cannot stop the church of Jesus Christ from fulfilling its mission on earth. Jesus has given His church spiritual keys that enable us to bind the forces of hell over a circumstance, and then, release the powers of heaven over them.

Thought for Today

The church of Jesus Christ is not an organization or a building—it is a living habitation of His presence. As a believer in Jesus Christ, you are a member of His glorious church.

Prayer Journal

_____

_____

_____

~ ~ ~ SEPTEMBER 29 ~ ~ ~

"He who overcomes, I will make him a pillar in the temple of My God, and he shall go out no more. And I will write on him the name of My God and the name of the city of My God, the New Jerusalem, which comes down out of heaven from My God. And I will write on him My new name" (Revelation 3:12).

The qualifying requirement for being made a pillar in the Lord's house is that we must be overcomers: We are overcomers in that we have been faithful to the Lord and to His assignment for our lives. We are overcomers in that we have stood upon the integrity of God's Word in faith, believing that what God has promised, He will surely do. We are overcomers in that we have shunned the values and ways of the world and have clung to the standards for living as set forth in the Word of God. We are overcomers in that we have submitted ourselves to the leadership of the Holy Spirit and have embraced His instruction on every matter. We are overcomers in that we have kept the commandments and have treated them as mandates, and not options. We are overcomers in that we have faithfully waged spiritual warfare against the devil and have not yielded to the temptation to quit the battle.

An overcomer is one of God's champions—someone, who against all odds, has risen above their adversity and stood strong for the Lord and His cause. The good news is that every believer can live in victory and be an overcomer, if they will but choose to be one.

Thought for Today

An overcomer is someone who has purposed to daily live in the power of the Holy Spirit. They realize that they have no strength, in and of themselves, so they rest in His strength.

Prayer Journal

_____

_____

_____

~ ~ ~ SEPTEMBER 30 ~ ~ ~

"He who overcomes, I will make him a pillar in the temple of My God, and he shall go out no more. And I will write on him the name of My God and the name of the city of My God, the New Jerusalem, which comes down out of heaven from My God. And I will write on him My new name" (Revelation 3:12).

The Lord promises that overcomers will become pillars in the house of the Lord. It should be the desire of every believer to be made a pillar in the Lord's house. In the Old Testament, pillars were used as markers and as monuments. As markers, they gave direction; and as monuments, they brought to remembrance the faithfulness of the Lord. Pillars were also used as supports within a building. Pillars were usually made of bronze, which symbolized that they had been tested and tried in the fires of life's trials.

The pillars in the house of the Lord are made up of overcomers. These are people who are proven, tested, and tried, in the trials of life, yet, without being shaken or moved by circumstances. These are people who have determined to finish their assignment no matter the cost. They are highly visible and they always seem to stand out above the crowd; they can be seen in the good times, as well as, in the bad times. Pillars are not loners for they know that they must work alongside others, and that the blending of their talents with those around them, will be a benefit to everyone.

Thought for Today

Pillars are considered to be burden bearers for they lend support to their part of the structure. A pillar will always be available to help support the weight of another who is in need of resting. Can anyone say of you that you are a pillar in the house of God?

Prayer Journal

_____

_____

_____

~ ~ ~ OCTOBER 1 ~ ~ ~

"One of the two who heard John speak, and followed Him, was Andrew, Simon Peter's brother. He first found his own brother Simon, and said to him, 'We have found the Messiah' (which is translated, The Christ). And he brought him to Jesus. Now when Jesus looked at him, He said, 'You are Simon the son of Jonah. You shall be called Cephas' (which is translated, A Stone)" (John 1:40-42).

Andrew, Simon's younger brother, was a new follower of John the Baptist and had just met Jesus. There was something unexplainable about Jesus that captured his heart, so much so, that he returned home to find Simon and requested he return with him. Andrew's claims of having found the Messiah must have intrigued Simon, as he followed Andrew to where Jesus was staying. When Simon first laid eyes on Jesus, he appeared to be like any other man. However, when Jesus laid His eyes on Simon, He did what no other man could have done; without being introduced, Jesus knew Simon's name—how did Jesus know his name? No one in that gathering knew him, except Andrew, or at least that is what Simon thought.

There is something wonderful in this encounter between Simon and Jesus that offers us great assurance and comfort. Jesus knew Simon's name long before his mother ever called it for the first time. Isaiah 49:1 tells us, *"The Lord has called Me from the womb; from the matrix of My mother He has made mention of My name."*

Thought for Today

Loved ones, the Lord knew our names long before we ever knew His. We are not just strangers in the crowd to Jesus, for He is intimately acquainted with us.

Prayer Journal

_____

_____

_____

~ ~ ~ OCTOBER 2 ~ ~ ~

"And he brought him to Jesus. Now when Jesus looked at him, He said, 'You are Simon the son of Jonah. You shall be called Cephas' (which is translated, A Stone)" (John 1:42).

Simon followed Andrew to meet Jesus and at the very moment their eyes met, Jesus spoke to him—calling him by his name. If that was not astounding enough for Simon, Jesus then called him by a new name *"Cephas,"* which translated means, *"A Stone."* All Hebrews knew the importance of a name, for it was given in a prophetic manner to give purpose and direction to one's life. Simon knew that the meaning of his current name was hard enough to live up to. The name Simon, means "obedient," and Jonah, means "dove." Simon was prophetically supposed to be like an "obedient dove." For Simon, this was all but impossible to live up to.

Every Christian can relate to Simon's bewilderment, considering the contrast between "who" we know ourselves to really be like, and the "person" the Holy Spirit promises to make us into. When Jesus named Simon *"A Stone,"* He was prophetically speaking of the strength and stability that would be built into Simon's life. Simon was aware that there was nothing in his life that was of "rock-like" quality. His strength was in his muscles only, and as to stability, it was a foreign concept. Yet, we know that even with his roller-coaster life of successes and failures, the prophecy of Jesus came true. Simon became everything Jesus said he would.

Thought for Today

Just as with His disciples, Jesus wants to build the same qualities of strength and stability into our lives. Do not get discouraged with who you are now, He is not finished yet.

Prayer Journal

_____

_____

_____

~ ~ ~ OCTOBER 3 ~ ~ ~

"For whatever is born of God overcomes the world. And this is the victory that has overcome the world—our faith. Who is he who overcomes the world, but he who believes that Jesus is the Son of God" (I John 5:4-5)?

We are made overcomers by placing our faith in Jesus and believing that He is the Son of God. Faith is a foundational, basic trust in Jesus which gives a daily expression as to Who He is, and to what He has done as our Lord and Savior. This faith will result in our overcoming all of the obstacles of life. Our faith in Jesus releases His creative power to work through us. The same creative power that Jesus used to shape the world is the same creative power He uses to shape us. Our expressed faith in Jesus, to shape our lives according to what He wills, stands in direct contrast to today's self-help theology of "I will make myself better."

In Revelation 3:12, Jesus promises to make pillars in the house of the Lord of those who overcome, *"He who overcomes, I will make him a pillar in the temple of My God."* The word "make" means to shape something already present and to bring into existence anything that may be lacking. Jesus is saying to us, "I'll take the raw material of your life and shape it. If something is missing, I'll create what is needed to finish the project." The verb "make" is in the future tense. Jesus is promising to shape and create until the project is completed.

Thought for Today

God is not giving up on shaping your life. He is determined to help you establish your purpose in the earth. Jesus will lovingly make of you what you will never have the capacity to make of yourself.

Prayer Journal

_____

_____

_____

~ ~ ~ OCTOBER 4 ~ ~ ~

"Now when the Day of Pentecost had fully come, they were all with one accord in one place. And suddenly there came a sound from heaven, as of a rushing mighty wind, and it filled the whole house where they were sitting. Then there appeared to them divided tongues, as of fire, and one sat upon each of them. And they were all filled with the Holy Spirit and began to speak with other tongues, as the Spirit gave them utterance" (Acts 2:1-4).

The process by which the Holy Spirit brings about a change is called discipleship. Discipleship is not merely the accumulation of knowledge, but is the process of learning how to live. Discipleship is not information that is truth, explained in facts; rather, it is incarnation, which is truth in flesh. Just as Jesus, the Living Word, became flesh, so the Holy Spirit wants to make the promises of God's Word become living flesh in our lives. In John 1:14, we read, *"And the Word became flesh and dwelt among us."* Everything that was real in Jesus, God wants to make real in us.

The entry point for the process of discipleship was the outpouring of the Holy Spirit on the Day of Pentecost. God was pouring the glory of heaven into human vessels which would then enable us to become all that God had purposed and intended. The Holy Spirit is given without measure, so that all believers can become recipients of God's power at whatever level they will allow.

Thought for Today

Every generation can be a recipient of this outpouring of heaven's glory into human flesh. We can experience the power of the Holy Spirit in transforming our humanity into all that the Word promises that we can become in Christ.

Prayer Journal

_____

_____

_____

~ ~ ~ OCTOBER 5 ~ ~ ~

"Then Peter said to them, 'Repent, and let every one of you be baptized in the name of Jesus Christ for the remission of sins; and you shall receive the gift of the Holy Spirit. For the promise is to you and to your children, and to all who are afar off, as many as the Lord our God will call'" (Acts 2:38-39).

God began the process of discipleship on the Day of Pentecost. The promise, of which the prophets spoke, was fulfilled through the outpouring of the Holy Spirit upon everyone who would receive Him. The Holy Spirit is given to all who desire a relationship with God and will come on His terms. Just as the Holy Spirit performed a biological miracle within Mary that resulted in the Incarnation of Jesus, He wants to perform a miracle within us that will bring Jesus into our lives and then, release Him through us to others.

God's terms for relationship are clear. First, we must repent of our sins and then the Holy Spirit will give birth to the life of Christ within us. The Holy Spirit nurtures and grows the life of Christ within us, and in doing so, He develops the nature and character of Christ in our lives. Discipleship requires a long-term commitment to the growth process. It will take time to grow in the Lord's love, grace, and character. Tragically, it is at this point of discovery that many Christians drop-out of the discipling process. They do not have the discipline to wait on the growth brought about on the Holy Spirit's terms, so they allow feelings to dictate their growth rate.

Thought for Today

The goal of the Holy Spirit is to grow the life, nature, character, and power of Christ within us. When we commit to walk as disciples, the Holy Spirit will then minister to others through us.

Prayer Journal

_____

_____

_____

~ ~ ~ OCTOBER 6 ~ ~ ~

"And let them make Me a sanctuary, that I may dwell among them" (Exodus 25:8).

Peter and Paul were convinced that salvation incorporated more than just the forgiveness of sin and one's going to heaven when they passed from this life. Salvation incorporated God's design to recover His original plan; that being, to dwell with man.

God's desire was to dwell with Adam, but He couldn't because of Adam's sin. God tried to reveal Himself as a loving God to every generation, but no one wanted Him. The plan of God, to dwell with man, was foreshadowed when He instructed Moses to build Him a dwelling place among the people. There, in the Tabernacle of Moses, God expressed His desire to be directly in the center of the lives of His people.

Jesus came to fulfill what God had foreshadowed in the Tabernacle of Moses. He came to dwell among men, so that through His power of salvation and the blessing of His incarnation, He could multiply His life and grace to all men. Peter tells us in I Peter 2:5, *"You also, as living stones, are being built up a spiritual house, a holy priesthood, to offer up spiritual sacrifices acceptable to God through Jesus Christ."* Peter likens us to living stones that need to be shaped and fitted together to make a dwelling place for the Lord in our hearts and lives. This shaping and fitting together to build the Lord's dwelling place, is the assignment of the Holy Spirit.

Thought for Today

God's desire is to dwell with you and to be the center of your life, not just a part of it. Make the Lord first priority in your schedule.

Prayer Journal

_____

_____

_____

~ ~ ~ OCTOBER 7 ~ ~ ~

"Then He got into one of the boats, which was Simon's, and asked him to put out a little from the land. And He sat down and taught the multitudes from the boat" (Luke 5:3).

One morning, after a night out fishing and not catching any fish, Simon, and the other fishermen were busy cleaning their nets. Each was looking forward to going home so they could rest. On this particular morning, Jesus approached Simon and asked if He could use his boat as a platform to preach from, to which Simon agreed. After speaking, Jesus asked Simon to take Him out fishing. At first, Simon protested for it was not the right time of the day to catch fish. However, Simon gave in, and as a result there was a miracle catch of fish. This event would forever mark Simon's life, so much so, that he left the fishing business that very day and followed Jesus into his destiny for the future.

It was not a mistake that Jesus chose Simon's fishing boat that morning. There were two fishing boats tied up, and Jesus could have requested to use either one; but it was Simon's boat that He wanted. We don't know everything that transpired between Simon's first encounter with Jesus and this particular day, but Jesus knew. Jesus was intimately acquainted with every one of Simon's actions and with the thoughts of his heart. Jesus knew that this was the right time to confront Simon and call him into his destiny that God had ordained.

Thought for Today

Jesus knows the perfect time to confront us and call us into our God-appointed destinies. We may feel that we couldn't possibly be ready, but Jesus knows us intimately and knows what is best.

Prayer Journal

_____

_____

_____

~ ~ ~ OCTOBER 8 ~ ~ ~

"And when they had done this, they caught a great number of fish, and their net was breaking. So they signaled to their partners in the other boat to come and help them. And they came and filled both the boats, so that they began to sink" (Luke 5:6-7).

Jesus made two requests of Simon, and Simon had a problem with both of them. First, Jesus requested that they go out to fish in the daytime. Simon knew that Jesus wasn't ignorant to the fact that after the sun was up, the fish simply were not to be found, or caught. Secondly, Jesus asked him to throw his net into the deep waters. Again, Simon knew that Jesus surely would have known that when fish were caught, they were caught in the shallow water, not the deep water. Simon gave Jesus a mild protest, but he wisely submitted to both requests, and a miracle catch of fish resulted.

It is interesting to note that Jesus chose to confront Simon with the call of God on his life, right in the place where the daily grind of his present life took place—in his boat with his fishing nets and friends. Most of us have the misconception that God only deals with us on matters of great importance during our high and holy moments. Yet, more often than not, Jesus will choose to confront and challenge us to take steps of faith right in the middle of our daily grind and routine. It is in these hectic moments, that Jesus calls us into deeper waters of commitment and devotion to Him, and to His purposes for our lives.

Thought for Today

Your obedience to do what Jesus tells you to do, when He tells you to do it, will position you for a miracle harvest. Remember, He knows more than you do.

Prayer Journal

_____

_____

_____

~ ~ ~ OCTOBER 9 ~ ~ ~

"When Simon Peter saw it, he fell down at Jesus' knees, saying, 'Depart from me, for I am a sinful man, O Lord!' For he and all who were with him were astonished at the catch of fish which they had taken; and so also were James and John, the sons of Zebedee, who were partners with Simon. And Jesus said to Simon, 'Do not be afraid. From now on you will catch men'" (Luke 5:8-10).

Simon obeyed the instructions of Jesus to let his nets down into the deep water and as a result, there was a miracle catch of fish. Simon was so humbled by this event, that he told Jesus, *"Depart from me, for I am a sinful man."* On the surface, this sounds like a repentant sinner seeking forgiveness, but a deeper look at his statement reveals that there is much more to be learned. Simon wasn't really asking Jesus to leave, nor was he confessing his sins to find forgiveness. Actually, Simon was afraid: he was afraid that Jesus had picked the wrong guy for the job. He was afraid that even if he was on his best behavior, he would never be able to measure up to such high expectations. What Simon was actually saying was, "You had better leave now. You don't know what I'm really like."

We can relate to Simon's concerns. We hear the Lord's call on our life and something inside us wants to step out in faith and step into what He wants us to do. However, deep in our hearts, we believe that He made a mistake in wanting us. We must always remember that Christ's call on our lives is never based on our abilities.

Thought for Today

There is no limit to what our Savior and Creator can work through us if we will surrender to His call on our lives, and let Him do things His way.

Prayer Journal

_____

_____

_____

~ ~ ~ OCTOBER 10 ~ ~ ~

"And when it was day, He called His disciples to Himself; and from them He chose twelve whom He also named apostles: Simon, whom He also named Peter, and Andrew his brother; James and John; Philip and Bartholomew" (Luke 6:13-14).

Jesus gathered His followers together, and from them, He chose twelve men to continually be with Him in ministry. Simon was among the twelve men chosen by Jesus. Simon was now faced with a decision of whether or not to submit to Jesus' choice for him to be more than just one in the crowd of followers. Simon had decided to leave his fishing business and follow Jesus, but now Jesus was asking for even a deeper commitment from him. Simon willfully submitted to being chosen as one of the twelve disciples.

God will never force anyone to do something that they do not want to do. What we become in life is a direct result of the choices that we have made. Whether or not we fit into the plan and purpose that God has for our lives, will hinge upon our willingness to submit to Him. Submission is not subjugation—forcing the will of one upon another. Submission is accepting your place in God's master plan. Submission is subordinating your plan to His plan and accepting your responsibility as His servant. Submission involves accepting His directives for living and obeying the directives of the Spirit.

Thought for Today

Once you decide to submit to God's plan for your life, you will never be able to go back to living your life as before—you can only drop out. If you return, you are willfully removing yourself from what you might have been had you stayed the course and fulfilled your calling in life.

Prayer Journal

_____

_____

_____

~ ~ ~ OCTOBER 11 ~ ~ ~

"Simon Peter answered and said, 'You are the Christ, the Son of the living God.' Jesus answered and said to him, 'Blessed are you, Simon Bar-Jonah, for flesh and blood has not revealed this to you, but My Father who is in heaven'" (Matthew 16:16-17).

It is human nature to want affirmation. We want people around us to affirm that we are doing well. As much as our human natures crave affirmation, it is not something that we are comfortable asking God to do. Even thinking about asking makes us nervous, as He might want to talk about some of those areas in which we know we are not doing so well. Simon was no different from us. He wanted to know how he was doing in becoming that "rock" which Jesus had prophetically spoken about him becoming.

Jesus had asked His disciples who people were saying that He was. Jesus then asked them who they thought He was. It was on this occasion that Simon received his first affirmation as to how well he was doing in becoming "rock-like." Simon boldly declared that he believed Jesus to be the Christ, meaning the Messiah, the Son of God. Jesus congratulated Simon for having spoken the correct answer. Jesus also told Simon, "What I promised would happen, is now taking place. The Holy Spirit is revealing truth to you and you perceive it correctly." What a tremendous promise this moment in Simon's life holds for us. What Jesus promises to do in us, He will actually do—no matter how long it takes.

Thought for Today

It will not happen overnight, but it will happen. God will fulfill every promise that He has made to us and will shape us into the person He intends for us to become.

Prayer Journal

_____

_____

_____

~ ~ ~ OCTOBER 12 ~ ~ ~

"Jesus answered and said to him, 'Blessed are you, Simon Bar-Jonah, for flesh and blood has not revealed this to you, but My Father who is in heaven. And I also say to you that you are Peter, and on this rock I will build My church, and the gates of Hades shall not prevail against it'" (Matthew 16:17-18).

Jesus asked His disciples who they believed Him to be, and Simon boldly declared that he believed Jesus to be the Christ, God's very own Son. Jesus gave Simon the affirmation that his heart was seeking. It was in this setting that Jesus called Simon, *"Peter,"* for the first time. In calling him *"Peter,"* Jesus was saying, "You are Peter and the rock I promised to make of you is now complete."

What did Jesus see in Peter that would cause Him to say, *"You are Peter?"* It wasn't because Peter had achieved a state of infallibility, for the record indicates how vulnerable Peter was to failure. Jesus saw in Peter a "living faith" that was born out of a "supernatural revelation." "Living faith" is more than a creed to live by. "Living faith" is a life-controlling conviction that is forever settled because of our conviction concerning the solid ground of changeless truth—God's Word. "Supernatural revelation" is more than theological insight. Supernatural revelation is being caught in the grip of the Holy Spirit and allowing Him to show us the tangible reality of invisible things. The Holy Spirit will give us "supernatural revelation" resulting in "living faith" which, in turn, will yield in total submission to God's purpose for our lives.

Thought for Today

Be settled in your faith to the point that you settle the question of whether or not you are going to walk with Jesus. Never, turn back.

Prayer Journal

_____

_____

_____

~ ~ ~ OCTOBER 13 ~ ~ ~

"Now I rejoice, not that you were made sorry, but that your sorrow led to repentance. For you were made sorry in a Godly manner, that you might suffer loss from us in nothing. For Godly sorrow produces repentance leading to salvation, not to be regretted; but the sorrow of the world produces death" (II Corinthians 7:9-10).

Repentance is often considered to be an initiation rite in turning from sin and coming to Christ for salvation. However, once we initially repent of our sin, we must realize that our repentance is not a climax—rather, it is a starting point for a lifetime of living before the Lord with a repentant heart. True repentance involves a reversal of one's perception and attitudes, which will always result in a reversal of one's actions and behavior. Repentance involves our acknowledging error, failure, or transgression, as soon as it is seen and acknowledging it for what it is. Genuine repentance will separate thinking from feelings. Repentance is often accompanied by an emotional response, as a result of Godly sorrow and grief.

We must separate repentance from a sense of condemnation and guilt. In answering a call to a lifestyle of repentance, we are not to nurture any guilt feelings. Our repentance is not by reason of our feelings, but by reason of our transgression of truth. Living a lifestyle of repentance requires our being available to the Holy Spirit for His correction, teaching, and the shaping of our lives.

Thought for Today

We are to be correctable because we need the Holy Spirit to admonish us. We are to be teachable, because we know so little about the issues of life. We are to be shapeable, because we are in need of a transformation.

Prayer Journal

_____

_____

_____

~ ~ ~ OCTOBER 14 ~ ~ ~

"From that time Jesus began to show to His disciples that He must go to Jerusalem, and suffer many things from the elders and chief priests and scribes, and be killed, and be raised the third day. Then Peter took Him aside and began to rebuke Him, saying, 'Far be it from You, Lord; this shall not happen to You!' But He turned and said to Peter, 'Get behind Me, Satan! You are an offense to Me, for you are not mindful of the things of God, but the things of men'" (Matthew 16:21-23).

Six months prior to the crucifixion, Jesus began to spend more time teaching His disciples about His death and subsequent resurrection. Yet, they couldn't comprehend how these things could be true. They were lost in the enchantment of the idea that Jesus, as the Messiah, would soon set up His kingdom and rule with loving justice, as well as, overrule the Roman injustice that abounded. They were totally oblivious to the cost of redemption.

Peter decided to set Jesus straight regarding His death, at which point, Jesus rebuked him and accused him of speaking on behalf of the devil. Actually, Peter was refusing to give place to the Cross, and in a sense, he was suggesting an alternative plan for salvation. For all practical purposes, he was saying, "You've done a good job, but we'll take it from here." Peter didn't understand that the Cross was the place where redemption was going to be accomplished and the place where the flesh would be put to death.

Thought for Today

The call to take up our cross is a call to take our place on Christ's Cross and die to our self. On the cross, we surrender and refuse to be dominated by our flesh.

Prayer Journal

_____

_____

_____

~ ~ ~ OCTOBER 15 ~ ~ ~

"And the Lord said, 'Simon, Simon! Indeed, Satan has asked for you, that he may sift you as wheat. But I have prayed for you, that your faith should not fail; and when you have returned to Me, strengthen your brethren'" (Luke 22:31-32).

It was a very sad night for Peter and the other disciples. Jesus had gathered with them to observe the Passover and He spoke to them concerning His death again. This night was especially painful for Peter as Jesus told him in the presence of the others, that before morning, he would deny knowing Him. Next, Jesus rebuked him for fighting in the Garden that night.

Later when Peter was in the courtyard of the high priest, they questioned him about his association with Jesus. Then, just before dawn, he failed as he had never failed before—with an oath, he denied ever knowing Jesus. Jesus' earlier warning to Peter came rushing back with gut-wrenching guilt. This moment so darkened his heart, that he couldn't remember the rest of what Jesus had said earlier that night. Immediately after Jesus told him of satan's desire to test him and of his subsequent denial, Jesus promised his failure wouldn't be fatal to his faith, because He had prayed for him.

We can all identify with Peter, as we all have promised the Lord that we would not fail, and then failed miserably. Yet, like Peter, our failure does not have to destroy our faith.

Thought for Today

The promise of Jesus that Peter's faith would not fail as a result of his failures, applies to us too. Jesus, our High Priest, is seated at the right hand of the Father in heaven praying for us.

Prayer Journal

_____

_____

_____

~ ~ ~ OCTOBER 16 ~ ~ ~

"Simon Peter said to them, 'I am going fishing.' They said to him, 'We are going with you also.' They went out and immediately got into the boat, and that night they caught nothing" (John 21:3).

Lost in the fog of self-doubt, Peter returned to being a fisherman. He was saying, "I'm going back to something I know." His return to fishing was not for the purpose of a night of sport, but he was trying to feel his way into his uncertain future. Peter's self-doubt and confusion was not from an uncertainty of whether Jesus had forgiven him for his denial. For you see, on His resurrection day, Jesus told the women at the tomb to go tell My disciples and Peter. From these words, Peter knew that he was still "on the team." However, that did not change his embarrassment or confusion over how he, of all the disciples, could have failed Jesus so miserably.

Now, sitting in a boat in the cool of the night, Peter is left alone with his thoughts. Perhaps Peter was thinking, "What am I doing out here, I can't even catch fish anymore? Jesus said to go to Galilee and He'd meet us there; well we're here and He's not—He hasn't come, and it's probably my fault. He probably doesn't want to ever see me again." Self-doubt must be conquered before we can move into the fulfillment of purpose that God has for each us.

Thought for Today

Have you failed? Because of your failure, are you filled with self-doubt? Are you wondering if it is your fault that things are not turning out as you had planned and hoped they would? Are you wondering if God the Father still considers you to be usable for His kingdom? Please stop wondering. Remember Peter's failure and how Jesus mercifully restored him—then rest in that assurance.

Prayer Journal

_____

_____

_____

~ ~ ~ OCTOBER 17 ~ ~ ~

"But when the morning had now come, Jesus stood on the shore; yet the disciples did not know that it was Jesus" (John 21:4).

Peter and a few of the other disciples had decided to return to being fishermen. This task was proving to be a frustrating decision, as they had fished all night and had not caught any fish. There is no doubt Peter reviewed some of the lessons for life that he had been taught while walking with Jesus, the Master.

Peter would never forget the stormy night when they thought they were not going to make it, and then they saw Jesus walking towards them on the water. He remembered Jesus' invitation for him to step out of the boat and walk on the water to Him. He remembered what it felt like to step on the water and walk on it as though it were pavement. He remembered the day that Jesus took the little boy's lunch and fed the multitudes. Looking at his hands, he remembered that he was one of the men through whom the miracle meal was distributed. He could not forget the night in the Garden when he had cut off the ear of a soldier who was attempting to arrest Jesus. He would never forget how he felt when Jesus picked up the severed ear and replaced it, healing the soldier's wound.

Thought for Today

Just as Peter walked on the water that night, Jesus still invites us to walk into a miracle and watch Him sustain that miracle for us. Just as Jesus took the little boy's lunch and multiplied it, Jesus still multiplies his blessings through the hands of those willing to serve others. Just as Jesus healed the ear of the soldier, Jesus still takes situations in which our zeal has cut and injured another, and he heals their wounds.

Prayer Journal

_____

_____

_____

~ ~ ~ OCTOBER 18 ~ ~ ~

"So when they had eaten breakfast, Jesus said to Simon Peter, 'Simon, son of Jonah, do you love Me more than these?' He said to Him, 'Yes, Lord; You know that I love You.' He said to him, 'Feed My lambs'" (John 21:15).

Jesus asked Peter a question that pierced his heart, *"Simon...do you love Me?"* The word for *"love"* that Jesus used in His question was "Agape," which means a divine or Godly love. Peter responded that he did indeed love Jesus; however, the word for *"love"* that Peter used was "Phileo," the love of a friend. Peter did not try to match terms with Jesus even though his love for Jesus had grown, not diminished. It was just that Peter had some nagging doubts about his capacity to love with faithfulness in light of his recent boasts and subsequent failure.

Jesus would ask Peter this same question three times. Each time Peter responded, Jesus spoke of his new assignment, *"Feed My lambs."* Jesus was conveying to Peter, "Your fishing days are over and from now on you will be a shepherd over My flock." This new assignment would require a new level of faith, for fishermen and shepherds are nothing alike. Fishermen brag about the "one that got away," while shepherds have to go out and find that "one." Fishermen can do their job and not even get their feet wet, but shepherds who do their job, cannot keep their feet clean. This new assignment for Peter would require his total dependency upon the Lord to accomplish it.

Thought for Today

Jesus asks about our love for Him before He asks if we will serve Him. Jesus knows that if our love is intact, our service will follow.

Prayer Journal

_____

_____

_____

~ ~ ~ OCTOBER 19 ~ ~ ~

"He said to him the third time, 'Simon, son of Jonah, do you love Me?' Peter was grieved because He said to him the third time, 'Do you love Me?' And he said to Him, 'Lord, You know all things; You know that I love You.' Jesus said to him, 'Feed My sheep'" (John 21:17).

Jesus only asked Peter one question, *"Do you love Me;"* but He asked it three times. Peter had denied knowing Jesus three times and now he was hearing himself say, three times, *"Lord...You know that I love You."* There was one loving affirmation for every damning denial Peter had spoken. Notice the questions that Jesus did not ask Peter that, if we had been Jesus, we would have asked him. Jesus did not ask Peter, "What great things are you going to do for Me to try to make up for your unfaithfulness?" Nor did Jesus ask Peter, "The next time you find yourself under pressure, do you think that you will be able to hold the line?" No, Jesus only wanted to know if Peter still loved Him.

Jesus never measures our potential by our past failures. He only measures our potential by the love we are willing to exchange in the present. Jesus did not want to know if Peter thought he would love Him three weeks from now, Jesus was only concerned with Peter's love at that moment. Dealing with Peter's failure was easy; however, dealing with his heart required an act of Peter's will.

Thought for Today

Jesus knows that if our love for Him is in its proper place, then in spite of our failures or our self-doubts (as to our capacity to follow through on our commitments), He can use us. He can take us further into His purposes for our lives than we had ever dreamed.

Prayer Journal

_____

_____

_____

~ ~ ~ OCTOBER 20 ~ ~ ~

"Not that I speak in regard to need, for I have learned in whatever state I am, to be content: I know how to be abased, and I know how to abound. Everywhere and in all things I have learned both to be full and to be hungry, both to abound and to suffer need. I can do all things through Christ who strengthens me" (Philippians 4:11-13).

When the Apostle Paul penned these words, he revealed that his circumstances did not control his sense of well-being. His security was derived from his dependence on Jesus Christ as his total and only source of supply for the needs of his life. His statement might seem trite, until you consider all that Paul had endured throughout his lifetime; hard times, persecutions, weariness, and now he was facing death. Yet, he claimed that he had been content through everything.

Ancient Roman coins bore the engraving of an ox looking at an altar and a plow and the inscription read, "Ready for Either." It represented an ox that lived prepared and was ready to go to the altar as a sacrifice if his master should lead him there, or he was ready to go to the field and pull the plow. Paul's trust in Jesus, as his Lord and Master, is much like that of the ox on the Roman coin. Paul lived prepared and ready for anything that Jesus asked him to do. Whether it was good times or bad, Paul derived his contentment from knowing that Jesus had led him to this moment and would bring him through.

Thought for Today

What Jesus did for Paul, He will do for us if we trust Him. Follow Paul's example—don't let circumstances dictate your contentment.

Prayer Journal

_____

_____

_____

~ ~ ~ OCTOBER 21 ~ ~ ~

"For to me, to live is Christ, and to die is gain" (Philippians 1:21).

Paul was nearing the end of his life and ministry on earth. Writing from a prison cell, Paul summarized the governing philosophy for how he lived his life; "As I live, I live for Christ and if I die living for Christ, I gain heaven and uninterrupted fellowship with Jesus, Whom I serve." Paul realized that his spirituality demanded a personal decision on his part. No one could be saved for him, nor could anyone fulfill his ministry. Paul knew he was responsible to walk upright and faithfully before the Lord and that one day, he would stand before his God and give an account for his life.

The life of Paul was centered on serving Christ and the family of God. Paul did not make the Lord just a part of his life, he placed Him on the throne of his life. The Lord received first consideration for every word that Paul spoke and for every action that he took. Paul did not divide his life into compartments of sacred and secular. His life only had one compartment, and that was sacred. Paul considered himself to be a prisoner of the Lord. While he may be bound in the iron chains of men, his heart had long ago been bound in the unbreakable chains of Christ's love. Paul also felt himself to be a debtor to mankind. He felt he owed a debt to every man to tell them of Christ's love and salvation. Paul lived prepared to die. He served God with such abandon, that his personal safety was of no concern to him. The cause of Christ consumed him.

Thought for Today

To what, or to whom, is your heart chained? What cause in life consumes you? I pray you will be consumed with, *"For to me, to live is Christ, and to die is gain."*

Prayer Journal

_____

_____

_____

~ ~ ~ OCTOBER 22 ~ ~ ~

"And let them make Me a sanctuary, that I may dwell among them...And there I will meet with you, and I will speak with you from above the mercy seat, from between the two cherubim which are on the ark of the Testimony, about everything which I will give you in commandment to the children of Israel" (Exodus 25:8,22).

Worship is a fundamental discipline of a disciple. A disciple must incorporate a daily and private devotional practice, and he must regularly participate in assembling with God's people in a local congregation. Many Christians have a misconception about the importance of church attendance. Some assume that it is to bolster church attendance records, while others assume that it is to build up the financial coffers. Many believe the preacher pushes church attendance so he can insure His job security.

Our assembling together is not man's plan—it is God's plan. God told Moses to raise an offering from the children of Israel and build Him a sanctuary that He might dwell among His people. It is from this sanctuary that God promised to meet with Moses and speak to the people. Our private times of worship will never take the place of our need to gather with the family of God. Our flesh man is always prepared to offer us a number of reasons why we shouldn't attend, but we must resist; there isn't a reason that is good enough for God.

Thought for Today

Resist the temptation of your flesh to stay away from church. In the environment of your obedience, and through the grace and compassion of God's people, the Lord will minister to you and meet the deepest longings and needs of your heart.

Prayer Journal

_____

_____

~ ~ ~ OCTOBER 23 ~ ~ ~

"Not forsaking the assembling of ourselves together, as is the manner of some, but exhorting one another, and so much the more as you see the Day approaching" (Hebrews 10:25).

Within this passage of Scripture, there is a prophetic directive calling the family of God to assemble together at appointed times. As we do so in faithfulness to God's Word, we demonstrate our discipline as a believer. Apparently, the early church had a problem with attendance. Some within the early church were treating the assembling together as optional. The early church had lost sight of the power that was connected in the assembling of the church. The warning in this verse, "be even more diligent as you see the signs of the times," was going unheeded by many.

The discipline of church attendance protects us against the "spirit" of the times. In Romans 12:1-2, we read, *"I beseech you therefore, brethren, by the mercies of God, that you present your bodies a living sacrifice, holy, acceptable to God, which is your reasonable service. And do not be conformed to this world, but be transformed by the renewing of your mind, that you may prove what is that good and acceptable and perfect will of God."* Church attendance also stirs our anticipation of Christ's return. II Timothy 4:8 tells us, *"Finally, there is laid up for me the crown of righteousness, which the Lord, the righteous Judge, will give to me on that Day, and not to me only but also to all who have loved His appearing."*

Thought for Today

Our gathering as the family of God is far more than a ritual exacted by man. Our assembling together is a life-giving source that will keep us as we *"see the Day approaching."*

Prayer Journal

_____

_____

_____

~ ~ ~ OCTOBER 24 ~ ~ ~

"For those who live according to the flesh set their minds on the things of the flesh, but those who live according to the Spirit, the things of the Spirit. For to be carnally minded is death, but to be spiritually minded is life and peace. Because the carnal mind is enmity against God; for it is not subject to the law of God, nor indeed can be. So then, those who are in the flesh cannot please God" (Romans 8:5-8).

We all have "one" and it gets us into trouble 100% of the time. I am speaking of our carnal, fleshly natures. Our flesh man and our spirit man are as different as night and day. They never agree on anything and argue about everything. Whenever our spirit man wants to do something that will please the Lord, our flesh man fights it. Our spirit man only cares about pleasing the Lord, while our flesh man could care less about pleasing God. Our spirit man is ready to obey God, while our flesh man insists on negotiating.

The flesh man hates going to church and looks for an out. Here are some common excuses that our flesh man uses to convince us not to go to church. There is the, "I need a break" excuse. There is the "If my heart is not in it, it's no use" excuse. There is the "I'd be a hindrance as my bad attitude will spoil it for everyone" excuse. There is the, "I'm sure that God won't talk to me today, because my spouse and I are fighting" excuse. Finally, here is the classic, "I don't want to, because I don't feel like it" excuse.

Thought for Today

We all have a flesh man, but our flesh man does not have to have us. You must purpose in your heart not to give a voice to your flesh man. Make your spirit man dominate.

Prayer Journal

_____

_____

_____

~ ~ ~ OCTOBER 25 ~ ~ ~

"And let us consider one another in order to stir up love and good works, not forsaking the assembling of ourselves together, as is the manner of some, but exhorting one another, and so much the more as you see the Day approaching" (Hebrews 10:24-25).

The *"Day approaching"* in this passage of Scripture, is a reference to the day of Christ's return to earth. While no one knows when that day will come, we are to live as though it were going to be today. Any day could be the day Jesus comes again. The Scriptures call us to tighten up our discipline of attendance, especially as we see prophetic signs being fulfilled concerning the return of Christ. As Christians, we are called to be obedient to God and His Word. We must reject the popular notion that church attendance is nothing more than mere ritual and traditions that have been set by men.

We need but look at the example that Jesus set for us regarding our corporate times of worship. Consider the worship habit of Jesus in Luke 4:16, *"So He came to Nazareth, where He had been brought up. And as His custom was, He went into the synagogue on the Sabbath day, and stood up to read."* It was the custom of Jesus to attend church on the day set aside for worshiping God. What is amazing about Jesus' custom is that He attended faithfully, even though the church He attended was spiritually dead—actually, it was rotten to the core. Jesus didn't let the spiritual temperature of others dictate the warmth of His own desire for God's presence.

Thought for Today

Have you made church attendance a custom? Don't let the spiritual deadness in others prevent you from receiving the abundant life Jesus has promised to you.

Prayer Journal

_____

_____

_____

~ ~ ~ OCTOBER 26 ~ ~ ~

"In all things showing yourself to be a pattern of good works; in doctrine showing integrity, reverence, incorruptibility, sound speech that cannot be condemned, that one who is an opponent may be ashamed, having nothing evil to say of you" (Titus 2:7-8).

Paul was very clear about how he believed Christians should live. He spent a great deal of time teaching the early church Christians concerning their conduct at home, at work, and at church. Paul states *"Imitate me, just as I also imitate Christ."* (I Corinthians 11:1). In other words, follow my example and you will do just fine. Paul believed that in every arena of life we should set a good example, and this included church attendance. Our obedience to assemble ourselves with other Christians will make room for God's grace to work among us. Our collective unity will release the anointing of the Holy Spirit, which in turn, will break yokes of bondage. In humility, we acknowledge that we need one another and we recognize that we are members of a living body. If we separate ourselves, we will cause ourselves to decay spiritually just as a severed limb naturally decays.

When we assemble, we acknowledge our accountability to the Body of Christ as we allow for a time and a place to receive correction. We show a practical availability to serve the Lord and others. We demonstrate our submission to Christ's rule through His church. We manifest a model pathway for others in discerning the "Lord's way," regarding the assembling together.

Thought for Today

Whether we like it or not, our life is the only Bible that someone is reading. How would someone fare if they followed your example?

Prayer Journal

_____

_____

_____

~ ~ ~ OCTOBER 27 ~ ~ ~

"Then Abram took Sarai his wife and Lot his brother's son, and all their possessions that they had gathered, and the people whom they had acquired in Haran, and they departed to go to the land of Canaan. So they came to the land of Canaan. Abram passed through the land to the place of Shechem, as far as the terebinth tree of Moreh. And the Canaanites were then in the land. Then the Lord appeared to Abram and said, 'To your descendants I will give this land.' And there he built an altar to the Lord, who had appeared to him" (Genesis 12:5-7).

Altars in the Old Testament served two fundamental purposes. First, they were elevated places of worship where sacrifices were presented to God. Secondly, altars were places where personal decisions and commitments were made that would shape the individual's character and therefore, chart a course for his life. The altars in Abraham's life were defining moments that marked his life and thereby, anchored his faith.

We need to renew our understanding as to our need to build altars within our hearts to the Lord as we offer the love and adoration of our hearts, for Who He is and for His faithfulness to us. Many have become so casual with the Lord—they run into His house on Sunday and pay their dues through the exacting of religious rituals, and never even notice if the Lord is there. Every single day, we need to kneel at the altar within our hearts and present our sincere praise and worship to the Lord.

Thought for Today

It is at the altar of our hearts, that we will make commitments and decisions that will shape our character and chart a course for life.

Prayer Journal

_____

_____

_____

~ ~ ~ OCTOBER 28 ~ ~ ~

"Then the Lord appeared to Abram and said, 'To your descendants I will give this land.' And there he built an altar to the Lord, who had appeared to him" (Genesis 12:7).

The altars in Abraham's life parallel our own experience with the Lord. Just as Abraham knelt before his private altars and dealt with God, so should we kneel at the altar of our hearts and let God deal with us, and us with Him. The first altar in Abraham's life can be called the altar of promise, for God promised Abraham, *"To your descendants I will give this land."* The Lord's promise to Abraham was made in the presence of Abraham's adversaries, for the Canaanites were dwelling in the land at the time. God declared His promised purposes to Abraham in spite of the adversaries attempt to stop the promises from being fulfilled.

All of the promises of God are made to us in the presence of our adversary, the devil. God, however, is not moved by the presence of an enemy. All of the efforts of the enemy cannot stop God's purposes from coming to pass for the one who will stand in faith and believe God. Abraham was not casual about the Lord's promise to him. He sealed this promise on an altar, as he secured his sacrifice as an act of his faith in the Lord and in His promise. When Abraham tied his animal sacrifice to the altar, he was tying it there with a rope, in the natural realm, and with his faith, in the realm of the spirit. Tie the promises of God to your heart in faith.

Thought for Today

What is secured by faith at an altar before God will be sealed at the throne of God? Your altar that is established in God's promises, will victoriously withstand every attack of the adversary.

Prayer Journal

_____

_____

_____

~ ~ ~ OCTOBER 29 ~ ~ ~

"And he moved from there to the mountain east of Bethel, and he pitched his tent with Bethel on the west and Ai on the east; there he built an altar to the Lord and called on the name of the Lord" (Genesis 12:8).

"Calling (called) on the name of the Lord" reveals Abraham's growing intimacy with the Lord. Every day, Abraham was learning something new about God, and his faith was growing. The name of the Lord represents the fullness of His person, His nature, and His character. Throughout the Old Testament, God progressively revealed Himself through His name. Like the facets of a diamond, the Lord revealed one aspect of Himself at a time. However, Abraham did not have the advantage of knowing all of the revealed names of God, as most were revealed after his death. Abraham also did not have the written Scriptures to study that would have given him insight as to who God was, and who He wanted to be in Abraham's life. Abraham was discovering God one day at a time, and it was during life's daily routine that God would speak to him, as well as, during his times of private devotion and worship.

We have the advantage of the Scriptures, as well as, the indwelling fellowship of the Holy Spirit to help us discover who God is, and who He wants to become in our lives. Abraham's faith was not the product of his exacting of a formula; rather, it was the result of his increasing intimacy with the Lord.

Thought for Today

Our walk with God should be an ever-increasing and ever-deepening experience of intimacy, which will result in the strengthening of our faith.

Prayer Journal

_____

_____

_____

~ ~ ~ OCTOBER 30 ~ ~ ~

"And he went on his journey from the South as far as Bethel, to the place where his tent had been at the beginning, between Bethel and Ai, to the place of the altar which he had made there at first. And there Abram called on the name of the Lord. Lot also, who went with Abram, had flocks and herds and tents" (Genesis 13:3-5).

God was keeping His promise to Abraham concerning giving him the land. Abraham was growing in his relationship with God and in his understanding of God. However, fear began to grip Abraham's heart and his faith in God's ability to protect him was challenged. Abraham chose to take matters into his own hands, and in fear for his life fled to Egypt. While in Egypt, Abraham learned first-hand the high cost of abandoning God's plan and taking matters into his own hands; while there, he nearly lost his wife, and his own life, to Pharaoh. However, God intervened and showed him great mercy. God caused Pharaoh to let Abraham's wife go, and let Abraham keep his life even after he had deceived Pharaoh. It was God, Who personally brought Abraham out of Egypt and restored him to the original plan for his life.

When he left Egypt, Abraham returned to the first altar where the Lord had first promised him the land and a future. Abraham recommitted his life at this altar, making it the altar of no return. Abraham never again left the land of God's purpose for him.

Thought for Today

We sometimes allow people or circumstances to cause us to stray from God's purposes for our lives. We need to come back to the place where we made our first commitments to the Lord. We need to renew our vows to Him.

Prayer Journal

_____

_____

_____

~ ~ ~ OCTOBER 31 ~ ~ ~

"And the Lord said to Abram, after Lot had separated from him: 'Lift your eyes now and look from the place where you are—northward, southward, eastward, and westward; for all the land which you see I give to you and your descendants forever. And I will make your descendants as the dust of the earth; so that if a man could number the dust of the earth, then your descendants also could be numbered. Arise, walk in the land through its length and its width, for I give it to you.' Then Abram moved his tent, and went and dwelt by the terebinth trees of Mamre, which are in Hebron, and built an altar there to the Lord" (Genesis 13:14-18).

What had been given to Abraham as a promise was now becoming a possession. God had captured Abraham's heart and imagination with His promises and now, God was commanding him to literally step forward in faith into the reality of the promises. God spelled it out for Abraham—all the land, as far as his eyes could see in every direction, was going to belong to him. However, in order to possess it, Abraham had to get up and walk into the land.

Just knowing that the promises of God exist and are intended for us is not enough to make them a reality in our lives. Like Abraham, we must walk into them by our faith. Through our faith in action, we confirm our acceptance of the implications of God's promised purposes for our lives. Also, through our faith, we commit our lives in a tangible way to the pursuit of the fulfillment of that promise.

Thought for Today

The discipline of worship calls us to private encounters with God. In these encounters, we experience defining moments with God that anchor our faith to our unfailing God.

Prayer Journal

_____

_____

_____

~ ~ ~ NOVEMBER 1 ~ ~ ~

"Now if you walk before Me as your father David walked, in integrity of heart and in uprightness, to do according to all that I have commanded you, and if you keep My statutes and My judgments, then I will establish the throne of your kingdom over Israel forever, as I promised David your father, saying, 'You shall not fail to have a man on the throne of Israel'" (I Kings 9:4-5).

God promised Solomon the perpetuation of his kingdom if he maintained the integrity of his heart, as did his father David. Integrity of heart requires being open and honest before the Lord, as well as, being sensitive and obedient to the Holy Spirit's prompting. Integrity of heart also demands responsiveness to the Holy Spirit's corrections without offering excuses or justifications.

David exercised total dependency on the Lord for His protection from every one of his enemies. In contrast to his father, Solomon exercised his skills of negotiation and sought protection of his borders through diplomacy. Solomon negotiated treaties with neighboring kings and ended up marrying the daughters of these various kings. Each foreign wife brought her gods with her, and Solomon built shrines throughout the land to these pagan gods. The end result of Solomon's actions was the decay of his kingdom. Every day of our lives, we find ourselves at the crossroads of diplomacy and dependence.

Thought for Today

If we choose diplomacy and manipulate our situations through our human reasoning and wisdom, we will suffer decay of the Lord's rule in the kingdom of our hearts. We will sacrifice our integrity of heart on the altar of human expediency.

Prayer Journal

_____

_____

_____

~ ~ ~ NOVEMBER 2 ~ ~ ~

"And you shall put in the breastplate of judgment the Urim and the Thummim, and they shall be over Aaron's heart when he goes in before the Lord. So Aaron shall bear the judgment of the children of Israel over his heart before the Lord continually" (Exodus 28:30).

God instructed that the high priest's heart be covered with the *"Urim and the Thummim"* whenever he went before the Lord. While we don't know exactly what the *"Urim and the Thummim"* actually was, we do know the meaning of the words and generally, how they functioned. The word *"Urim"* means "lights," and the word *"Thummim"* means "completeness." They were consulted whenever the high priest needed direction from the Lord for the nation of Israel. Standing before the curtain of the Holy of Holies, the high priest would inquire of the Lord and wait for His answer. Again, we don't know exactly how the answer was manifested; however, the assumption is that within the *"Urim"* there was evidence of the radiant warmth of the Lord's presence and in the *"Thummim"* there was a sense of peace and assurance.

In the New Testament, every believer has been made a priest unto the Lord and is charged with the responsibility of maintaining their hearts. The New Testament counterpart for the word "integrity," is the word, peace. As priests, we are to let peace be the deciding factor in all of our decisions, thoughts, and actions.

Thought for Today

Whenever we choose to exercise our wills and human reasoning, our hearts will become fragmented. The Holy Spirit is grieved at times by our choices, and will signal us that we are grieving Him.

Prayer Journal

_____

_____

_____

~ ~ ~ NOVEMBER 3 ~ ~ ~

"And God said to him in a dream, 'Yes, I know that you did this in the integrity of your heart. For I also withheld you from sinning against Me; therefore I did not let you touch her'" (Genesis 20:6).

Abraham and his wife Sarah had an agreement between them in their nomadic travels. They had agreed that if a territorial king wanted to add her to his harem, she would spare Abraham's life by claiming to be his sister. Such a situation arose, as Abimelech, King of Gerar, noticed and desired Sarah. God steps in to protect Abraham and Sarah from their own fear and lack of faith. God visited King Abimelech in a dream and quickly got his attention by telling him he was a dead man. After learning the reason for such a statement, Abimelech appeals to the innocence of his intent and claims he was acting out of the integrity of his heart. God agrees with Abimelech and lets him off the hook.

Living with integrity of heart requires our being totally honest with God in all areas of our lives. Integrity of heart demands that we are responsive to the dealings and corrections of the Holy Spirit without offering excuses or attempting to justify ourselves, or our actions. One of the benefits of walking before the Lord with integrity of heart is that, as with Abimelech, the Lord will prevent us from becoming innocently entangled in someone's lies. Another benefit of integrity of heart is that, as with David, the borders of our lives will be protected from the enemy's unwelcome encroachment.

Thought for Today

God protects and delivers those who walk before Him with a heart of integrity. He saves us from all the devices of evil and from the detours of self-confusion.

Prayer Journal

_____

_____

_____

~ ~ ~ NOVEMBER 4 ~ ~ ~

"Teach me Your way, O Lord; I will walk in Your truth; unite my heart to fear Your name" (Psalms 86:11).

The word "integrity" is actually built from the root thought found in two words. The first word is "integer." It means a whole number, such as the numbers: one, two, or three, as opposed to fractions. The word "integer" conveys the idea of completeness and wholeness. The second word is "integration," which carries the meaning of parts that are fitted together to bring about completeness and wholeness. Integrity of the heart requires the maintenance of one's heart before the Lord. Therefore, the heart must be pure and honest.

David asked God to bind the fragments and pieces of his heart together in such a way that he would be kept aligned with God, His Word, and His ways. David asked God not to let his heart become divided by the temptation to yield to the negativity of life's circumstances. David resisted giving into sin's temptation as he wanted to keep his heart from coming apart at the seams. In Psalms 119:10, we read, *"With my whole heart I have sought You; Oh, let me not wander from Your commandments!"* Sin will fragment our hearts and cause us to loose our integrity. The Lord promises that when we seek Him with a whole heart, meaning a heart of integrity, that we will be able to find Him.

Thought for Today

God promises us that if we will live with integrity of heart before Him, He will prevent us from becoming snared in confusion. God promises to preserve our lives against the enemies encroachment, and He will perpetuate His blessings in our lives.

Prayer Journal

_____

_____

_____

~ ~ ~ NOVEMBER 5 ~ ~ ~

"Or do you think that the Scripture says in vain, 'The Spirit who dwells in us yearns jealously?' But He gives more grace. Therefore He says: 'God resists the proud, but gives grace to the humble'" (James 4:5-6).

Many Christians have a misconception of what it means to be enthusiastic in their walk with God, especially as it relates to expressing one's self in worship. They believe that enthusiasm is being superficially exuberant and is nothing more than the working of one's self into a state of frenzy. They assume this enthusiasm is just a lot of wild gestures and loud shouting. What is amazing is that we readily embrace and endorse such behavior as a normal response to occasions, such as sporting events, but reject it as a proper response to spiritual matters. The word "enthusiasm" comes from the Greek word "Entheos," which means "full of God." One showing their enthusiasm is one that is so full of God, that their behavior is therefore dominated by Him. Enthusiasm makes a person vibrantly alive with a resource from another realm other than the natural.

Enthusiasm challenges our inclination towards becoming reserved and sedate in our response to the Holy Spirit. We are tempted to keep our enthusiasm under control in an effort to maintain a sense of respectability and dignity. In our sophisticated society, it is easy to assume that God equates our reserve with reverence.

Thought for Today

What we call dignity; God calls pride. Our pride will always repel His presence. Do not hide your enthusiasm for God behind a wall of pride.

Prayer Journal

_____

_____

_____

~ ~ ~ NOVEMBER 6 ~ ~ ~

"But the natural man does not receive the things of the Spirit of God, for they are foolishness to him; nor can he know them, because they are spiritually discerned" (I Corinthians 2:14).

Many churches are making a gross error in what they have allowed themselves to become in an effort to evangelize the lost. The feeling today is that in order to evangelize the lost, we must pamper the lost. They assume by toning down their enthusiasm, God will be made palatable to the unsaved. As a result, we end up toning down our expressions of praise and worship, as well as, toning down our message in preaching our convictions and lifestyle as mandated in the Word of God. We do everything that we can to keep from offending the world in our behavior and message, in order to get them to accept us and our message of salvation.

Church is not for people; it is for God. We have not gathered to please men, but to please God. Our concern should not be whether or not we will offend sinners: our concern should be whether or not we will offend God. If we fail to preach that sin is sin, hell is hot, and eternity is forever, we will be greasing the road to hell with our compromise. Our flesh will always seek to control what it deems to be fanatical responses, and will always seek to avoid confrontation by trying to tone down the hot issues.

Thought for Today

The world will always reject our expressions of true worship. They will deem us to be fanatical, foolish, and irrelevant to the present day. The world will never embrace or understand our enthusiasm for our God until they personally get a glimpse of His greatness for themselves.

Prayer Journal

~ ~ ~ NOVEMBER 7 ~ ~ ~

"On the last day, that great day of the feast, Jesus stood and cried out, saying, 'If anyone thirsts, let him come to Me and drink. He who believes in Me, as the Scripture has said, out of his heart will flow rivers of living water.' But this He spoke concerning the Spirit, whom those believing in Him would receive; for the Holy Spirit was not yet given, because Jesus was not yet glorified" (John 7:37-39).

This event, the celebration of the Feast of Tabernacles, took place approximately six months before the crucifixion. The Feast of Tabernacles was an annual commemoration of the Israelites' forty year journey through the wilderness, and was celebrated with a week of feasting. They built shelters out of branches to sleep in, which would serve as a reminder of how God had led them and provided for them in the wilderness. The Feast included an event called the "Water Pouring Ceremony." This event reminded the people of God's supernatural provision of water in their journey through the desert wastelands. The priest stood at the top of the Temple steps and poured water out of large urns. As the water cascaded and splashed down the steps, the people rejoiced and lifted their voices in praise.

Jesus used this occasion to prophetically promise a day when His followers would be called to live in the Holy Spirit's fullness. He also pointed beyond the initial experience, to a lifestyle of living in the Holy Spirit's resources, where rivers of life would be released.

Thought for Today

Being open to the Spirit of enthusiasm calls us to readily welcome the overflow, vibrancy, warmth, and expressiveness of the Holy Spirit's fullness.

Prayer Journal

_____

_____

_____

~ ~ ~ NOVEMBER 8 ~ ~ ~

"He who believes in Me, as the Scripture has said, out of his heart will flow rivers of living water" (John 7:38).

Jesus used the occasion of the "Water Pouring Ceremony," on the last day of the Feast of Tabernacle celebration, to make a prophetic forecast of a day when His followers would be called to live in the Holy Spirit's fullness. Jesus pointed to an initial experience with the Holy Spirit in bringing us to salvation, and then pointed to His baptizing us into the fullness of the Holy Spirit. He also pointed to the Holy Spirit's desire to release His resources through us. Jesus spoke of *"rivers of living water,"* referencing the Holy Spirit that would flow out of our lives. The word *"rivers"* is plural and speaks of streams of refreshing and of the power that the Holy Spirit wants to release through anyone who will allow Him to do so.

The Holy Spirit wants to release through us, rivers of praise and worship. On the Day of Pentecost, the Holy Spirit released His supernatural language of praise and worship. This was recognized and acknowledged by the unbelievers who heard them speaking and praising God. In Acts 2:11 we read, *"We hear them speaking in our own tongues the wonderful works of God."* Some people have assumed that the disciples were preaching in tongues, which is not the case. They were praising God in languages that the Holy Spirit was supernaturally releasing through them. These languages came forth as rivers of praise and worship.

Thought for Today

The Holy Spirit gives us access to the dynamic privilege of praising God through His supernatural gifting of language. Let *"rivers of living water"* flow from your heart today.

Prayer Journal

_____

_____

_____

~ ~ ~ NOVEMBER 9 ~ ~ ~

"He who believes in Me, as the Scripture has said, out of his heart will flow rivers of living water" (John 7:38).

On the last day of the Feast of Tabernacles, Jesus boldly proclaimed that the Holy Spirit would be released in, and through, His followers as *"rivers of living water."* Living in the fullness of the Holy Spirit will develop a lifestyle in which there will be an ongoing release of the Holy Spirit's resources. One such release will be rivers of witnessing. Jesus promised that the Holy Spirit would testify of Him and that this would be accomplished through us. John 15:26-27 says, *"But when the Helper comes, whom I shall send to you from the Father, the Spirit of truth who proceeds from the Father, He will testify of Me. And you also will bear witness, because you have been with Me from the beginning."* The fullness of the Holy Spirit will release a desire and readiness to share the love of Jesus. As we witness, rivers of ministry will be released.

The Holy Spirit will release sign-gift ministries to people around us in need of divine grace. In Mark 16:17-18 we read, *"And these signs will follow those who believe: In My name they will cast out demons; they will speak with new tongues; they will take up serpents; and if they drink anything deadly, it will by no means hurt them; they will lay hands on the sick, and they will recover."* Hurting people matter to Jesus. He wants to release through us the Holy Spirit's rivers of ministry to heal those who are hurting.

Thought for Today

We are the agents through whom the Holy Spirit wants to release His abundant resources. Through Him, we can touch and change the lives of people around us who are in need.

Prayer Journal

_____

_____

_____

~ ~ ~ NOVEMBER 10 ~ ~ ~

"There are diversities of gifts, but the same Spirit. There are differences of ministries, but the same Lord. And there are diversities of activities, but it is the same God who works all in all. But the manifestation of the Spirit is given to each one for the profit of all" (I Corinthians 12:4-7).

The Holy Spirit has placed His gifts within each and every believer. Not everyone has the same gifts, which brings a wonderful diversity to the family of God. While we may not all have the same gifts, we all are expected to use the gifts that we have under the direction of the Holy Spirit, so that the Body of Christ can be built up and edified. The fullness of the Holy Spirit rekindles our desire for His gifts. It also renews our availability to be His messengers of delivery that give away God's gifts of goodness, mercy, and blessings to others.

Today, with just a phone call, we are able to have a pizza delivered to our door. When the pizza arrives, we appreciate the efforts of the delivery person, but it is the pizza that we are really wanting. We are much like the pizza delivery person, in that, we are to deliver the blessings of God to people around us as we allow the Holy Spirit to release His river of gifts through us. This places us in a position of responsibility to be sensitive to the Holy Spirit. Through His prompting, we will recognize a need and then, if we are open to being used, the Holy Spirit will release His gifts through us to touch those around us.

Thought for Today

Be sensitive and open to the Holy Spirit's desire to release His gifts in you so that the Body of Christ can be edified through you.

Prayer Journal

_____

_____

_____

~ ~ ~ NOVEMBER 11 ~ ~ ~

"Likewise the Spirit also helps in our weaknesses. For we do not know what we should pray for as we ought, but the Spirit Himself makes intercession for us with groanings which cannot be uttered. Now He who searches the hearts knows what the mind of the Spirit is, because He makes intercession for the saints according to the will of God" (Romans 8:26-27).

The Holy Spirit is anxious to get involved in every area of our lives in which we will let Him have access. Sometimes, we are confronted with circumstances that are so overwhelming to us, that we are at a total loss as to know how to approach God in prayer. This is when the Holy Spirit rushes to our aid and begins to intercede to the Father on our behalf. He knows the perfect will of God for every situation; thus, He knows how to lead us in prayer. Living in the fullness of the Holy Spirit releases His assistance in helping us to pray in power over situations we're not sure how to pray about. He brings His ability to strengthen our inability.

One of the assignments of the Holy Spirit is to make us like Jesus. He does this by growing the life of Christ within us, thereby reproducing the Lord's nature and character. We read in Galatians 5:22-23, *"But the fruit of the Spirit is love, joy, peace, longsuffering, kindness, goodness, faithfulness, gentleness, self-control. Against such there is no law."*

Thought for Today

Water is absolutely necessary to bring about the increase of fruit-bearing in agriculture. The same is true spiritually, as the overflow of the Holy Spirit's fullness will produce fruit in our character and conduct.

Prayer Journal

_____

_____

_____

~ ~ ~ NOVEMBER 12 ~ ~ ~

"Blessed are the undefiled in the way, who walk in the law of the Lord! Blessed are those who keep His testimonies, who seek Him with the whole heart! They also do no iniquity; they walk in His ways. You have commanded us to keep Your precepts diligently" (Psalms 119:1-4).

No one would deny the value of a proper diet and physical exercise in maintaining one's health. The challenge is not in the knowledge of its benefit rather, it is in the discipline of developing the habit. Spiritual health is derived in the same manner. It requires a proper diet of feeding on the Word, coupled with a daily discipline of exercising, or heeding the Word. Again, as with the physical, the challenge is not in the knowledge of its benefit, rather, it is in the discipline of developing the habit. This discipline requires more than mere inspiration—it demands an action of our wills, and a determination of our spirits.

A daily habit of reading the Word will ensure that we are certain about the path of our lives. In Psalms 119:6, we read, *"Then I would not be ashamed, when I look into all Your commandments."* The Word helps us avoid confusion and embarrassing mistakes in life. The Word will also give direction to the path our lives take. In Psalms 119:105, the Psalmist tells us, *"Your word is a lamp to my feet and a light to my path."* The Word gives direction to our immediate steps, as well as, reveals our future.

Thought for Today

The Word serves as a lamp to our feet, which gives us details for daily living. The Word also serves as a light to our paths, which grants us discernment for tomorrow.

Prayer Journal

_____

_____

_____

~ ~ ~ NOVEMBER 13 ~ ~ ~

"Trust in the Lord with all your heart, and lean not on your own understanding; in all your ways acknowledge Him, and He shall direct your paths" (Proverbs 3:5-6).

Making God's Word a daily priority will result in God charting a course for our lives. Our daily reading of the Word of God makes a statement to God; "Lord, Your Word is a foundational priority in all matters of my life." The Word of God imparts wisdom to us about our lives. In Psalms 19:7, we read, *"The law of the Lord is perfect, converting the soul; the testimony of the Lord is sure, making wise the simple."* The word *"simple"* is a reference to an inexperienced person and is not a slur referencing one's being stupid or ignorant. Actually, the verse promises that God will grant us wisdom in matters for which we have no knowledge, experience, or expertise.

Daily reading the Word places wisdom on deposit which the Holy Spirit will call to our remembrance when we are in need. Wisdom on deposit nourishes our spirits and provides for spiritual strength and wisdom. God's Word will also keep us pure in our path of life. *"How can a young man cleanse his way? By taking heed according to Your word. With my whole heart I have sought You; Oh, let me not wander from Your commandments! Your word I have hidden in my heart that I might not sin against You"* (Psalms 119:9-11)! The Word purifies our hearts and acts as a preventative against sin.

Thought for Today

The famous preacher D. L. Moody once remarked, "This holy book will keep you from sin, and sin will keep you from this holy book." These are true and wise words to heed.

Prayer Journal

_____

_____

_____

~ ~ ~ NOVEMBER 14 ~ ~ ~

"This Book of the Law shall not depart from your mouth, but you shall meditate in it day and night, that you may observe to do according to all that is written in it. For then you will make your way prosperous, and then you will have good success" (Joshua 1:8).

God intends for us to live in victory every single day of our lives. However, victory is not something that we can achieve in our own strength. The victory that God has purposed for us comes as a result of our adhering to the precepts and principles of His Word. Our victory is assured, if we are obedient to structure our lives according to the standards of the Word. Many Christians claim to live according to God's precepts, when in truth, they merely pay lip service to the Word. They assume that God will understand the reasons for their compromise and will also overlook their disobedience.

God promises us that His presence, His power, and His purposes, have always been linked to the precepts of His Word. In Colossians 3:16, we read Paul's admonition, *"Let the word of Christ dwell in you richly."* Paul also tells us that the Word will have a mighty impact on our lives and on the lives of those around us. In Colossians 1:29, we read, *"According to His working which works in me mightily."*

Thought for Today

The promise of our success will be realized on the same terms as in the life of Joshua. We are to keep the Word in our thoughts, in the meditations of our hearts, and on our lips. Most importantly, we are to let the Word work in us so we can impact the lives of others.

Prayer Journal

_____

_____

_____

~ ~ ~ NOVEMBER 15 ~ ~ ~

"Assuredly, I say to you, this generation will by no means pass away till all things take place. Heaven and earth will pass away, but My words will by no means pass away. But take heed to yourselves, lest your hearts be weighed down with carousing, drunkenness, and cares of this life, and that Day come on you unexpectedly. For it will come as a snare on all those who dwell on the face of the whole earth. Watch therefore, and pray always that you may be counted worthy to escape all these things that will come to pass, and to stand before the Son of Man" (Luke 21:32-36).

Our daily interaction with the Word of God will keep us sensitive to sin. The Word will keep us from falling asleep in indifference as the hour darkens, and the spirit of our age attempts to lull us into carnality and sensual indulgence. The Word helps us stay alert and ready for the return of Christ.

God's Word is also our shield as we read in Romans 10:17, *"So then faith comes by hearing, and hearing by the word of God."* Our faith is the fundamental means of resisting the devil and shielding our lives from his attacks. Our faith is formed and fashioned in only one way—our hearing the Word of God. We need to feed on the Word as a daily habit and then heed the Word as a sensitive hearer. The Word is the standard by which everything in life, both now and eternally, is gauged. As we commit to the Word, it becomes the foundation for every step we take in life.

Thought for Today

Make a commitment to read the Word every day as you find a time that best fits your schedule. As you read, ask the Holy Spirit to open your understanding.

Prayer Journal

_____

_____

_____

~ ~ ~ NOVEMBER 16 ~ ~ ~

"Therefore submit yourselves to every ordinance of man for the Lord's sake, whether to the king as supreme, or to governors, as to those who are sent by him for the punishment of evildoers and for the praise of those who do good. For this is the will of God, that by doing good you may put to silence the ignorance of foolish men—as free, yet not using liberty as a cloak for vice, but as bondservants of God" (I Peter 2:13-16).

The discipline of submission is one of the most difficult of all the Biblical mandates in a disciple's life. We have all heard horror stories of the abuse that surrounds the subject of submission. We have been told how the Scriptures have wrongly been applied in order to satisfy a desire to dominate another. For many, submission means to be under the dominating control of someone else, and it suggests the loss of one's right to think and act.

Submission, as taught in the Scriptures, is far removed from any notion that we must loose our identity and bow our will to the will of another. Submission is the mutual yielding to one another in the love of the Lord; whereby, we seek out each other's best interests. An alarming number of Christians, in an attempt to be exempted from abuse, have developed a "Lone Ranger" mentality. They boast, "I'll do whatever I want, because I'm free in Christ." Please understand that our freedom in Christ isn't a program of self-rule. Our freedom in Christ is meant to free us from practicing sin and from conforming to the world's value systems.

Thought for Today

Submission is not a "bad" word. Our freedom in Christ frees us from the death and decay of an independent spirit.

Prayer Journal

~ ~ ~ NOVEMBER 17 ~ ~ ~

"The centurion answered and said, 'Lord, I am not worthy that You should come under my roof. But only speak a word, and my servant will be healed. For I also am a man under authority, having soldiers under me. And I say to this one, 'Go,' and he goes; and to another, 'Come,' and he comes; and to my servant, 'Do this,' and he does it.' When Jesus heard it, He marveled, and said to those who followed, 'Assuredly, I say to you, I have not found such great faith, not even in Israel'" (Matthew 8:8-10)!

While the word "submission" isn't specifically mentioned in this passage, the concept of submission is portrayed. The centurion stated he was *"a man under authority"* and that he administered his authority according to a specific order. It was his understanding and acceptance of his role, which released the authority over others that he exercised. He recognized that his authority was not self-derived; rather, it was delegated through an appointed order.

The centurion spoke to Jesus and drew this analogy, "Just as I have military authority, You have spiritual authority—speak the word and it will be done." Jesus confirms the man's faith and commends his understanding. The centurion's servant was healed by a release of faith which was born out of his perspective on submission to authority in his life. We would be wise to ask the question, "What areas in our lives are waiting for healing and wholeness that could be dealt with if we were submitted like the centurion?"

Thought for Today

The centurion related to an order of authority over himself. We also must discipline ourselves to accept and respond to the divinely appointed points of order that are given to us by God.

Prayer Journal

_____

_____

_____

~ ~ ~ NOVEMBER 18 ~ ~ ~

"Giving thanks always for all things to God the Father in the name of our Lord Jesus Christ, submitting to one another in the fear of God" (Ephesians 5:20-21).

The word "submit," literally and culturally, is a term related to the military arrangement of troops and the chain of command; thus, the order of authority. In the military, the chain of command is not designed to reduce one's significance, while inflating the significance of another. However, the acceptance of authority will assist in effectively resisting and overthrowing the enemy.

The Bible clearly defines a God-ordained order for every facet of our lives: in the church, in the home, in the workplace, and in our marriages. Submission to God's arrangement and order is not to rank certain people above others, but it is to serve the interests of all. Through our submission, we can live in God's intended victory in every arena of our lives. Society interprets "submission," as subjugation and domination through tactics of intimidation. Cults use brainwashing techniques to gain control over the mind and ultimately, over the person. However, Scriptural submission can never be forced or required—only volunteered. Submission is always an inner attitude of the heart and is meaningless, if our hearts resent or resist it. If our hearts do not willingly submit to God's prescribed order, we will stop the release of God's power and blessings in our lives.

Thought for Today

Scriptural submission calls us to make a deep commitment to discover our place within God's order. We must yield to the Holy Spirit's teaching and flow in His order of authority to others.

Prayer Journal

_____

_____

_____

~ ~ ~ NOVEMBER 19 ~ ~ ~

"Wives, submit to your own husbands, as is fitting in the Lord. Husbands, love your wives and do not be bitter toward them. Children, obey your parents in all things, for this is well pleasing to the Lord" (Colossians 3:18-20).

Our application of submission will give evidence to the degree in which we are willing to live in a spirit of submission.

As a husband, how do you relate to your wife; as a servant, or as a tyrant? Are you a responsible leader, or an irresponsible child? As a wife, how do you relate to your husband; as a supporting partner, manifesting a unique strength and love; or as a nagging complainer and one jockeying for position and control? As a parent, how do you relate to your children; as a role model, serving their need for a picture of what they can become in Christ? Are you an "interested-in-you" parent who is caring, correcting, affirming, and disciplining when it is necessary? As an employee, how do you relate to your job, fellow workers, and your boss; as a trustworthy participant in your share of the task and as a dependable, on-time, "you can count on me" worker; or as a passive, disinterested, "only-as-much-as-I-gotta-do" pain to have around? As a Christian, how do you relate to your church family; as a supporting giver, an active servant, a right-spirited member, and a team player with the leadership? Or are you, an "I'll attend, but don't ask me to do anything," and "If I don't like something, I'll be sure to let you know" type of person?

Thought for Today

It is only by our willingness to learn, and then grow in a spirit of submission, that we will become all that we have been destined to be in Christ.

Prayer Journal

_____

_____

_____

~ ~ ~ NOVEMBER 20 ~ ~ ~

"But they did not receive Him, because His face was set for the journey to Jerusalem. And when His disciples James and John saw this, they said, 'Lord, do You want us to command fire to come down from heaven and consume them, just as Elijah did?' But He turned and rebuked them, and said, 'You do not know what manner of spirit you are of. For the Son of Man did not come to destroy men's lives but to save them.' And they went to another village" (Luke 9:53-36).

Sin is the result of a decision to reject one's place in God's order. Prior to being cast out of heaven for his rebellion against God, Lucifer attempted to exercise his will over the will of God as we read in Isaiah 14:14, *"I will ascend above the heights of the clouds, I will be like the Most High."* Sin is always the result of stepping out of God's prescribed order.

Jesus models for us how to live a submitted life, through His submitting Himself to people that misunderstood Him. He tirelessly gave Himself to help them understand His desire to touch them with His love and grace. When the Samaritans rejected the ministry of Jesus, James and John wanted to call down fire from heaven on them. Jesus rebuked them and let them know that such retribution was not His plan. Jesus wanted His disciples to know that they were of a different spirit. The spirit of His kingdom was not to exercise the power to prove spiritual superiorty, or to prove that you have all the right answers.

Thought for Today

The spirit of His kingdom is to exercise the power of love, which over time will bear the fruit of trust and responsiveness.

Prayer Journal

_____

_____

_____

~ ~ ~ NOVEMBER 21 ~ ~ ~

"So also Christ did not glorify Himself to become High Priest, but it was He who said to Him: 'You are My Son, today I have begotten You'" (Hebrews 5:5).

Jesus' submission, to the Father's will, resulted in His provision for the redemption of mankind. Jesus submitted to the Incarnation, as He laid down His rights as the Creator and King of the universe and submitted to being born in a lowly stable. Jesus submitted to being identified with mankind as we find in Matthew 3:13, *"Then Jesus came from Galilee to John at the Jordan to be baptized by him."* The on-lookers on the bank of the Sea of Galilee no doubt assumed that Jesus' submission to John's baptism was an act of repentance, for all the others John baptized, were baptized for repentance.

Jesus submitted to suffering in life. Hebrews 5:8 tells us, *"Though He was a Son, yet He learned obedience by the things which He suffered."* Again in Hebrews 12:3, we read, *"For consider Him who endured such hostility from sinners against Himself, lest you become weary and discouraged in your souls."* Jesus accepted rejection without retaliating; He accepted loneliness without whining; and He accepted being struck without striking back. Jesus also submitted to death, as found in Philippians 2:8, *"And being found in appearance as a man, He humbled Himself and became obedient to the point of death, even the death of the cross."* Jesus accepted the spearing of His body while praying, "Father forgive them, for they don't understand."

Thought for Today

The key to living a submitted life is to follow Jesus' example of praying, "Father, not My will, but Thine be done."

Prayer Journal

_____

_____

_____

~ ~ ~ NOVEMBER 22 ~ ~ ~

"Likewise you younger people, submit yourselves to your elders. Yes, all of you be submissive to one another, and be clothed with humility, for 'God resists the proud, but gives grace to the humble'" (I Peter 5:5).

The Bible clearly states that there is a God-ordained order for every facet of our lives and that no one is permitted to stand in a spirit of independence. The submitted disciple learns that there is a tactical advantage and a mutual protection through committed involvement within a church family. This commitment includes service to the church family, as well as, acceptance of one's accountability to the church family.

We are to be submitted unto God, the Father. In Hebrews 12:5-9 we read, *"And you have forgotten the exhortation which speaks to you as to sons: 'My son, do not despise the chastening of the Lord, nor be discouraged when you are rebuked by Him; For whom the Lord loves He chastens, and scourges every son whom He receives.' If you endure chastening, God deals with you as with sons; for what son is there whom a father does not chasten? But if you are without chastening, of which all have become partakers, then you are illegitimate and not sons. Furthermore, we have had human fathers who corrected us, and we paid them respect. Shall we not much more readily be in subjection to the Father of spirits and live?"* The proof of God's love for us, as our Father, is seen in His loving correction.

Thought for Today

The Father disciplines us not to destroy us, but to release us through our obedience into the fullness of His purposes.

Prayer Journal

_____

_____

_____

~ ~ ~ NOVEMBER 23 ~ ~ ~

"Most assuredly, I say to you, he who believes in Me, the works that I do he will do also; and greater works than these he will do, because I go to My Father" (John 14:12).

Jesus encourages our expectation for fullness in our spiritual lives and ministries. Being able to flow in the quality of Jesus' ministry requires the quality of Jesus' submission to the Father's will. Long before Jesus became the "Great Shepherd," He submitted to being the "Lamb of God." We will never know the fullness of our life and ministry until we learn to live with a spirit of submission to God.

The spirit of submission is not cowardly. The Holy Spirit will not produce passive and insensitive people who submit to anything. We are not to submit to Satan, as found in I Peter 5:8-9, *"Be sober, be vigilant; because your adversary the devil walks about like a roaring lion, seeking whom he may devour. Resist him, steadfast in the faith, knowing that the same sufferings are experienced by your brotherhood in the world."* I Corinthians 9:27 tells us we are not to submit to our flesh, *"But I discipline my body and bring it into subjection, lest, when I have preached to others, I myself should become disqualified."* Paul tells us in Galatians 2:4-5 that we are not to submit to legalism; *"This occurred because of false brethren secretly brought in (who came in by stealth to spy out our liberty which we have in Christ Jesus, that they might bring us into bondage), to whom we did not yield submission even for an hour, that the truth of the gospel might continue with you."*

Thought for Today

Living a submitted life does not mean that we are to be mindless robots. Quite the contrary, we are to live a life of expectancy.

Prayer Journal

~ ~ ~ NOVEMBER 24 ~ ~ ~

"Now I plead with you, brethren, by the name of our Lord Jesus Christ, that you all speak the same thing, and that there be no divisions among you, but that you be perfectly joined together in the same mind and in the same judgment. For it has been declared to me concerning you, by those of Chloe's household, that there are contentions among you. Now I say this, that each of you says, 'I am of Paul,' or 'I am of Apollos,' or 'I am of Cephas,' or 'I am of Christ.' Is Christ divided? Was Paul crucified for you? Or were you baptized in the name of Paul" (I Corinthians 1:10-13)?

The religious ads in most newspapers are like reading the entertainment section as churches promote their programs. A great deal of advertising is consumed trying to convince people that "our church" is better than "your church." The result is that churches end up trading members until something bigger and more exciting comes to town. Some misguided Christians actually believe that their church is better than all other churches in town, causing them to operate in a spirit of spiritual superiority. How confusing this must be to the unsaved in our community as they see fighting among the Christian community, however civil it may appear to be.

The only reason we should separate is if a church preaches another way to salvation other than through the Cross. We must stop criticizing differences in our methods and seek to strengthen each other. We must unify around the common goal of reaching the lost.

Thought for Today

The spirit of submission is never competitive and always seeks to bring out the best in another. We are one family—united in Jesus Christ.

Prayer Journal

_____

_____

_____

~ ~ ~ NOVEMBER 25 ~ ~ ~

"For since the creation of the world His invisible attributes are clearly seen, being understood by the things that are made, even His eternal power and Godhead, so that they are without excuse, because, although they knew God, they did not glorify Him as God, nor were thankful, but became futile in their thoughts, and their foolish hearts were darkened. Professing to be wise, they became fools" (Romans 1:20-22).

Thankfulness is a trait that is generally not found among mankind. Failure to give the Lord thanks for His abundant provision and faithfulness is one of our greatest failures. One of the first virtues that we teach our children is to say "thank you." We know that if our children do not learn to be grateful when something is given to them, or done for them, they will develop the warped view of life that everything is owed to them. Ungratefulness hardens the heart.

A grateful heart can be developed by realizing that God is good all of the time and that He is deserving of our thanks. In Psalms 106:1, we read, *"Praise the Lord! Oh, give thanks to the Lord, for He is good! For His mercy endures forever."* Thanksgiving is the gateway into His presence. Psalms 100:4 instructs us, *"Enter into His gates with thanksgiving, and into His courts with praise. Be thankful to Him, and bless His name."* David assumed that the family of God would live before the Lord with grateful hearts. David states in Psalms 140:13, *"Surely the righteous shall give thanks to Your name; the upright shall dwell in Your presence."*

Thought for Today

God has been faithful to you even when you have not been faithful to Him. Live in an attitude of gratefulness.

Prayer Journal

_____

_____

_____

~ ~ ~ NOVEMBER 26 ~ ~ ~

"Bless the Lord, O my soul; and all that is within me, bless His holy name! Bless the Lord, O my soul, and forget not all His benefits: Who forgives all your iniquities, Who heals all your diseases, Who redeems your life from destruction, Who crowns you with lovingkindness and tender mercies, Who satisfies your mouth with good things, so that your youth is renewed like the eagle's. The Lord executes righteousness and justice for all who are oppressed. He made known His ways to Moses, His acts to the children of Israel. The Lord is merciful and gracious, slow to anger, and abounding in mercy" (Psalms 103:1-8).

One sure way to develop a grateful heart is to stop and count the Lord's blessings. He has loaded our lives with His benefits. He forgives our sins, no matter what we have done. He heals our sicknesses, regardless of the disease. He redeems our lives from destruction and crowns us with His lovingkindness and mercy. He satisfies the longings of our hearts and renews our strength. He defends us and sets us free from the enemy's oppression.

We are truly a blessed people. Therefore, we need to offer the Lord the sincere gratitude of our hearts every day. The devil wants us to become so focused on our needs, that we cannot see God's faithfulness and goodness. He knows that if he can change our focus from seeing the goodness of God, he can also stop our praise and thanksgiving to God. Ungratefulness opens us to defeat.

Thought for Today

Take time today to list the blessings of God in your life. Thank Him for being so good to you. Thank Him for His faithfulness to meet your every need, just as He promised.

Prayer Journal

_____

_____

_____

~ ~ ~ NOVEMBER 27 ~ ~ ~

"Through the Lord's mercies we are not consumed, because His compassions fail not. They are new every morning; great is Your faithfulness. 'The Lord is my portion,' says my soul, 'Therefore I hope in Him!' The Lord is good to those who wait for Him, to the soul who seeks Him. It is good that one should hope and wait quietly for the salvation of the Lord" (Lamentations 3:22-26).

With the dawning of each new day, the Lord renews His commitment to demonstrate His faithfulness to us. The Lord is ever compassionate towards us, and through His mercy, He delivers us from every snare that the devil has set for us. It is the faithfulness of God that secures our hope in His love, in His mercy, and in His ability to save us. If the Lord were not faithful to us, our hope would be destroyed and our hearts would grow sick with grief. In Proverbs 13:12, we read, *"Hope deferred makes the heart sick, but when the desire comes, it is a tree of life."* When the trials of life assail us, we can rest assured the Lord will not fail us in our time of need. Regardless of how long it takes for the Lord's hand to manifest, we know that He will answer our cry for help.

God is faithful to us, because He is faithful to keep the promises of His Word. In Ezekiel 12:25, we are promised, *"'For I am the Lord. I speak, and the word which I speak will come to pass; it will no more be postponed; for in your days, O rebellious house, I will say the word and perform it,' says the Lord God."*

Thought for Today

Anchor your life to the Word of God. You must never forget that God is faithful to keep His promises to you. *"The Lord is good to those who wait for Him."*

Prayer Journal

_____

_____

_____

~ ~ ~ NOVEMBER 28 ~ ~ ~

"If his sons forsake My law and do not walk in My judgments, if they break My statutes and do not keep My commandments, then I will punish their transgression with the rod, and their iniquity with stripes. Nevertheless My lovingkindness I will not utterly take from him, nor allow My faithfulness to fail. My covenant I will not break, nor alter the word that has gone out of My lips. Once I have sworn by My holiness; I will not lie to David: His seed shall endure forever, and his throne as the sun before Me; It shall be established forever like the moon, even like the faithful witness in the sky" (Psalms 89:30-37).

God made a promise to David that his seed would endure forever, and that his throne would not pass away or be given to another. God is fiercely protective of His Word. Circumstances do not alter the promises of God. If the descendants of David proved to be unfaithful to God, God promised that He would remain faithful to them. God declared that once He has spoken and made covenant with someone, that He would not go back on His Word and what He had promised. God also declared that He would not lie to David. God said what He meant and nothing will ever change it.

What great hope and assurance this gives us. God is not moved by our circumstances and He will not alter His promises to us to suit the situation. We can know that every promise God has made to us will be kept, no matter what. There has never been a circumstance that would cause God to fail in keeping His Word.

Thought for Today

We have all been unfaithful to God; however, God promises that our unfaithfulness to Him will not change His faithfulness to us.

Prayer Journal

_____

_____

_____

~ ~ ~ NOVEMBER 29 ~ ~ ~

"Rejoice always, pray without ceasing, in everything give thanks; for this is the will of God in Christ Jesus for you" (I Thessalonians 5:16-18).

Paul instructs us to give the Lord thanks in the midst of everything. This verse has often been misinterpreted to mean that we are to be thankful for everything that comes into our lives. That would mean we would have to assume that everything that happens is the will of God for us. In other words, if we are sick, we are to thank God for the sickness; or if we can't pay our bills, we are to thank God that we are broke. Nothing could be further from the truth. God is not the author of our problems—He is the solution.

Paul is telling us that no matter what may come our way we are to thank God in the midst of it. What are we to thank God for? We are to thank God, that even though we are sick, He is our healer. We are to be thankful that He will never leave us nor forsake us. We are to be thankful that nothing can separate us from His love.

Dr. Alexander Whyte was a pastor known for always finding something to give thanks for in his prayers. One Sunday, his church members thought he would fail to find something on such a stormy day for which to give thanks. Dr Whyte started his prayer with, "I thank Thee Lord that it is not always like this." We can give thanks to God, because He is in the midst of everything with us.

Thought for Today

We must decide not to dwell on our problems. We need to remain thankful to God in the midst of our trials which will cause us to shift our focus towards God, and His promise to deliver us.

Prayer Journal

_____

_____

_____

~ ~ ~ NOVEMBER 30 ~ ~ ~

"Then as He entered a certain village, there met Him ten men who were lepers, who stood afar off. And they lifted up their voices and said, 'Jesus, Master, have mercy on us!' So when He saw them, He said to them, 'Go, show yourselves to the priests.' And so it was that as they went, they were cleansed. And one of them, when he saw that he was healed, returned, and with a loud voice glorified God, and fell down on his face at His feet, giving Him thanks. And he was a Samaritan. So Jesus answered and said, 'Were there not ten cleansed? But where are the nine? Were there not any found who returned to give glory to God except this foreigner'" (Luke 17:12-18).

The reputation of Jesus' ability to heal the sick had spread to this small village. Ten men, suffering from the dreaded disease of leprosy, had lost everything. They had lost their families, their friends, their businesses, and their places in the community. The news reached them that Jesus, Who had healed others, was passing through their village. As Jesus passed by, they cried out for His mercy and He heard their cry for help. Jesus healed them of their disease and sent them to the priest to be declared clean and restored to society. All ten were healed, but only one came back to Jesus to say "thank you." The other nine were absent and Jesus noticed.

We get upset with the other nine lepers and accuse them of blatant ingratitude. Before we take a vote to stone them, we need to check our record of giving thanks to God for what He has done. If we are honest, we will recognize we also have been guilty.

Thought for Today

Do not take God's blessings for granted—offer Him your gratitude.

Prayer Journal

_____

_____

_____

~ ~ ~ DECEMBER 1 ~ ~ ~

"Be anxious for nothing, but in everything by prayer and supplication, with thanksgiving, let your requests be made known to God; and the peace of God, which surpasses all understanding, will guard your hearts and minds through Christ Jesus" (Philippians 4:6-7).

Many Christians remind me of the over-indulged child at Christmas, who after ripping his last package open loudly exclaims, "Is that all?" God has been so good to us, that many are spoiled and as a result, they are unthankful. Being thankful is not automatic—it is a choice that we make. A close examination of the Scriptures will reveal that our thanksgiving is to precede our petitions. We read in Psalms 100:4 *"Enter into His gates with thanksgiving, and into His courts with praise. Be thankful to Him, and bless His name."* We are to come before His presence with our offerings of thanksgiving and then, after blessing His name, we are to present Him with our petitions.

Paul tells us that we are to balance our petitions with giving thanks. Every prayer that we pray is to be tempered with our thanksgiving. The fruit of such balance in prayer is the manifestation of God's peace, giving rest to our hearts and minds. The greatest miracles that Jesus performed were accomplished as a result of His giving thanks to God the Father, rather than just petitioning Him.

Thought for Today

There is a level of spiritual maturity that comes when we believe God's promises implicitly; this allows us to rest in the knowledge that God has foreseen our need. We can then spend our energies "thanking Him" for His provision and for His faithfulness.

Prayer Journal

_____

_____

_____

~ ~ ~ DECEMBER 2 ~ ~ ~

"For I received from the Lord that which I also delivered to you: that the Lord Jesus on the same night in which He was betrayed took bread; and when He had given thanks, He broke it and said, 'Take, eat; this is My body which is broken for you; do this in remembrance of Me.' In the same manner He also took the cup after supper, saying, 'This cup is the new covenant in My blood. This do, as often as you drink it, in remembrance of Me.' For as often as you eat this bread and drink this cup, you proclaim the Lord's death till He comes" (I Corinthians 11:23-26).

On the night that Jesus instituted the Lord's Supper, He told His disciples that they were to observe communion in remembrance of Him. What was it that Jesus wanted us to remember? Jesus wanted us to remember that we are to acknowledge, that through the Cross, His perfect work of salvation was made complete. Through the Cross, we have been given full justification. Justification not only renders us as forgiven, but in God's eyes, we will be regarded as "never-having-sinned" at all.

Through the Cross we are vested with full dominion over all the powers of hell. This dominion will render every bondage of the soul and the spirit to be broken, and will bring us deliverance from every hellish affliction. Through the Cross, we are granted full availability to the Lord's healing touch in every dimension of our person.

Thought for Today

The Cross supplies us with the release of God's love poured forth by His Spirit to fill our souls with peace. The Cross also brings reconciled peace and restored unity to strained human relationships.

Prayer Journal

~ ~ ~ DECEMBER 3 ~ ~ ~

"But the angel said to him, 'Do not be afraid, Zacharias, for your prayer is heard; and your wife Elizabeth will bear you a son, and you shall call his name John. And you will have joy and gladness, and many will rejoice at his birth. For he will be great in the sight of the Lord, and shall drink neither wine nor strong drink. He will also be filled with the Holy Spirit, even from his mother's womb. And he will turn many of the children of Israel to the Lord their God. He will also go before Him in the spirit and power of Elijah, to turn the hearts of the fathers to the children, and the disobedient to the wisdom of the just, to make ready a people prepared for the Lord" (Luke 1:13-17).

A priest by the name of Zacharias, and his wife Elizabeth, received a prophetic word from God, breaking a four-hundred-year period of silence. Zacharias and Elizabeth were faithful to serve God in spite of the fact that their most pressing need had not been met by God. They continued to walk with God, even though there was no evidence that their prayers were heard. They were not sure God noticed their service, or if He was present with them at all times.

The angel Gabriel slipped through the shroud of silence and announced to Zacharias God's re-entry into human affairs. Gabriel told Zacharias that God had heard his prayers and He was going to give them the son they had prayed for. He announced that their son would be a source of joy to them because he would have a heart to serve God, and that God would use him mightily.

Thought for Today

Elizabeth became pregnant, as promised. Answered prayer will silence critics. Don't defend yourself—let God be your defense.

Prayer Journal

_____

_____

_____

~ ~ ~ DECEMBER 4 ~ ~ ~

"And it happened, when Elizabeth heard the greeting of Mary, that the babe leaped in her womb; and Elizabeth was filled with the Holy Spirit. Then she spoke out with a loud voice and said, 'Blessed are you among women, and blessed is the fruit of your womb! But why is this granted to me, that the mother of my Lord should come to me? For indeed, as soon as the voice of your greeting sounded in my ears, the babe leaped in my womb for joy'" (Luke 1:41-44).

Just as the angel Gabriel had visited her cousin Elizabeth to announce her miraculous pregnancy, so Gabriel had visited Mary with similar news. Mary, now also miraculously pregnant, went to share in Elizabeth's good news and to share some news of her own. The moment Elizabeth heard Mary's greeting, she was filled with spiritual discernment, as *"the baby leaped in her womb and Elizabeth was filled with the Holy Spirit."* Elizabeth not only blessed Mary, but the child that was in her womb as well. Elizabeth knew there was power in the house and she was filled with praise.

Elizabeth declared the Lordship of Jesus in referencing Mary as the *"mother of my Lord."* As we declare His Lordship, His power will transform our circumstances to His Word. Elizabeth's baby, John, also responded with joy to the presence of Jesus. John's response is proof that there is always room for expressions of joy, regardless of how dark and restrictive our circumstances have become.

Thought for Today

Even though you may be in a time where there seems to not be any answers—never let your circumstances shut out the penetrating presence and promises of our Lord.

Prayer Journal

_____

_____

_____

~ ~ ~ DECEMBER 5 ~ ~ ~

"And behold, there was a man in Jerusalem whose name was Simeon, and this man was just and devout, waiting for the Consolation of Israel, and the Holy Spirit was upon him. And it had been revealed to him by the Holy Spirit that he would not see death before he had seen the Lord's Christ. So he came by the Spirit into the temple. And when the parents brought in the Child Jesus, to do for Him according to the custom of the law, he took Him up in his arms and blessed God and said: 'Lord, now You are letting Your servant depart in peace, according to Your word; For my eyes have seen Your salvation'" (Luke 2:25-30).

When Simeon, the old prophet, claimed that God had promised him *"that he would not see death before he had seen the Lord's Christ,"* most people just rolled their eyes and walked away. Then one day, the Holy Spirit led him to the Temple just as Mary and Joseph were coming in to present Jesus according to the requirements of the Law. The presence of Jesus gave Simeon the gift of peace to face his approaching death. Simeon realized that in holding the "Prince of Peace" in his arms, that in reality, the "Prince of Peace" was holding him.

Anna was also in the Temple that day when Jesus arrived with Mary and Joseph. Anna was a dedicated prayer warrior, who never left her post. The presence of Jesus released in her a renewed compassion for people and the courage to share her faith in God.

Thought for Today

The presence of Jesus will always give us peace in the face of an uncertain future. His presence will also renew in us a compassion for others.

Prayer Journal

_____

_____

_____

~ ~ ~ DECEMBER 6 ~ ~ ~

"Behold, the virgin shall be with child, and bear a Son, and they shall call His name Immanuel, which is translated, 'God with us'" (Matthew 1:23).

The Christmas story actually begins on a wordless page—the dividing page between the Old and New Testaments. This page is the break between "Law and Grace." This page also represents four hundred years of prophetic silence in regards to God's next move into the affairs of humanity. One has to wonder if God ever became exasperated with the fallen kings and false prophets of the Old Testament, to the point that He was growing weary of His pledge to redeem Adam's fallen family. In the midst of great unfaithfulness to God, there were some who remained faithful and devout. People like Zacharias and Elizabeth, Joseph and Mary, and Simeon and Anna. All of these people remained faithful to God in spite of the long spiritual drought.

Submitting to Caesar's census, Joseph and Mary came to Bethlehem where she gave birth in a stable. As instructed by the angel Gabriel, they named the baby "Jesus" and called Him *"'Immanuel,' which is translated, 'God with us.'"* The Messiah was no longer a prophetic promise—He was a living reality. Sometimes we tend to grow weary of waiting on God to fulfill His promises to us. In our weariness, if we are not careful, we will let our faithfulness to the Lord suffer. God has never failed to keep His Word of promise to anyone.

Thought for Today

In the fullness of God's time, deliverance came. Within Mary's womb, God built the bridge of redemption, one cell at a time.

Prayer Journal

_____

_____

_____

~ ~ ~ DECEMBER 7 ~ ~ ~

"Then Herod, when he saw that he was deceived by the wise men, was exceedingly angry; and he sent forth and put to death all the male children who were in Bethlehem and in all its districts, from two years old and under, according to the time which he had determined from the wise men. Then was fulfilled what was spoken by Jeremiah the prophet, saying: 'A voice was heard in Ramah, lamentation, weeping, and great mourning, Rachel weeping for her children, refusing to be comforted, because they are no more'" (Matthew 2:16-18).

King Herod, twisted with an evil heart, had requested that the wise men return after they had visited this supposed new infant king. They were to inform him of the baby's whereabouts, so that he might show his respect. Warned by God, the wise men returned home another way leaving Herod very angry. The darkest chapter in the Christmas story took place as Herod, in a sweeping decision to get rid of this infant king, ordered his soldiers to march through Bethlehem's nursery and murder all baby boys under two.

Joseph and Mary were warned by God in a dream to flee to Egypt in order to escape Herod. It is an irony that God chose to hide His Son in Egypt, for Egypt was where Pharaoh had murdered baby boys in an attempt to kill Moses—God's chosen deliverer in the Old Testament. In Bethlehem, weeping filled the air, while in heaven there was great rejoicing over heaven's newest residents.

Thought for Today

Satan's plan did not work—Jesus, our Deliverer, was kept safe in Egypt. God will always keep His promises and then He will protect the promises He has kept.

Prayer Journal

_____

_____

_____

~ ~ ~ DECEMBER 8 ~ ~ ~

"Now in the sixth month the angel Gabriel was sent by God to a city of Galilee named Nazareth, to a virgin betrothed to a man whose name was Joseph, of the house of David. The virgin's name was Mary. And having come in, the angel said to her, 'Rejoice, highly favored one, the Lord is with you; blessed are you among women'" (Luke 1:26-28).

Throughout history, God has used various forms of communication to deliver His messages of love and hope. One of the ways God has spoken to mankind in the past was through angels. Today, we live in a society that has a tremendous fascination with angels. In the Scriptures, messages from angels always revealed the loving purposes of God, His living promises, and His transforming power. Gabriel delivered God's plan and purpose to the young virgin, Mary. She was fearful at first, but as Gabriel unfolded the plan of God to her, Mary's heart was filled with hope and promise.

Salvation involves two desires of God. First, He desires to live within us, and secondly, He desires to extend His life and kingdom through us. Knowing these two desires of God, many Christians have made the mistake in thinking that they can fulfill God's desires through their trying harder, or being more disciplined in their walk. The efforts of our flesh will never please God.

Thought for Today

We must allow the life of Christ to be formed in us and then, through the power of the Holy Spirit, let His life be delivered through us to others. When this happens, we find victory over habitual sins; we find love that drives out our fears; and we find God's provision for all of our needs.

Prayer Journal

~ ~ ~ DECEMBER 9 ~ ~ ~

"For whatever things were written before were written for our learning, that we through the patience and comfort of the Scriptures might have hope" (Romans 15:4).

God used various ways to communicate in the Old Testament. Today, He speaks to us through Jesus, through the ministry of the Holy Spirit. The Holy Spirit communicates in various modes, but predominately speaks through the Word. We would be wise to understand that the messages that were spoken to the people by God are also written for us. Consider some of the angels' messages given in the Bible.

Angels came to Abraham and Sarah to announce that the child they had desired would be born just as God had promised. The message to us is that God still desires to fulfill our deepest longings. In Psalms 37:4, we read, *"Delight yourself also in the Lord, and He shall give you the desires of your heart."* Angels appeared to Jacob, ascending and descending on a ladder reaching into heaven, and he received God's promise about his future. The message to us is that God still desires to lead us into the fullness of His purpose. The Angel of the Lord (Jesus) joins the three Hebrew children in the fiery furnace and brings deliverance while vindicating their cause. The message to us is that God still desires to bring us through life's trials and vindicate our stance of faith. An angel led Peter out of King Herod's innermost prison to freedom. The message to us is that God still desires to set us free from all of life's prisons.

Thought for Today

God desires for us to live within His purposes. What the angels spoke to men of old can still be embraced as relevant to us.

Prayer Journal

_____

_____

_____

~ ~ ~ DECEMBER 10 ~ ~ ~

"He will be great, and will be called the Son of the Highest; and the Lord God will give Him the throne of His father David. And He will reign over the house of Jacob forever, and of His kingdom there will be no end" (Luke 1:32-33).

The angel Gabriel's message to Mary contains God's message, which is full of promise to us today. Gabriel said that, *"He will be great."* The message and promise to us is that Christ in us will meet and exceed all of our expectations. He will satisfy our deepest longings in life. In Ephesians 3:20, we read, *"Now to Him who is able to do exceedingly abundantly above all that we ask or think, according to the power that works in us."* Gabriel also said that, *"The Lord God will give Him the throne."* The message and promise to us is that Jesus' presence in our lives will release His power to rule over all that opposes us. II Corinthians 2:14, tells us, *"Now thanks be to God who always leads us in triumph in Christ."*

Gabriel said to Mary *"of His kingdom."* The message and promise to us is that His kingdom is manifested as His ruling grace that expels whatever seeks to defeat or discourage us. Isaiah 54:17 promises us, *"No weapon formed against you shall prosper, and every tongue which rises against you in judgment you shall condemn. This is the heritage of the servants of the Lord, and their righteousness is from Me."* Speaking of Christ's kingdom, Gabriel said *"there shall be no end."* The message and promise to us is that Jesus has come to abide within our hearts forever.

Thought for Today

When our physical life is over, Jesus will escort us into His heavenly home which He has personally prepared for us.

Prayer Journal

_____

_____

_____

~ ~ ~ DECEMBER 11 ~ ~ ~

"And having come in, the angel said to her, 'Rejoice, highly favored one, the Lord is with you; blessed are you among women!' But when she saw him, she was troubled at his saying, and considered what manner of greeting this was" (Luke 1:28-29).

The process of life can be summed up in two words: conception and delivery. Conception and delivery involve the receiving of a seed that, at the time of delivery, brings forth life and fruitfulness. This is true whether we are speaking of a baby or an idea. Our understanding of Mary's miracle is vital to our grasping the processes of life. Through Mary's miracle, we can understand how we can break through the limitations of our circumstances. We can partner with God when we open ourselves to His creative power and to His redemptive grace.

God created everyone with a hunger for living life with meaning. A meaningless life is a powerless life. Without meaning, we are powerless to change our negative circumstances. Without meaning in our lives, we are powerless to deal effectively with our frustrations and to overcome our failures. Mary's miracle unveils the pattern by which we can be freed from the trap of a meaningless and powerless life. The first step in filling our lives with meaning and power is to be open to God's redemptive possibilities in every area of our lives.

Thought for Today

We all crave significance. However, in and of ourselves, we will never know the significance that God has intended and purposed for us to enjoy. Ask God what He has purposed for your life—even before the foundation of the world.

Prayer Journal

_____

_____

_____

~ ~ ~ DECEMBER 12 ~ ~ ~

"Then Mary said to the angel, 'How can this be, since I do not know a man?' And the angel answered and said to her, 'The Holy Spirit will come upon you, and the power of the Highest will overshadow you; therefore, also, that Holy One who is to be born will be called the Son of God'" (Luke 1:34-35).

Mary's immediate response to the angel Gabriel's announcement to her was the question, "How can this be? I haven't had a physical relationship with a man, which makes this impossible to be true." We can relate to Mary's concern and question, for we also respond in much the same way she did when we are confronted with God's desire to do a redemptive work in our lives. We often say, "Lord, how can this be, it's not humanly possible." Gabriel's answer to Mary unveils the answer to all of life's dilemmas, "This will be a creative work of the Holy Spirit and not a work of yours." The same Holy Spirit, Who brought life and order out of emptiness, chaos, and darkness, wants to move into the emptiness, chaos, and darkness of our lives and bring forth His life of redemption.

Gabriel said that to accomplish this redemptive work, the Holy Spirit would *"come upon her."* The term *"come upon"* means that a greater power will overcome a weaker vessel. Gabriel also used the term *"overshadow"* to describe the work of the Holy Spirit. This term indicates the spreading of wings and is symbolic of the "aboveness and mightiness" of God.

Thought for Today

God spoke His desire to Mary and the Holy Spirit administered His power to fulfill that Word. When God speaks His desire over your life, will you allow the Holy Spirit to create a life-change in you?

Prayer Journal

_____

_____

_____

~ ~ ~ DECEMBER 13 ~ ~ ~

"For unto us a Child is born, unto us a Son is given; and the government will be upon His shoulder. And His name will be called Wonderful, Counselor, Mighty God, Everlasting Father, Prince of Peace. Of the increase of His government and peace there will be no end, upon the throne of David and over His kingdom, to order it and establish it with judgment and justice from that time forward, even forever. The zeal of the Lord of hosts will perform this" (Isaiah 9:6-7).

There is an order to God's redemptive plan. The first point of order is to receive the Holy Spirit. In John 20:22, we read, *"And when He had said this, He breathed on them, and said to them, 'Receive the Holy Spirit.'"* Our receiving the Holy Spirit requires our being open before Him. The second point of order is to receive the Holy Spirit's power. In receiving the Holy Spirit, we have access to His unlimited power, but we must open our lives to Him so that He can release His power through us. In Acts 1:8 Jesus promised, *"But you shall receive power when the Holy Spirit has come upon you; and you shall be witnesses to Me in Jerusalem, and in all Judea and Samaria, and to the end of the earth."* The third point of order is to receive the love of the Holy Spirit. We are to be filled with His love, which becomes the motivator for our service to the Lord. In Romans 5:5 we are reminded, *"Now hope does not disappoint, because the love of God has been poured out in our hearts by the Holy Spirit who was given to us."*

Thought for Today

Regardless of how dark our circumstances may be, God's Word declares His plan for us and the Holy Spirit administers the power that brings the fulfillment of His Word to our lives.

Prayer Journal

_____

_____

_____

~ ~ ~ DECEMBER 14 ~ ~ ~

"Then Mary said, 'Behold the maidservant of the Lord! Let it be to me according to your word.' And the angel departed from her" (Luke 1:38).

Gabriel's announcement to Mary was filled with great promise. However, Mary's response was crucial to the fulfillment of Gabriel's announcement. Mary humbly consented in two very important areas. First, she had to consent to the expressed will of God and to His promise. Secondly, she would be required to consent to God's terms of fulfillment.

We must also consent to the same two areas in order to receive anything from God. We must consent to God's expressed will and promise for our lives as declared in His Word, whether or not we understand what is transpiring in our life. We also must consent to God's terms for fulfillment of His plan. We want all of God's promises to be fulfilled in our lives, but at times we are not agreeable to the terms Hes has established. We want to know the details of His plan for our lives, but we don't want to discipline ourselves to pray. We want the Lord to bless us financially, but we don't want to tithe. We want the Lord to bless all of our endeavors, but we do not want to be held accountable for our actions or our attitudes. Nothing will ever change in our lives until we completely surrender to His terms.

Thought for Today

Our surrender is evidenced by our obedience to the Word of God. In order for God to perfect that which concerns us, we must be willing to relinquish the control of every area of our life so that He can do His perfect work in us.

Prayer Journal

_____

_____

_____

~ ~ ~ DECEMBER 15 ~ ~ ~

"And Mary said: 'My soul magnifies the Lord, And my spirit has rejoiced in God my Savior. For He has regarded the lowly state of His maidservant; for behold, henceforth all generations will call me blessed. For He who is mighty has done great things for me, and holy is His name. And His mercy is on those who fear Him from generation to generation. He has shown strength with His arm; He has scattered the proud in the imagination of their hearts. He has put down the mighty from their thrones, and exalted the lowly. He has filled the hungry with good things, and the rich He has sent away empty. He has helped His servant Israel, in remembrance of His mercy, as He spoke to our fathers, to Abraham and to his seed forever'" (Luke 1:46-55).

Pregnancy is the ultimate analogy for everything in life. Everything starts with a seed of possibility and proceeds to a living reality. The process of conception, to the time of delivery, is God's operational order of doing things. The most incredible and important pregnancy in all of history was Mary's. Out of the dusty and drab town of Nazareth, God brought forth His life through a virgin named Mary.

This holds great promise for us, for it proves that God is willing to bring His life into the most barren of settings. Every area in which the devil has attempted to dry up our hope of recovery, the Lord desires to step in and bring us to completeness through releasing His life in us. In bringing His life into our barrenness, He breathes hope into the most unpromising situations that we face.

Thought for Today

Mary's miracle unlocks the truth that Jesus has come to birth His miracles in us. God desires for us to be open to His creative work.

Prayer Journal

_____

_____

_____

~ ~ ~ DECEMBER 16 ~ ~ ~

"And Mary said: 'My soul magnifies the Lord, and my spirit has rejoiced in God my Savior. For He has regarded the lowly state of His maidservant; for behold, henceforth all generations will call me blessed. For He who is mighty has done great things for me, and holy is His name'" (Luke 1:46-49).

Mary's first response to Gabriel's announcement was one of disbelief. She simply could not understand how such a thing could be possible, since she had never been intimate with a man. Gabriel's response to Mary was that while this may be impossible in the human realm, it was not impossible for God. God desires to do great and mighty things in our lives; yet, like Mary, we often close the door to God's promises because of unbelief. We simply cannot see some things working out as we have deemed them to be impossible in human terms, or improbable, at best.

God still wants to work the "Mary-kind" of miracle in people today. He wants to pour His promises and power into the most unlikely people and do so, in the most unlikely of places. Anyone who has lost their love, their hope, their faith, and their strength, is a candidate for God's miracle intervention. God wants to intervene into every arena of our lives, including our marriages, our families, our businesses and our relationships. His intervention will release His abundant life, His hope, and His power, which will bring about the necessary changes we believe Him for.

Thought for Today

What God did in the physical and biological realm, He still wants to do spiritually in every area of our lives. He created life, hope, and promise, where none existed before.

Prayer Journal

_____

_____

_____

~ ~ ~ DECEMBER 17 ~ ~ ~

"Then Peter opened his mouth and said: 'In truth I perceive that God shows no partiality. But in every nation whoever fears Him and works righteousness is accepted by Him'" (Acts 10:34-35).

God desires to do in us spiritually, what He did biologically within Mary; however, most Christians do not feel qualified for such interaction with God. One problem is that many do not believe that God is available to them on a personal level. They believe that God sort of watches out for the big picture, but not for the intimate details of their lives. They believe that miracles only happen to the "Saint Mary's" of our world, and even if there is more than one "Saint Mary," they are sure it is not them and that they do not qualify for the miracles of God.

A visitation from God doesn't require some kind of self-accomplished goodness on our parts. A visitation from God only requires that we are open before the Lord. In Mary's miracle, heaven penetrated the earth with a power Who can change lives—past, present, and future. A young Jewish virgin was met with God's divine grace, resulting in the Incarnation of the world's Savior. Mary's miracle presents the possibilities that God will incarnate His purpose and power into anyone who will open themselves to Him, as Mary did. Mary's miracle was never intended to be Mary's alone. It establishes the pattern for all of God's promises and possibilities to be realized in each us.

Thought for Today

God is not a respecter of persons. What He was willing to do for one, He is willing and able to do for all who will come before Him with open hearts.

Prayer Journal

_____

_____

_____

~ ~ ~ DECEMBER 18 ~ ~ ~

"I, the Lord, have called You in righteousness, and will hold Your hand; I will keep You and give You as a covenant to the people, as a light to the Gentiles, to open blind eyes, to bring out prisoners from the prison, those who sit in darkness from the prison house" (Isaiah 42:6-7).

Spiritual blindness will hinder our faith to believe God. God desires to open our eyes, so that we can be open to His miracle grace and power. To be open before the Lord, we must allow the Holy Spirit to break through the intellectual membrane of doubt that separates our minds from our hearts. We must allow the Holy Spirit to have access to the areas, in which daily realities create restrictions that either disintegrate our dreams, or incarcerate our hopes. We must stop believing wrongly that "this is what God intends for my life."

The Holy Spirit invites us to live beyond life's limitations. To do so, requires more than having a mere positive mental attitude, or visualizing better things, or thinking good thoughts while wishing upon a star. Understand that Mary's miracle didn't come by human seed or from some kind of mystic meditation. She was not intimate with a man, nor did she obtain some grand level of spiritual awareness through intellectual enlightenment. Mary simply opened herself spiritually to God. God wants to bring His redemptive promises to you so that they might grow within you and then, when grown, be delivered through you to change the world around you

Thought for Today

Mary's type of miracle is God saying, "I'm not finished creating yet. Don't shut the door of your heart and close Me out. Nothing is impossible to Me!"

Prayer Journal

_____

_____

_____

~ ~ ~ DECEMBER 19 ~ ~ ~

"Now the birth of Jesus Christ was as follows: After His mother Mary was betrothed to Joseph, before they came together, she was found with child of the Holy Spirit. Then Joseph her husband, being a just man, and not wanting to make her a public example, was minded to put her away secretly. But while he thought about these things, behold, an angel of the Lord appeared to him in a dream, saying, 'Joseph, son of David, do not be afraid to take to you Mary your wife, for that which is conceived in her is of the Holy Spirit. And she will bring forth a Son, and you shall call His name Jesus, for He will save His people from their sins'" (Matthew 1:18-21).

The event of Mary's pregnancy was very traumatic for her beloved Joseph. Suddenly, he was confronted with the possibility of her unfaithfulness, coupled with the requirement of the Law to have her put to death. That she was pregnant was hard enough to take, but then to be asked to believe such a bazaar explanation was almost too much for him to bear. Furthermore, Joseph was confronted with the concept of the Trinity for the first time. Joseph's belief system was rooted in the Old Testament concept of "The Lord our God is one God." God was not asking Joseph to understand what was happening; however, he was inviting him to participate in His plan by faith. God had one question for Joseph, "Will you trust and obey Me, even though you don't understand?" Joseph trusted and obeyed God and did not let confusion, doubt, or his lack of understanding, disrupt his trust in God or his obedience to God's instructions.

Thought for Today

God is still looking for Joseph's today. He is looking for people who will trust and obey, whether or not they understand or agree with God's instructions.

Prayer Journal

_____

_____

_____

~ ~ ~ DECEMBER 20 ~ ~ ~

"Now there were in the same country shepherds living out in the fields, keeping watch over their flock by night. And behold, an angel of the Lord stood before them, and the glory of the Lord shone around them, and they were greatly afraid" (Luke 2:8-9).

The shepherds were watching over the Temple flock that was destined for ritual sacrifice. Angels, robed in the glory of the Lord, suddenly appeared to the shepherds. They were both alarmed and filled with reverence at the sight of the angels. After the angels calmed their fears, they made an announcement to the shepherds, which was one of the greatest announcements ever made on the earth. The angels announced that a Savior, the Messiah, was born in Bethlehem. The shepherds made their way to Bethlehem and found the baby, just as the angels had said they would. They left Bethlehem rejoicing and praising God.

Why did the angels choose to visit and give the subsequent announcement to the shepherds, and not to King Herod or one of the religious leaders? The shepherds were not men of influence, either in society or in religious circles. They were just common men, doing their jobs. Perhaps, the reason they were chosen for a heavenly visitation, was that no one else would have understood the significance of such an announcement. These shepherds knew the requirements of the Law regarding every father being responsible to provide a sacrificial lamb for the sins of his family. They were responsible to watch over the lambs of earthly fathers.

Thought for Today

The angel's announcement disclosed that God was providing a sacrificial Lamb. No wonder the shepherds could rejoice.

Prayer Journal

_____

_____

_____

~ ~ ~ DECEMBER 21 ~ ~ ~

"Then the angel said to them, 'Do not be afraid, for behold, I bring you good tidings of great joy which will be to all people. For there is born to you this day in the city of David a Savior, who is Christ the Lord'" (Luke 2:10-11).

When the shepherds first saw the angels, robed in the Glory of God, they were very alarmed and yet, filled with reverence at the same time. The first thing that the angels spoke to the shepherds was, *"Do not be afraid."* In other words, do not be fearful of us. The broader meaning, that is applicable to us, is that we do not have to live in fear any longer since Jesus has come to us. Fear is the harness the devil uses to manipulate peoples' lives. The good news is that Jesus has come to deliver us from all of our fears. In II Timothy 1:7, we read, *"For God has not given us a spirit of fear, but of power and of love and of a sound mind."* The angel also told the shepherds that *"I bring you good tidings of great joy."* The news the angels were bringing was the greatest news that anyone will ever hear. The best part about this news is that it applies to each one of us. We are all included in God's plan for redemption.

When the angel mentioned the *"city of David,"* the shepherds knew that he was referencing the city of Bethlehem. The shepherds knew that the prophets of old had prophesied that the Messiah would come out of the city of Bethlehem. God was proving something else—He was proving that He would keep His Word of Promise.

Thought for Today

We have all been included in God's plan to redeem and reclaim His family. God will not fail to keep His promises to you. Stand fast on His Word.

Prayer Journal

_____

_____

_____

~ ~ ~ DECEMBER 22 ~ ~ ~

"But He was wounded for our transgressions, He was bruised for our iniquities; the chastisement for our peace was upon Him, and by His stripes we are healed" (Isaiah 53:5).

The angel's announcement recorded in Luke 2:11 reads, *"For there is born to you this day in the city of David a Savior, who is Christ the Lord."* When the shepherds heard the term, *"Savior,"* they fully understood what it meant. They understood the word *"Savior"* to mean a deliverer from sin's oppression. These shepherds watched over the Temple flocks that were destined for sacrifice as "yearly saviors." Each year, fathers were to select a lamb to present as a sacrifice for the sins of their family. This ritual had to be repeated every year in order to fulfill the requirements of the Law. Isaiah the prophet foretold of the Messiah's sacrifice for sin and that His sacrifice would be once, and for all.

Jesus Christ was God's anointed Messiah that everyone had been waiting for. The prophets of old longed to see the arrival of the Messiah, but only through the eyes of their faith did they behold Him. As the Messiah, Jesus would hold the answers to all of the questions and dilemmas of life. Jesus is also "Lord," and as Lord, He is the supreme ruler with absolute authority and power. He is eternal and there will never be another to replace Him. He is Lord in heaven, and in earth.

Thought for Today

We mistakenly try to fill our lives with things that we assume will fill the void and satisfy the longing in our hearts. However, nothing will ever take the place of Jesus. He is the One we are looking for, and only He can satisfy our souls.

Prayer Journal

_____

_____

_____

~ ~ ~ DECEMBER 23 ~ ~ ~

"So all this was done that it might be fulfilled which was spoken by the Lord through the prophet, saying: 'Behold, the virgin shall be with child, and bear a Son, and they shall call His name Immanuel,' which is translated, 'God with us'" (Matthew 1:22-23).

God had long ago promised that He was going to provide a Savior Who would be resident among mankind. When Jesus was born, He was called *"'Immanuel,' which is translated, 'God with us.'"* In Jesus, God had kept His promise of old to provide a resident Savior among men. While Mary rejoiced at this event, Joseph was hurt and confused. However, God responded to Joseph with compassion and sent an angel to tenderly reassure him. The angel's message assured Joseph, that this child Jesus, Who was to be mankind's Savior, was actually, the "Great I Am," and "Jehovah," the God of his fathers.

Now Joseph was faced with a personal dilemma. A battle raged between his flesh and his spirit for Joseph was just and devout, he loved God, and was faithful in his service to Him. Joseph's theological training forbade him to have other gods in his life. In Isaiah 45:22, we read, *"Look to Me, and be saved, all you ends of the earth! For I am God, and there is no other."* For the first time, Joseph was exposed to the Trinity and the intricate workings of God. The angel's announcement revealed that God would manifest Himself in the flesh of a man, through His Son Jesus, and that this would be the work of God and the Holy Spirit.

Thought for Today

Joseph was not asked to comprehend it, but he was asked to participate by faith. God never seeks our understanding, only our trust.

Prayer Journal

_____

_____

_____

~ ~ ~ DECEMBER 24 ~ ~ ~

"Jesus said to him, 'Have I been with you so long, and yet you have not known Me, Philip? He who has seen Me has seen the Father; so how can you say, 'Show us the Father?' Do you not believe that I am in the Father, and the Father in Me? The words that I speak to you I do not speak on My own authority; but the Father who dwells in Me does the works'" (John 14:9-10).

Adam's sin separated him, and all of mankind, from God; therefore, Adam died spiritually. The fellowship that Adam had enjoyed with God was broken and his worship of God stopped. Throughout the generations that followed, God attempted to reveal Himself to man in order to reestablish their relationship and renew their fellowship. However, generation after generation rejected God's attempt at reconciliation.

God's final revelation of Himself was through His Son, Jesus. God became a man to walk among us and reach mankind. Jesus came as a baby, revealing that man had nothing to fear—as a baby, He was not a threat to anyone. One of the reasons that Jesus came was to reveal the Father. Man had totally lost touch with who God was and who He wanted to be in their lives. Jesus came to show the love and compassion that consumed God's heart. He wanted to erase man's fear of approaching God and having fellowship with Him. Jesus also came to reconcile man to God through His death. The Cross of Jesus closes the gap between man and His God.

Thought for Today

Jesus completely reveals to us what the Father is like and how much He loves us. Christ's birth, and subsequent death on the Cross, removed the sin barrier and opened the way to God.

Prayer Journal

_____

_____

_____

~ ~ ~ DECEMBER 25 ~ ~ ~

"'For there is born to you this day in the city of David a Savior, who is Christ the Lord. And this will be the sign to you: You will find a Babe wrapped in swaddling cloths, lying in a manger.' And suddenly there was with the angel a multitude of the heavenly host praising God and saying: 'Glory to God in the highest, and on earth peace, goodwill toward men'" (Luke 2:11-14).

The most significant birth in all of history was the birth of Jesus Christ. Jesus came to reveal the Father and to remove man's fear of having intimate fellowship with God. Through His death, Jesus removed the sin barrier that separated man from coming to God. Jesus' death opened the only way man can come to God and be restored in relationship and fellowship. Jesus said in John 14:6, *"I am the way, the truth, and the life. No one comes to the Father except through Me."* All the religions of the world can't produce a way to God—only Jesus can.

Mankind not only lost their concept of who God was, but due to his separation from God, man lost his desire to know God. Jesus came to restore man's desire for God. In Galatians 4:4-6, we read, *"But when the fullness of the time had come, God sent forth His Son, born of a woman, born under the law, to redeem those who were under the law, that we might receive the adoption as sons. And because you are sons, God has sent forth the Spirit of His Son into your hearts, crying out, 'Abba, Father!'"* Jesus resides within us and causes our hearts to cry out to the Father for His fellowship.

Thought for Today

God's desire for us is simple. God has always believed, "If you only knew Me, I know that you would love Me."

Prayer Journal

_____

_____

_____

~ ~ ~ DECEMBER 26 ~ ~ ~

"But God has revealed them to us through His Spirit. For the Spirit searches all things, yes, the deep things of God" (I Corinthians 2:10).

In the Old Testament, there were two ways to be led by the Spirit. The first way involved what was called "fleecing." To fleece the Lord meant to ask God for a specific sign that confirmed an action or belief. If the fleece or sign was as asked for, then one would believe that God had granted the sign as a means of giving His direction to that individual. Moses, in an attempt to prove to Pharaoh that God had sent him to lead the Israelites out of Egypt, performed a number of signs and wonders: however, the magicians of Pharaoh's court duplicated some of them. Fleecing God today, or asking for direction through a sign, is very risky because the devil can duplicate the sign requested; thus giving a false direction.

The second way to be led by the Spirit, involved the ministry of the prophets. Men sought God's guidance through the voice of the prophets, and it was through the prophets that God gave His primary instructions to His people. The reason that God used the prophets was that the Holy Spirit was not yet given to all men; therefore, only a restricted few had this privilege. Today, we do not need to place a fleece before the Lord, or rely solely on the prophetic gifts, in order to gain God's direction and leadership in our lives. We have all been given access to the Person of the Holy Spirit, Who reveals the things of God to our spirits.

Thought for Today

The Holy Spirit has been given to every person who will receive Him. The Holy Spirit's assignment is to reveal the secrets of God.

Prayer Journal

_____

_____

_____

~ ~ ~ DECEMBER 27 ~ ~ ~

"The spirit of a man is the lamp of the Lord, searching all the inner depths of his heart" (Proverbs 20:27).

When we are led by the Spirit it is our spirits that receive the revelation and direction from God, not our minds or our bodies. God will talk to us—Spirit to spirit. The number one way to be led by the Spirit is through an "inward witness." God will give us a check in our spirits when His answer is "no" to any given situation. If we run this red light of the Spirit, we will ultimately open ourselves to an attack from the devil. We must remember that God knows what we do not know, and He always has our best interest at heart. Just as a parent has to say "no" to a child at times for the good of the child, so God also says "no" to His children, through a check or red light in our spirits.

God will give us an ease or calm, or even an excited anticipation in our spirits, when His answer is "yes" to a situation. When we have these types of witnesses in our spirits, we are assured that God is saying "yes" to our direction. If we will follow this leading or witness in our spirits, we will open ourselves to God's very best for our lives. We must learn to follow the "inward witness." We will walk in a state of confusion if we look to our five senses for signs or confirmation of God's leadership in our lives. We are New Testament believers with a direct line to the Father: therefore, we do not need Old Testament guidance.

Thought for Today

We need to daily submit ourselves to the expert leadership of the Holy Spirit. It is His assignment to bear witness with our spirits as to the direction He is leading us.

Prayer Journal

_____

_____

_____

~ ~ ~ DECEMBER 28 ~ ~ ~

"I tell the truth in Christ, I am not lying, my conscience also bearing me witness in the Holy Spirit" (Romans 9:1).

We all have an "inward voice," which is the voice of our spirits. We call this inner voice by various names; such as, the "still, small voice in our hearts," or we call it our "conscience." We must realize that as Christians, we have the "life" of God within our spirits, and His "life" always produces His light in which we are to walk. We need to confess, "The life of God in my spirit dominates me: therefore, I purpose in my heart to walk in the light of that life." In John 1:4-5, we read, *"In Him was life, and the life was the light of men. And the light shines in the darkness, and the darkness did not comprehend it."* God dwells in our spirits by the Person of the Holy Spirit and He communicates to us through our spirits.

In order to be successfully led by the Holy Spirit, we must keep our hearts (spirits) tender. We are warned in Proverbs 4:23, *"Keep your heart with all diligence, for out of it spring the issues of life."* To succesfuly be led by the Spirit, our heart must remain tender and free from condemnation resulting from unrepentant sin. I John 3:21-22 tells us, *"Beloved, if our heart does not condemn us, we have confidence toward God. And whatever we ask we receive from Him, because we keep His commandments and do those things that are pleasing in His sight."*

Thought for Today

God's desire for us is that every area of our lives will be under the leadership of the Holy Spirit. The Holy Spirit will always lead us by speaking to our spirits: He doesn't guide us through our minds, senses, or bodies.

Prayer Journal

_____

_____

_____

~ ~ ~ DECEMBER 29 ~ ~ ~

"Yours, O Lord, is the greatness, the power and the glory, the victory and the majesty; for all that is in heaven and in earth is Yours; Yours is the kingdom, O Lord, and You are exalted as head over all" (I Chronicles 29:11).

It is the nature of God to give. To Adam—God gave a wife. To Noah—God gave a rainbow. To Israel in the wilderness—God gave a pillar of fire by night, a cloud by day, and manna for breakfast each morning. To a lost and dying world that He loved—God gave a Savior in His Son, Jesus. God loves to give. One day, Jesus turned to His disciples and told them that the Kingdom of God belonged to them. Luke 12:32 says, *"Do not fear, little flock, for it is your Father's good pleasure to give you the kingdom."*

Consider the natural kingdom of God as found in Psalms 24:1, *"The earth is the Lord's, and all its fullness, the world and those who dwell therein. For He has founded it upon the seas, and established it upon the waters."* The world systems may be presently ruled by the devil, but the earth, and all that dwell therein, belong to God. Everywhere you look in God's creation, His fingerprint is seen. Consider the great spiritual kingdom of God. This kingdom is filled with blessings and benefits for all who believe in Jesus as their personal Lord and Savior. We are blessed with the Lord's presence. He promises never to leave or forsake us. If everyone else in our life walks out, Jesus promises to stay.

Thought for Today

We have been blessed with the Lord's provision and with the privilege of living in His Kingdom. The resources of heaven are ours through Christ. Do not take His blessings for granted.

Prayer Journal

_____

_____

_____

~ ~ ~ DECEMBER 30 ~ ~ ~

"Behold, I give you the authority to trample on serpents and scorpions, and over all the power of the enemy, and nothing shall by any means hurt you" (Luke 10:19).

A man in Dallas, Texas, gave this testimony about his two daughters. They had been shopping and it was late. As they approached their car, they saw two men leaning up against it, each with a wicked smile on his face. As they put the key into the door, one man said, "You're not going anywhere." The girls quickly got in and attempted to start the car, but it wouldn't start. They joined hands and prayed, "Lord, please start this car." Turning the key again, the car started and they sped off leaving the two men in amazement. When they arrived home they told their father of the car not starting. The next morning he checked it—the battery was gone. The car had started without a battery.

Many do not believe this testimony could be true. However, Jesus demonstrated the power of God everywhere He went. One day, He gave His disciples the power of God to be exercised over all the power of the enemy. If we can't believe this story, then why do we believe that Moses parted the Red Sea, or Joshua commanded the sun to stand still, or any of the other miracles in the Bible? We believe the miracles of the Bible, but we can't believe that God can start a car without a battery? We serve a mighty God!

Thought for Today

If God commands a man to see without eyes—he will see. If God commands a man to hear without ears—he will hear. If God commands a car to start without a battery—it will start. Place your trust and faith in God. He is a miracle worker.

Prayer Journal

_____

_____

_____

~ ~ ~ DECEMBER 31 ~ ~ ~

"I am the Lord, that is My name; and My glory I will not give to another, nor My praise to carved images" (Isaiah 42:8).

God said *"My glory"* is the one thing I will not share with anyone. However, it is the one thing that we try the hardest to take away from Him—preachers and church people are guilty. God begins to do a work among His people and we insist on taking credit for it. In the Old Testament, the glory of God was evidenced by His manifest presence. The saddest story in the Bible is the story of the Ark of the Covenant being stolen by the Philistines. The Ark was the place where God would manifest His glorious presence and communicate with His people. With the Ark gone, so was the glory of God's presence. At first, the Israelites were heartbroken, but as time went on, they simply adjusted their lives and soon forgot about the Ark. Years later, a young king by the name of David, purposed in his heart to get the Ark and bring it back home.

After all God had done for the Israelites, and after witnessing God's mighty miracles on their behalf, one would have to ask, "How could you just adjust your life and go on as if God's presence didn't matter?" Before we pass judgment on the Israelites, we must realize that, at times, we have done the same thing. Our churches have become so carnal, that if the Holy Spirit left town on Saturday, the church wouldn't know the difference on Sunday.

Thought for Today

Far too many have known what it is to walk in the fullness of the Holy Spirit, only to become entangled in the affairs of life. Sadly, they never even miss His fellowship. In the New Year purpose to live in God's presence and give Him the glory for everything.

Prayer Journal

_____

_____

_____

www.ingramcontent.com/pod-product-compliance
Lightning Source LLC
Chambersburg PA
CBHW031612160426
43196CB00006B/104